THE HUNGER HABIT

THE HUNGER HABIT

WHY WE EAT WHEN WE'RE
NOT HUNGRY
AND HOW TO STOP

Judson Brewer, MD, PhD

AVERY

AN IMPRINT OF PENGUIN RANDOM HOUSE

NEW YORK

AVERY

an imprint of Penguin Random House LLC
penguinrandomhouse.com

Most Avery books are available at special quantity discounts for bulk purchase for sales promotions, premiums, fund-raising, and educational needs. Special books or book excerpts also can be created to fit specific needs. For details, write SpecialMarkets@penguinrandomhouse.com.

Library of Congress Cataloging-in-Publication Data has been applied for.
ISBN 9780593543252
Ebook ISBN 9780593543276

Printed in the United States of America
1st Printing

Book design by Lorie Pagnozzi

CONTENTS

PART 3: A Bigger Better Offer: Days 17–21

To Jacqui, Rob,
and to all who have had fraught relationships with food

INTRODUCTION

JACQUI'S STORY

Jacqui, a forty-something dog-loving yoga and mindfulness instructor, felt like a fraud. Even as she led her students through classes on acceptance and equanimity, she was hiding the fact that her own heart was far from tranquil. Beneath her calm exterior, she was battling a toxic cycle of shame numbed by secret eating, which cycled back and fed more shame. She feared she was losing not just the battle, but the war—the war with herself.

Jacqui's complicated relationship with food went as far back as she could remember. As a child, she had been a slow and picky eater. Her well-meaning parents used to encourage her to eat more and be quick about it, so she tried to please them by picking up the pace and quantity of the food she ate. When Jacqui hit puberty, her body started filling out along the lines of the rock star Pink's. When Jacqui looked in the mirror, she didn't feel like a rock star; instead, she felt dismay. She didn't want to look curvy or muscular. She wanted to look willowy and ethereal, more Gwyneth Paltrow than Pink. Jacqui wasn't overweight, but like so many adolescent girls bombarded by images of slender celebrities and models like Kate "nothing tastes as good as skinny feels" Moss, she felt life would be happier *if only* she could be thinner. To reach her goal, she started restricting the amount and types of food she ate. Instead of ordering fries and a soda when she went out with friends, she'd order salad and drink water. Her careful food choices did leave her thinner, but not necessarily happier.

During her teenage years, Jacqui started spending more time with her friend Alice. Alice had recently lost a family member and was going through a period of depression. Jacqui could relate. She seemed to feel bad about herself all the time. Together, the friends realized they could numb some of their miserable feelings with food—a lot of food, eaten all at once. They began bingeing wildly, smothering their negative emotions with chocolates, cake, and fries—all foods Jacqui had been so careful to avoid in her quest for a thinner body. Because bingeing didn't solve all their problems, Jacqui and Alice also added cigarettes and alcohol for good measure.

As Jacqui got older, she went back to eating less and less so she could maintain what she felt was a normal weight. Before long, her focus on restricted eating became a full-time obsession. She thought about food, especially the food she was keeping herself from eating, all day every day. It was as if her brain had been hijacked by these intrusive thoughts. She needed to take control again before she crashed, so she doubled down on her careful eating. She got so good at restricting what she ate, she could go the entire year following a strict diet, but then would have an epic blowout binge at Christmas.

Restricting her eating to this extreme worked—sort of. Jacqui stayed slim and told herself she was in control of her food, which made her feel in control of her life. That lasted until she quit smoking at the age of thirty. Without the help of nicotine as a stimulant and appetite suppressant, she quickly put an additional 40 pounds on her five-two frame, and her feelings of failure came rushing back.

Family and friends didn't help matters. She caught them looking at her critically when they thought she wouldn't notice and could swear they were whispering judgmentally about her behind her back. Some-times they didn't even bother to hide it. One particularly harsh day, a family friend poked her in the stomach and said, "Wow, look how much weight you've piled on." As cruel as the world could be to her, it was nothing to how Jacqui heaped shame upon herself. There were times where she felt utterly worthless.

Jacqui couldn't keep going this way. By the time she was thirty-five, her restrict/binge/restrict cycle shortened from a year to months to weeks to daily. Monday morning would be her restrictive period, when she carefully counted calories and managed what she ate, but by three o'clock in the afternoon, all bets would be off. She would gorge on whatever she could get her hands on—doughnuts, chips, Chinese takeout—and then start over again the next day. Her restriction would inevitably collapse back into the bingeing—and self-judgment. As bad as she felt about her weight, she felt worse about the fact that she had let herself get so out of control. Bingeing again was the only way for her to escape those terrible feelings, if only for a moment.

After a nighttime binge, she would wake up choked with guilt. She would turn to her partner in bed and ask, "What's wrong with me?" She felt like a failure. She felt broken. And what's worse, she couldn't see a way out of the cycle.

Jacqui is far from alone in her tortured relationship with food.

In my practice as a psychiatrist, I have seen as many different ways to have a bad relationship with food as I have patients. Many of my patients have become so hopelessly out of touch with their bodies, they cannot even tell if they are hungry or are simply eating their emotions. Some people come to me because they cannot seem to resist eating a "bad" food no matter how hard they try. Others just can't stop eating once they've taken that first bite. More than one patient has come to me desperate to control their "mindless eating." I've seen people who micromanage each morsel they put in their mouths, carefully counting out seven almonds at exactly eleven A.M., weighing their kale salad, scrupulously avoiding sugar . . . until seven P.M., when they'll tear open a bag of potato chips and devour the whole thing. For many, thoughts of food crowd out nearly everything else, making it difficult for them to notice, let alone enjoy, what is going on in their lives. To cope, some of my patients try to impose strict rules for themselves—no oil, no salt, no sugar, no fast food—only to find that these rules make them feel as if they've constructed a cell and locked themselves up—in *food* jail.

As varied as the specifics are, these patients all have one thing in common—they feel bad about themselves. Actually, they feel *terrible* about themselves. They suffer from a rogues' gallery of feelings ranging from frustration, guilt, and annoyance to despair, disgust, and self-loathing.

It is painful for me to observe my patients in such agony. Typical diet advice makes the solution to their problems sound so simple: eat fewer calories. However, I have patients who come into my office week after week carrying their diligently recorded accounts of what they've eaten and how much they've exercised, and they are as miserable as ever. The reality is, for most people no amount of calorie counting makes a difference.

In medical school I had been taught that good eating and "weight management" is nothing more than a question of *calories in, calories out*. All I had to do was point out to my patients that if their relationship with food was bad, they could just eat more salad and lay off the cake while exercising more, and voilà, they'd lose weight. One of my medical school professors stated it matter-of-factly, as if it were one of Newton's laws of motion. Follow the formula and the results were guaranteed. My patients didn't need a juicer or an elaborate meal plan. They didn't even need me. They needed a calculator.

But it turned out that real life is not so simple.

When I started my psychiatric practice, I could not immediately see what was happening with my patients that made them feel so dreadful. I've seen people in deep anguish because their struggles with food are every bit as vexing and destructive as those of my patients with other afflictions—including addictions to heroin, gambling, sex, or alcohol. The difference, of course, is unlike drinking alcohol or smoking cigarettes, which are optional behaviors (at least at first), eating is essential for our survival. There had to be a better way to handle food issues.

I did what I was trained to do as a researcher: I investigated the problem. I started by looking carefully at the standard approaches to changing how people eat. Caloric restriction, low-carb, keto—no matter what diet or trend or nutritionist's advice, by and large they had one thing in common: *shoulding*. Nearly every suggested approach came back to my trusty medical school lecture: you *should* eat fewer calories, you *should* eat healthier food, and you *should* exercise more. It had become clear to me: my patients already knew what they *should* do. They just couldn't do it—and on top of that felt guilty for not being able to follow their doctors' advice. What was keeping them from doing what they knew they should do?

Then I had a realization (the first of many things that I learned from my patients): many of my patients were unhappy with more than just their eating. They were unhappy because it felt like they had brought the problem upon themselves. They were full of shame and self-recrimination. This wasn't the case with my patients who suffered with anxiety. When someone has anxiety, they experience it as something happening *to* them. But eating is different. We experience eating as something we *do,* and unhealthy eating habits as something we have inflicted upon ourselves. We feel bad for ourselves when we experience anxiety, but we judge ourselves for having a difficult relationship with food (and for many of us, that self-judgment doesn't stop at eating). In some cases, when we have a pattern of unhelpful eating, it shows up in our bodies, which compounds the issue. In a world that celebrates thinness and self-control, those who carry a few unwanted pounds can feel like they are wearing a sandwich board announcing their failure to achieve either one. The board reads: "Go ahead and judge me: I must be lazy and have no self-control." That societal judgment applies to basically everything that sets eating habit loops in motion, from genes to trauma to engineering food to—and note the irony here—societal judgments that tell us that we are lacking and should buy or be X, Y, or Z to be happy.

If you, too, have tried to improve your relationship with food, my guess is you already know what you *should* do. And like my patients, you probably feel like you have failed when you don't or can't.

It's not your fault. You have not failed. You are not hopeless or weak or any of the other terrible things you might have told yourself as you ate yet another bite you knew you "shouldn't." It's not you. There is nothing to feel guilty or ashamed about. It's the system we've built that has failed. It has failed you by focusing on the wrong things— willpower, measuring, self-control—instead of addressing the true root of the problem: unhelpful habits.

IT'S NOT YOU, IT'S YOUR HABITS

It was a study unrelated to eating that cracked the code for me and revealed that habits are a huge source of our eating issues.

In addition to being a psychiatrist, I am also a neuroscientist. I've spent decades researching how and why we form habits and what we can do to break them. In the early 2000s, I created a mindfulness program for smoking cessation and got some eye-popping results. In one of my lab's clinical trials, people who used my program were five times better at quitting smoking than those who used "gold standard" cognitive therapy.

We were thrilled by this outcome, of course, but also confused, because during that study, we uncovered another surprising finding. Some pilot testers reported they were changing their eating habits in addition to their smoking habit. Conventional wisdom would have predicted they would gain weight, as Jacqui had, due to increased snacking (remember, nicotine is an appetite suppressant). The typical person who quits smoking gains about 10 to 15 pounds when lighting up a cigarette triggered by anxiety, boredom, or restlessness is replaced by a trip to the kitchen. But these testers weren't gaining weight. They were *losing weight*. Using a *smoking program*. It seemed the practices they were using to ride out cravings to smoke were also helping them with their urges to eat.

I dove into the scientific research about eating habits to find out what the heck was going on. It turned out that the reason we were seeing improvements came down to empowering people to change habits. They weren't trying to force themselves to avoid snacking or certain foods. *They were changing their relationship to food and eating*. This was potentially big news. After decades of research, we now knew the methods for rewiring the brain to change old habits and replace them with new ones.

If issues related to food could be attributed to habitual behaviors, that meant that if we could apply these methods to my patients' habits, they could change how they ate, and in turn change how they felt about themselves.

We could use neuroscience principles to teach people how their minds work, and in the process work with their minds to overcome long-standing habitual eating patterns—from boredom to bingeing. People could learn to rewire their brains to change their relationships to food, potentially permanently. Break the habits, break the cycles. When we learn to be at peace with ourselves, the war naturally stops.

This was extremely exciting.

My team and I set about developing a program that would walk people through the process of changing their eating habits. We created an app-based program that brought together a basic training in habit change with an online community (called Eat Right Now) and began testing it. The results of our trials were very encouraging. The program worked the same way as our smoking studies. In a study led by Dr. Ashley Mason at the University of California, San Francisco, participants dropped their craving-related eating by 40 percent. It seemed that this theory could work. Whether it was binge eating, emotional eating, mindless eating, automatic eating, or overeating, focusing on these as unhelpful habits helped them approach them as habits, and step out of the cycle.

And the changes went deeper than simply how people ate. The program changed how people felt—not just about how they ate, but also about how they saw themselves. People who had felt controlled by their eating for decades no longer struggled to eat healthfully. Instead of trying to avoid forbidden foods, they could eat a healthy amount and stop. As one patient said, "I feel like I have my life back." They were changing their relationship to eating and ending the war with themselves.

The change in habits was gratifying, but it was the change in how my patients felt about themselves that made it clear I had to write this book. Some of them were stopping bingeing. Some were losing weight, which was helping their physical health. Others were letting go of unhelpful restrictive eating patterns that were causing major suffering for them. But most important, people who used the program became empowered instead of hopeless and replaced their self-loathing with self-compassion. They weren't just more in control, they were happier.

UNWINDING YOUR EATING HABITS

In this book, I'm going to take everything I've learned over the past two decades of studying habit change and show you how to abandon unhelpful habits and create helpful ones. You might have noticed I've avoided using the words *bad habits*. I'm not a huge fan of *good/bad* language because it causes us to praise and blame ourselves for something that our brains do at a very basic survival level. So as one of the first changes you'll make, I'll ask you to use the words *helpful* and *unhelpful* instead of *good* and *bad*.

The object here is not to lose weight—unless that's what you want. The plan you'll find in this book is designed to break you out of food jail so that you feel you control your eating—not that your eating controls you. Critically, this comes without making a constant, exhausting, and ultimately futile effort to overcome your habits using willpower. This might sound inconceivable, but when you learn how your brain works, you can learn to work with it to change your eating patterns in a way that renders the word *control* obsolete and irrelevant.

Using a powerful combination of habit change science and mindfulness practice, you will learn to use your brain to heal your relationship with yourself. You are on a path to self-compassion, which will help you break free from the cycle of emotional eating and shame. If you are simply looking to break some entrenched eating habits, we've got you covered there, too.

THE BOOK

In the first three chapters, we'll look at how our brains form habits, why they are so hard to break, and what you need to know about your brain to equip you for success. In the rest of the book, I'll take you step by step through a 21-day challenge—a program to help you unwind your food habits by working with, not against, the all-powerful organ responsible for healthy eating: your brain. (It brings a smile to my face when one of my patients or members of our program lights up with joy when they talk about how much easier it is to work *with* their brain.) The challenge is split into three parts based on what I've found in my research studies, which show a surprisingly consistent progression of behavior change: (1) identifying eating habit patterns; (2) interrupting them using awareness (not willpower); and then (3) leveraging the power of your brain to step out of old and into new habits that nurture us mentally and physically.

I will offer you science-backed ways to forge new, healthier habits that underlie practices such as mindful eating and intuitive eating—you'll learn how awareness is an extremely powerful tool as exemplified by these approaches. And when I say *science-backed*, I mean science that my lab has actually performed, not just someone else's studies or reports that I read about and am now summarizing in this book. Along the way, you may find that you become more present in your life when you are not obsessed with food. A quick word about who this book is *not* for. If you have a serious restrictive eating disorder such as anorexia or bulimia nervosa, unfortunately this book is not for you. Please work with your doctor or mental health clinician to support you.[1]

Throughout, I will use examples from my clinic, my lab's research

---

1 A really helpful resource is https://www.nationaleatingdisorders.org.

studies, and the many people who have used the Eat Right Now program to highlight the science that I have, well, scienced. (But don't worry, I will not be trying to sell you the app. Everything you need is in the book.)

It is possible that eating food can be a source of self-care and health, a pleasure, and an occasion to connect, not a referendum on your character. This book has one aim: to help you change your relationship with eating. At the end, you will know how your mind works, so you can work with it. You will be back in touch with your body, so that you can listen to its vast stores of wisdom. And you will stop letting food rule you, so you will have space for the rest of your life. End the war, begin the peace.

Let's get started.

CHAPTER 1

How Did We End Up in This Mess?

WE DON'T EVEN KNOW IF WE'RE HUNGRY

There I was, just after five P.M. on a Thursday evening. I was standing in front of a whiteboard, surrounded by a semicircle of women sitting in chairs. Each of these women had come to my clinic because they were struggling with binge eating.

Armed with a lot of knowledge about eating disorders I had learned in my recently completed residency and how they overlapped with addiction, I was attempting to help these patients work with Binge Eating Disorder (BED). They were all speaking in coherent sentences. And yet as they spoke, it felt like I was talking to people from another planet.

As a person who has not struggled with his weight, I had been protected my entire life from food-related issues. I had never been teased or subjected to fat jokes. As a male, I didn't have to face the daily stigma or "norms" that society pressured women in particular to conform to so they would look a certain way. In general, I ate when I was hungry and stopped when I was full. One of the few exceptions was a little problem I had with gummy worms (and if I'm honest, occasional half-gallon ice cream binges), which I'll get to in chapter 9.

I was largely blind to what my patients were struggling with; I couldn't see the world from their perspective. So I asked them to put me in their shoes. Starting before the first bite. I asked them to sketch the details for me. What urged them to eat? What were their cravings like? When did they eat?

They all started talking at once, describing the different times and triggers that led to a binge. They talked about time of day, different emotions, and people. They recounted how cravings and urges—which I will use interchangeably in this book, as they describe the same restless drive to do something—pushed or pulled them into the kitchen to find something to relieve their discomfort, whether it was an emotion or simply a desire to make the craving itself go away. I picked up a dry-erase marker and wrote what I could catch from the chorus of voices as fast as I could on the whiteboard.

Again, I understood everything they were saying, and yet I was still confused. They were talking about the people, places, and things emblematic of the overlap between binge eating and addiction. But no one had mentioned actual hunger. It was like they had skipped a critical step in baking a cake, moving from the list of ingredients to pulling the cake out of the oven.

I had them slow down. Once they began taking turns speaking, one sentence in particular grabbed my attention: "I just eat when I have a craving."

A glimmer of understanding flashed through my brain.

I asked another question: "What are the cravings like when you're hungry?"

Looking confused, one woman ventured, "I don't know. I just eat when I have a craving."

"But how do you know when you're hungry?"

With this question, she and the whole group went silent.

I asked them, "How do you know when you have an urge to eat because you are hungry as opposed to something else?"

More stunned silence. They didn't know. Hungry? Angry? Lonely? Tired? Bored? Sad? Distracted? Excited? All of these had one thing in common—they caused a craving. And that craving urged them to eat. No questions asked. These cravings had nothing to do with what their stomachs were telling them. It's as though the wires connecting their brains to their stomachs had been crossed with their emotional wiring. And worse, they seemed to be walking around much of the time with their brains disconnected from their bodies.

I had assumed that our most basic of survival mechanisms, hunger, was so rock solid, so clear, so *obvious*, that we immediately knew it when we felt it. I was dead wrong. Hunger could be colored, shaped, shifted, disguised, and even merged with other cravings. And for people who have ignored true physical hunger with dieting and restricting for a long time, this disconnect between brain and body can be especially significant. Cravings that come from very different spaces and places all converge in one place: the urge to eat. Just because I could distinguish between when I was hungry and when I was stressed didn't mean that everyone else in the world could.

My brain exploded.

Right then I had a huge lightbulb moment that would forever change how I viewed eating, one that would lead me along a path of discovery in my lab that would even change how I treated common clinical issues such as anxiety and depression.

My clinic patients—and by extension all of us who struggle with unhealthy eating patterns—needed to find a way to interrupt their habit loops by relearning how to pay attention to their brains and bodies, so they could rewire those mixed-up neural synapses. The good news was that I happened to be researching how to tap into the power of reinforcement learning as a way to help people overcome addictive behaviors. I had been developing programs that helped people leverage the very things that these women in my clinic needed to nurture and develop: awareness and self-kindness.

TRACY'S STORY

I met Tracy in 2013. In her mid-twenties, she was in graduate school at Yale, studying to get her master's degree in public health. She showed up at a Monday-evening meditation group I was leading on campus. One evening she hung around after the meditation group finished. After everyone had left, she told me that weekly meditation was having a big impact on her life, and she wanted to learn more. I agreed to take her on as a student. When I work with students, I usually start with struggles that they are facing in their lives. I ask them to identify where they might be suffering. They can use this knowledge as grist for the mill as they set about learning how their minds work, so that they can then learn to work better with these issues.

Tracy was struggling with anxiety but didn't even know it at first.

Tracy began this exploration and quickly made a connection between eating and intense studying. She noticed she relied on carrots to help her with her statistics class. Kind of. As she put it, "I'm not a numbers person, so that was the most difficult class in grad school for me." Stress and anxiety led to her "pounding carrots and anything crunchy" as she worked on her biostatistics assignments.

To be clear, to anyone who has struggled with the "eat carrots instead of cake" and "calories in, calories out" issue, pounding carrots sounds a lot like a first-world problem. If only they could just get in the habit of pounding carrots! The reason I bring Tracy's story up here is that the pounding is the problem. How we eat is more important than what we eat. If we don't understand and face upstream issues, we'll forever waste tons of energy downstream and end up frustrated and defeated, wondering why all of our effort isn't showing sustained results.

It wasn't about the carrots. It wasn't about being hungry. She simply had "anxious energy" in her body and needed to crunch on something. She also noticed that process of crunching on something had to be repetitive to help soothe her as she was doing her homework. She needed to be able to easily reach, grab, and crunch, without the process taking brain space away from her studying. As she learned how to explore her own experience with eating, she discovered something big. She reflected later, "That was the first time in my life I realized I had anxiety." She hadn't associated anxiety with eating carrots. She simply crunched carrots as she did her work.

This realization was the beginning of transforming her relationship to both anxiety and food. Like my patients who were struggling with binge eating, Tracy wasn't eating when she was hungry. She was feeding a feeling.

How important is this evolutionary hiccup?

When we link our evolutionary survival engine up to the mood train, the train can quickly build steam and momentum until it is out of control. Driven by an antsy feeling, we feel a magnetic pull to the kitchen late at night for a snack. We don't even know if we're hungry (and we often aren't), we just know we want SOMETHING. We gobble down cookies in the break room not because our stomachs are grumbling but because we're afraid of being downsized. We add another scoop to our bowl of ice cream after being ghosted by a romantic interest because nothing heals—or at least distracts from—feeling rejected like Ben & Jerry's or Häagen-Dazs ice cream.

The Hungry Ghost

Later in our work together, Tracy told me another illuminating story:

As she started to try to change her eating habits, she mapped out a pattern around how she handled self-care. She told me when she was struggling with something, she would want to get herself a treat. Treats usually came in the form of carb-filled and sugar-laden foods like cookies or pastries. She had been trying to shift to healthier options (carrots didn't make the cut for the self-care category). One afternoon, when she was feeling anxious, she bought some blackberries as a treat for herself.

You might be thinking, *Great! She switched to something healthy!* First-world eating problem. But now zoom in on what happened next. She bought them, sat down in the in-store café, and . . . promptly "downed them."

She told me she tried to enjoy them, but there was still an inexplicable urgency to her eating that drove her to eat past the point where her planning brain knew she had already had enough. She had this feeling that the intensity of consuming the entire pint was going to make her feel good.

The berries *did* taste good. But unfortunately she didn't find what she was looking for at the bottom of the container. There was something deep in her core that wasn't addressed by gobbling the entire pint. She reflected, "Eating fast and getting to the bottom of the carton of berries didn't satisfy whatever that feeling was." She described having a hole that she still wanted to fill, a discomfort she wanted to ease.

I have never downed a pint of blackberries, but I could relate to the hole that Tracy was talking about. It is very common. You can see how it is an unfortunate offshoot of our brain's survival mechanisms getting off track. The wires that should be helping us eat when we're hungry and stop when we're full get crossed with attempts at soothing our emotions. Ironically, whenever we want to eat for emotional reasons—this is called hedonic hunger—we pull out a shovel and dig that hole deeper.

This bottomless pit was identified thousands of years before modern psychology and neuroscience had even been conceived. I remember first hearing about it when a Buddhist teacher described the image of what is called a hungry ghost.

Imagine a ghost with a regular-sized mouth—whatever *regular-sized* is in ghost terms—leading to a long and narrow esophagus that shuttles food down to a ginormous stomach. No matter how much or how fast it eats, it can't possibly fill its belly. Therefore, the ghost never feels full.

Whenever we eat because of emotion, boredom, or any circumstance where we aren't actually hungry, we become that hungry ghost. Our actual stomachs don't feel empty because we don't need food in those moments. But we've learned to stuff down our feelings with food. So we want food. And because we are feeding our wants instead of meeting our needs, we never fill that void. In Tracy's words, "My issue isn't going to be solved right now because I'm eating."

As someone in the Eat Right Now community recently posted: "Inhaling sugar buries whatever thoughts/feelings/unpleasant body sensations generated the inhaling impulse . . . too much regret, indignation, shame. The immediate reward is an escape from those feelings etc., & a transition to the next activity without addressing any of that icky stuff. The downside is exactly that, plus nagging health concerns, plus the regret & self-hate cycle."

Emotional eating of this sort—like Tracy pounding carrots when studying or sucking down blackberries past the point of satiety—is EXACTLY THE OPPOSITE of how our brains and bodies evolved to work together to keep us alive. Our brain overrides our body's signals so that we crunch and munch to the point where it is hard to tell when and if we are actually hungry.

Unfortunately, knowing that we eat our feelings doesn't magically make us strong enough to stop doing it. Our puny prefrontal cortex, which is the seat of self-control, is no match for our brawny survival brain. And anyone who has tried to force themselves to stop an emotional eating habit following the "calories in, calories out" formula that I learned in medical school knows this.

THE FOOD INDUSTRY PROFITS WHEN YOU PICK UP THE CHIP

To make matters worse, our ability to make good survival food choices is sabotaged by more than just our brain. Food can be—and is—tweaked every which way so that we inevitably fail the old Lay's potato chip challenge, "Betcha can't eat just one!" (Fun trivia fact: Lay's came up with this slogan in 1963, the same year Weight Watchers was founded.) The food industry works hard to manipulate edibles so that they can win that bet. And they've done a pretty good job at tweaking things to make sure the house—in this case their industry—always wins. In a jaw-dropping exposé of food industry practices, Michael Moss, an investigative reporter for *The New York Times*, wrote an article called "The Extraordinary Science of Addictive Junk Food." The cover art for this piece was a picture of a Doritos chip with the following formula written across it:

$$\frac{\text{Salt} + \text{Fat}^2}{\text{Satisfying Crunch}} \times \text{Pleasing Mouth Feel} = \text{A Food Designed to Addict}$$

I like this picture for a number of reasons, one of which is highlighted by another headline in the satirical journal *The Onion*: "Doritos Celebrates One Millionth Ingredient." *The Onion* goes on to "report" that the "new ingredient, disodium guanylate, is expected not only to act as an additional emulsifying agent but also to make the big taste of Doritos even bigger."

Satire aside, refined sugar and overeating contribute to negative health effects like diabetes and obesity. Obesity gets the distinguished *dis*honor of currently being the runner-up to smoking as the most preventable cause of death in the United States.[1] When our ancestors looked up into the night sky searching for signs of the future, they couldn't have seen in the stars chemically altered foods leading to modern epidemics like obesity and diabetes. And never in a million years would they have seen that in today's world companies would be dedicating billions of dollars to manufacture food-like objects with the sole purpose of getting us to eat more and more of them.

There is an entire industry that spends billions of dollars designing food, from convenience to look, smell, taste, and of course, mouthfeel, with one purpose in mind: consumption. The more you eat, the more money they make.

Moss's article and his even more detailed book, *Salt Sugar Fat: How the Food Giants Hooked Us*, are illuminating. I won't go into the specifics because all you really need to know is this: food is increasingly designed for one thing—addiction. The food industry treats food more like a chemistry experiment than a form of nutrition. With the

---

1 It is important to point out here that science in general is nuanced. Research that aims to estimate attributable causes of things like death is an imperfect science in itself, especially when trying to isolate a single variable like obesity (which in itself—while a medical term—can be hurtful). This can lead to an overestimation of how much obesity directly contributes to death.

profit motive in mind, it manipulates us to eat (and buy) foods that aren't even good for us. For example, chemists and food researchers have found what they termed our "bliss point," which is the optimal balance of salt, sugar, and fat that flips our brains into a frenzy of desire. The industry also found that tailoring to convenience and a feeling of autonomy also made snacking more habit forming. Lunchables, anyone? Yes, my college students recall how they loved them as kids, even though they didn't taste very good. Now they know why.

Convenience, food engineering, and emotions add up to make it really easy to get locked into poor eating habits. And then our brain comes in and says, *Yup, this is working. Let's keep going with this strategy,* making it REALLY HARD to try—or even imagine trying—something else.

My clinic patients in the semicircle were pointing to the now-perennial problem of how society is selling us the "solution" to our worries: eat your feelings. Eating can distract us or give us some brief relief when we feel down or bad, but tapping into these survival mechanisms sets us up for trouble in the future. The more the food/mood wires get crossed, the more these behaviors become habits. And instead of uncrossing them, we blame ourselves, which triggers shame and guilt, as we think something is wrong with us. Don't worry, there *is* a way out of this mess. It starts with learning how our brains work.

CHAPTER 2

How Food Habits Form

When Jack first entered my psychiatric clinic, he struck me as the kind of person you hope to sit next to on an airplane—courteous and respectful, but not in-your-face friendly. I usually start off with something welcoming and authentic to kick off a first meeting with a patient, so after we settled in—it was during the pandemic, so we settled in as best we could via video—I asked, "How can I help?" He paused and a little self-consciously said that he struggled with his eating.

Okay, I thought, *that could be a million things.* People don't usually start by going to a psychiatrist for trouble with food. I tried not to jump to any conclusions about what he was grappling with or how he had tried to work with it in the past. I asked him to continue.

Jack answered by describing his relationship with Corn Nuts. Corn Nuts are prepared by soaking whole corn kernels in water for up to three days, roasting or deep frying them, and then adding salt—a *lot* of salt. This tasty snack originated south of the U.S. border: it is called cancha in Peru and chulpi in Ecuador. Here, you can find them packaged in plastic bags in gas stations, convenience stores, and the snack aisle of the grocery store.

Jack's relationship with this salty snack went way back—he had been eating them since he was about ten years old. Now in his sixties, he told me he ate Corn Nuts "about a hundred at a time." That's probably a slight exaggeration, but he was getting the idea across that he didn't just nibble on a few at a time. If you've ever had a Corn Nut, you might wonder, "How did he *do* that?" Corn Nuts are *very* salty. If I tried to eat even a few handfuls at a time, I would need to wash them down with a gallon of water. However much I suspected Jack was exaggerating—aiming to break the stereotype of doctors constantly interrupting their patients—I kept my mouth shut and kept listening. I could sense that he was leading up to something important.

"I have automatic eating," he announced. "I just shovel it in. I'm not processing. I'm just doing it." Jack continued, mentioning how he typically ate pasta: "If it was pasta and it was there, I'd just eat it."

Jack seemed to have a similar brain-body disconnection as my binge eating clinic patients, but instead of bingeing, he had wired himself up for automatic eating.

"So pasta has a pull?" I asked, to make sure I was understanding.

"Pasta and ice cream. Bagels and things like that. I'd go to the bagel shop, eat one, and eat two more on the way home. That's a lot of bagels. Then I'd feel unwell, but go back and do it again [on another day]."

Interesting. I was beginning to see why he had come to see me. I asked him when he found himself eating like this. He talked about eating when he felt depressed or anxious or stressed, and then he paused for a second and added, "Actually, I eat when I'm feeling good as well." After covering almost all the categories of non-hunger-based eating, he summed it up: "I have an urge, and the food satisfies the urge, so I just eat."

And as is true of my patients with Binge Eating Disorder, Jack's inability to control what he ate was hurting his mental and physical well-being. He didn't want to be eating Corn Nuts by the truckload;

he just couldn't help himself. His brain made him do it. What's going on here?

YOUR SURVIVAL BRAIN AND YOUR PLANNING BRAIN

Like every beast with a brain, we have a primary goal: to survive. Our oldest and deepest neural systems are designed to keep us alive and able to procreate. This ancient part of our brains includes the system responsible for such non-cerebral but crucial functions as breathing and regulating body temperature and, of course, eating and not being eaten. These are immediate needs. If we're being chased by the proverbial saber-toothed tiger, we'll need to deal with that pronto, not sit around weighing options and comparing possible outcomes before deciding to *RUN!* I call this part of our brain our *survival brain.*

When it comes to food, our survival brain has one mission: keep the body alive. For our caveperson ancestors, this meant foods that provided quick, easily digested calories were at the top of their preferences. That hasn't changed from hundreds of thousands of years ago. Have you ever seen a YouTube or social media video showing a baby's first taste of ice cream? As soon as the ice cream hits the tongue, the baby gets this "Wow!" look on her face and immediately grabs the cone and tries to eat more. That moment of amazement sets off a big spritz of the hormone dopamine in the reward centers of baby's brain, sending a loud and clear signal to baby: *Remember what you just ate.* In just a few seconds, the baby learned something that will likely follow her for the rest of her life: "I like ice cream." Or from a survival brain perspective, "This easily digestible substance is packed with a high density and optimized ratio of fat and sugar. Eat as much as you can. And don't forget what it looks like."

The remembering aspect is key: memory is critical for learning—and planning.

The Prefrontal Cortex Is for Planning

Sometime in the last million years, humans evolved a new layer on top of our primitive survival brain, called the prefrontal cortex (PFC). I call this our *planning brain*. From an anatomical perspective, this "newer" brain region is located just behind our eyes and forehead. The newer part of the brain helps us survive in a different way. Involved in creativity and planning, the PFC is less focused on the here and now and more focused on predicting what will happen in the future based on past experience.

The planning brain uses the memories our survival brain logged to make predictions. This is called predictive processing. Predicting the future can help us survive by simulating what might happen before we try it out in real life. When, for example, we are making a choice whether to go to this or that part of the savanna to find food, our planning brain simulates what might happen based on what has happened in the past. If we went to a certain spot—say, a tree by the river—and found berries and no tigers, and then continued on to another spot—say, a big boulder on a hill, where we saw a bunch of tigers but no food—the next morning when we wake up and are hungry, our brains could draw on those past experiences to simulate going to both spots and make a pretty simple choice: the tree by the river is the place to go because that is where I found berries and no tigers yesterday.

Having a planning brain that predicts everything from what a cat should look and act like to how a piece of cake should taste saves us a lot of time and energy. But it can also lead us astray, as we will soon find out. First, let's see how Jack's eating became automatic.

POSITIVE REINFORCEMENT: HOW WE LEARN TO REMEMBER WHERE TO FIND FOOD

Through millions of years of evolution, we humans have kept the most basic survival mechanisms—eat and not be eaten—because they work really well. When it comes to dictating our behaviors, nothing has improved on what neuroscientist and Nobel laureate Eric Kandel (and others) dubbed *reinforcement learning*.

Reinforcement learning has two related components: positive and negative reinforcement. In terms of food, positive reinforcement can be summed up as learning to find food sources so that we can remember where they are in the future and can go back and eat some more. When our ancient ancestors were foraging for food and found a good source, their stomach would send a dopamine signal to their brains saying, "Hey, this is good stuff. Don't forget this spot. Come back tomorrow when you are hungry again." This type of learning is so important that we have multiple places in our bodies that send these signals to our brains so that we don't miss the message.

It takes only three elements for us to learn through positive reinforcement: a trigger/cue, a behavior, and a result/reward. Remember the baby who tasted ice cream for the first time? When the baby eats the ice cream, the brain takes note of the reward: *This is gooood.* With positive reinforcement, we learn to repeat behaviors that help us survive. Often these are described as *approach behaviors* because we learn to approach the good stuff. Trigger: See ice cream. Behavior: Eat ice cream. Result: Yum! Repeat.

Now put yourself in Jack's shoes or, better yet, his survival brain. His brain learned that Corn Nuts were packed with calories—that bliss point of easily digested carbs, fat, and salt. He developed the habit of see Corn Nuts, eat Corn Nuts. Automatic snacking as a habit.

NEGATIVE REINFORCEMENT: HOW WE LEARN TO AVOID BEING EATEN

Our ancestors may have spent most of their days finding food and remembering where to find food, but they also had another major preoccupation: not becoming food themselves. They learned this through the process of negative reinforcement. Negative reinforcement largely works the same way as positive reinforcement. It has the trigger/behavior/result sequence. But instead of learning to promote behavior that is rewarding (pleasant experience), we learn to prevent situations that feel punishing (unpleasant experience). When our ancestors headed out to explore a new part of the savanna or forest, they didn't know if predators were also exploring the same area, so they had to be extra vigilant, always on the lookout for danger. If they heard a rustling in the bushes and saw a tiger, they learned to run (behavior) the next time they heard rustling (trigger) so that they didn't get eaten (certainly an unpleasant "punishment").

I'm going to geek out for a moment. We might learn to avoid anti-survival behaviors even more quickly than we learn to favor the pro-survival approach behaviors. When it comes to eating something new, if it tastes rotten or very bitter—a sign of danger or poison—we might spit it out before we are even consciously aware of what we are doing. Unlike how we respond to chocolate or a fine wine, we don't have time to savor the notes of something that could kill us. "Hmm, was that an oaky finish?" Or "Wow, cyanide *does* taste like almonds!" would be more of a last thought than a tasting note. We don't taste all of the nuanced flavors of poison because we are busy getting it out of our mouths. With foods that aren't going to kill us, we have time to linger. In other words, when it comes to eating, learning through negative reinforcement might happen more quickly than positive reinforcement. Think of the last time you tasted something disgusting. If it was really bad, you might have done the same thing: spat it out before you were even consciously aware that you had (give yourself a break; you have no control over the behavior, this is your brain helping you survive). In short, we register yuck (disgust) much more quickly than yum (pleasant).

Let's go back to Jack. Corn Nuts were his automatic eating habit. Did negative reinforcement drive his stress, anxiety, and other eating habits as well?

How Negative Reinforcement Taught Us to Eat Our Feelings

If you've ever heard the phrase *eat your feelings,* you might be surprised to learn that our body's initial impulse when we feel fear or stress is to *stop* eating. As a way to keep ourselves as light and nimble as possible, we humans evolved in such a way that we don't actually have enough blood to service all of our organs at the same time. Like an airplane that takes in only enough fuel to get to its destination (plus a little more for emergencies), the average human body has only 10 pints or roughly 5 liters of blood—that's about 8 percent of our weight. The rest is mostly water (some 60 percent), muscle, fat, and bone.

Unlike an airplane, which uses fuel only for one main purpose—to keep the engines running—our bodies use blood for everything from helping our stomachs digest food to delivering oxygen to our muscles. We've evolved an exquisite system so that our organs can communicate with one another and act according to our needs. When one organ system is in short supply of blood, it sends out signals so that other systems can shunt blood in the right direction. For example, if we are hungry, our stomach calls out to our muscles to send blood its way so it can digest the food it is about to receive. Our muscles are happy to take a break in situations like this. Their version of a BACK IN 15 MINUTES sign on the shop door is to make their blood vessels smaller, so that blood is redirected to our gastrointestinal tract.

Your body will keep happily directing its blood supply to your digestive system when it's hungry—unless another system sends out the emergency alert and calls for some of the blood to be directed its way.

Let's say that you are at work or school or even at home. It's lunchtime and you're hungry, so you take out your sandwich and sit down to eat. Blood to gut, no problem. Suddenly you start to smell smoke and the fire alarms go off—and your brain takes note. What happens? You have an *Oh, sh*t, something's wrong* moment. When your muscles put out that SOS signal, your brain and stomach immediately agree: "Lunch is over!" Your stomach closes down its blood vessels and sends all the blood it can to your muscles. This helps you jump up and run.

The feeling that lunch is over or at least postponed indefinitely until you get to safety has a technical term: *anorexia.* If you look up *anorexia* in the dictionary, it is defined as "a lack or loss of appetite for food." Add the term *nervosa* after it—*anorexia nervosa*—and you get "an emotional disorder characterized by an obsessive desire to lose weight." I bring this up to highlight how our bodies are set up to deal with stress by naturally shutting down hunger signals. This is an important piece of the puzzle.

The problem is that our brains don't know the difference between a genuine threat to our survival, like a car coming right at us in the wrong lane, and a cultural pressure, like our boss yelling at us. When it encounters a stressor, the brain reads "danger" and needs a way to deal with it. Our brain lumps fear and pain into that general category of unpleasantness. Fear is unpleasant. Pain is unpleasant. *Emotional* pain is unpleasant.

Esther, one of the people in our Eat Right Now program, shared her experience with how stress killed her appetite. Typically she struggled with binge eating when she was stressed, but this day was different: "I had a super stressful day today. I ate two eggs and some pumpkin seeds for breakfast and another two eggs for lunch. I couldn't eat the rest of the day because of the tremendous amount of adrenaline pumping through my body in response to the intense stress. I find this very interesting. I think that in the past I might have binged because of the stress, and today I couldn't bring myself to eat." She was surprised that her normal adaptive response of a loss of appetite had popped up out of the blue. It must have been strong enough in this situation to have outcompeted her learned behavior of stress eating that had been dominating her life.

Michelle had a similar response to going to the doctor. "Today I went to the doctor for a physical. I absolutely HATE going to the doctor . . . I was so anxious all morning about the visit—couldn't eat my breakfast or drink my tea (caffeine was def not going to help anything—I would have rocketed straight to the moon) or meditate or do any of the good things I normally do to start my morning. I even had to change the shirt I was wearing before I left the house because I had sweated through it!"

As you can see, our modern stressors can shut down our appetites as fast as any saber-toothed tiger. All of this happens rapidly and doesn't require learning. It is a hardwired adaptive survival mechanism that our body has in place to help us address clear and present danger. And when we're not under threat, from an evolutionary perspective, hunger is a scream and fullness is a whisper. That is to say, when food sources aren't guaranteed from day to day or even week to week, it is better to load up on calories in anticipation of not eating for a while.

In a cruel twist, what has happened over time in the absence of immediate threat and the presence of ready access to high-calorie foods is that instead of avoiding pain by channeling our blood supply to our legs and lungs so we can outrun the tiger, we learn to numb emotional pain with some pleasure or distraction. With emotional pain, we aren't physically in danger, but it sure hurts a lot. Because we're not in danger, we don't need to run, but our brain tells us to run away from the pain; it tells us to do something to make it stop. This is where negative reinforcement comes in and crosses the food wires with the mood ones in our brains.

Emotional pain can feel really painful, but it isn't the same as bleeding from a large artery: we aren't in an immediately life-threatening situation like being in front of a hungry tiger or a fast-approaching bus, so our brain knows we don't have to run, but it wants to do SOMETHING. So when we are stuck in a negative emotion, our brain says, "I know how to help make this painful feeling go away so that you'll feel better." If we were more rational beings, our thinking and planning part of the brain, the prefrontal cortex (the various parts of our brain don't really work in isolation, but for illustrative purposes, go with me on this) might say, "Hey, let's do some research and figure out the best way to handle your emotional needs. How about some psychotherapy to help you understand where your feelings are coming from? Or some cognitive behavioral therapy to help you develop some coping strategies? Or maybe some existential therapy to help you see your position in the world and what it means to be alive?"

Unfortunately, since our prefrontal cortex is the youngest and weakest part of the brain, when strong emotions arise, it goes offline. This leaves the older—not necessarily wiser—survival brain networks to do the heavy lifting.

When we're sad or mad, our survival brain starts searching for something that will perk us up or distract us from our anger. Unfortunately, one of the few tricks it has up its sleeve is an exquisite taste for food to entertain us, distract us from our woes, make us feel better right now.

Remembering that ice cream tastes good, our survival brain tells us to ignore the fact that we're not hungry and to go ahead and have a scoop. We quickly learn that the pleasantness of eating this sweet treat feels better than wallowing in our emotions. Our brain makes a note of this and stores it away for later. This is one of the important ways that our brains start to connect food with feelings. If you feel bad, your brain can step in and remind you that eating feels good, or at least blanks out the bad feelings—temporarily.

Anytime you choose to eat something to comfort your feelings, your survival brain and your planning brain get their wires crossed. You might have planned to eat healthily or cut down on your snacking, but instead, you've been seduced by the comforting power of habit. That well-intentioned "I'm going to lay off the snacks" leads you to be constantly thinking about food.

Here's another way to think about it: When you get stressed, your survival brain grabs the steering wheel from the PFC, which has only recently gotten its learner's permit, aiming to steer you to safety until the danger has passed. Once you're safely at the side of the road, you pull out some cupcakes to soothe yourself. The more you do this, the more it becomes a habit.

We have a hardwired tendency to turn away or distract ourselves from unpleasant emotions because we'd like to avoid the pain they cause. When there is stress flooding the brain, distraction makes us feel better in the moment, but this has the unintended consequence of keeping us from working on whatever caused it.

Shortly, you'll learn how to tap into the power of your brain to change this. You can rewire your brain to break out of food jail or wake up and stop mindlessly snacking. You can learn to hear and listen to those quiet but present fullness signals that your body is sending. But first, let's look at how the food/mood habit got so much power in the first place.

Rob first came to see me when he was about forty years old and 180 pounds overweight. He was referred to my clinic because of the severe panic attacks that he would get while he was driving. I wrote about his story in my book *Unwinding Anxiety* under the pseudonym Dave because at the time he was concerned that if he used his real name, it might affect his employability. I'm happy to say that Rob has done so well with working with his anxiety that he now coaches others who have severe anxiety, and he always *leads* with his story.

At the time, Rob had a pretty clear-cut case of anxiety. From the moment he walked into my office, he *looked* anxious. (This was BC—before COVID-19—so we actually got to meet in person.) His shoulders were up by his ears, his hands were always clenched into fists, and his breath came in short panting bursts. Rob's coping mechanism was eating fast food as a way to numb himself from his anxiety. He had reinforced this habit for decades.

Rob was in fifth grade when his anxiety got so bad that he started having panic attacks. "No one really knew what was wrong with me. I would just go to school and have anxiety and panic all day, and then I would just come home and just binge and just numb myself out. That was my way of trying to fix it."

Like so many others, he told me how he would use dieting and exercising when he was a kid and also later in life as a way to repair things. "I would start losing weight and I would work out, and I would just get all the weight off [30 to 40 pounds], and then something would happen in my life that would trigger that whole cycle again. Usually it was anxiety and panic." He described "dipping out" of his life for long periods of time, learning to eat not only to numb anxiety and panic but also to avoid "loneliness and everything else."

Many of my patients have turned to drugs as a way to escape from themselves. Rob turned to fast food. His behavior mirrored that of his friends (and my patients) who battled with drug or alcohol addiction. He would secretly eat fast food in his car and throw out all the garbage to hide his behavior from his family and friends, telling himself, "I'm going to start [eating better] tomorrow. I'm going to start tomorrow." And like many people with addictions that they call their "habit," Rob's habit was eating at him, pun intended. His health was suffering—he had blood pressure, sleep, and liver problems that were caused by his extra weight—and he saw no way out.

FORMING HABITS FAST

Imagine waking up in the morning, stumbling out of bed, and then not being able to stand up because that "how to walk" memory sequence in your brain has been erased. Now think of all the neat tricks that your brain has automated for you over the course of your life and add them up. You might start with your morning routine: putting on clothes, brushing your teeth, taking a shower, making coffee, making breakfast, eating breakfast (no bibs needed because you remember how to get the spoon in your mouth on the first try!). This list can easily get into the hundreds and even thousands of actions if you think of all the things that you don't have to think about doing anymore. Why? Because they're habits. And that's a good thing.

Basically, our brain figured out how to automate activities that follow the same sequence so that we can conserve our energy to learn new things. Neat trick. This process is so streamlined that if I try to consciously tie my shoes, I can't do it. By trying to walk myself through the process, I trip myself up. How about you? If you tried to explain to me how to tie my shoe, how easy would it be to do?

Our brains are so quick at learning habits that some behaviors can be set in a single trial—one and done. Do it once, and because it was so rewarding—like babies eating ice cream—it is now a habit. Most of the time, this is fine, but in the case of food, it can lead to trouble.

Here's a simple definition of *habit* that you can set in your brain as you go through this book: "a settled or regular tendency or practice, especially one that is hard to give up." You settle into a morning routine or the habit of tying your shoes once you've done it a few times. At that point you don't have to remember how to do it, because you can do it asleep, or at least half-asleep. Set and forget.

Habits are related to but different from skills that we learn. Skills are a bit more complex than the few steps that never change when we tie our shoes. Once we learn a skill—like riding a bicycle or playing a musical instrument—we can pick up where we've left off and keep improving it over time until we have some level of mastery. We can also lose a skill if we haven't practiced or performed the behavior in a while.

Our brain also does a lot of predictive processing to save energy on a moment-by-moment basis. Our brain extrapolates from past experience that a behavior will yield similar results in the future. If it was good in the past, it will likely be good in the future. This is where the habit formation of set and forget comes in: set the habit, forget about the details, and save your energy to learn new things. It turns out that this process is also critical for everything from making a decision at the grocery store to eating our feelings to breaking out of food/mood and other habitual eating cycles.

As Jack found out with Corn Nuts and other automatic eating, and you yourself know from your own experience, forming habits isn't always beneficial. While I'd say some 95 percent of habits are helpful (not having to relearn how to make coffee every morning), the other 5 percent can be problematic. If you develop a habit like smoking cigarettes, mindlessly snacking, or overeating, it can lead to all sorts of health problems such as cancer or diabetes.

But even less serious habits can have significant consequences. Being overly rigid or locked in to a habit moves us in the opposite direction of survival. If you have ever left work with the firm intention of stopping by the grocery store only to wake up from autopilot when you get home and curse yourself for forgetting, you know that habits can be mildly annoying. If you get stuck in a seemingly endless procrastination habit loop triggered by stress or anxiety, it can not only make you even more anxious, but it can affect your school or work performance, which can then have significant downstream effects such as jeopardizing your grade point average or employment.

So how does our brain learn what habits to set up in the first place?

The Orbitofrontal Cortex: The Decider

One very important part of the PFC is the orbitofrontal cortex, or the OFC for short. The OFC is constantly comparing everything that we do to determine whether it helps or hinders our survival. Whenever we try something new—whether it's trying a new flavor of ice cream, listening to a new song, or engaging in any new behavior—the OFC compares that new flavor (or behavior) to whatever past flavor (or behavior) was most similar. It makes a call on which one is better and then inserts the new flavor (or behavior) into an ever-expanding reward hierarchy it can reference the next time it has to make a decision. Think of the OFC as the decider. It decides what we do, but not in some random, whimsical, or peremptory way. It has a plan. And that plan is based on how behaviors feel when we do them.

Reward Hierarchies

One of the OFC's chief responsibilities is to set up reward hierarchies to determine how rewarding a behavior is. Thanks to our caveperson ancestors, the OFC has only one rule: if A is more rewarding than B in terms of survival, when given a choice, pick A. Every time we face a choice between two behaviors, the OFC is right there determining what might be best for us—at least right now.

Let's go back to the baby's eating a food for the first time to see how establishing a reward hierarchy works. Let's say that baby had never tasted ice cream *or* broccoli before. We already know what happens after she takes a bite of ice cream. Now imagine her parents doing the same experiment but with broccoli. She might take a bite and enjoy it, or it may end up spewed down her bib as she gives you a "why are you torturing me?" scrunched-up face. If baby is presented with both options at the same time, ice cream wins. Every. Time.

What's going on in our brains in these broccoli vs. ice cream moments? The OFC is comparing the calorie content of ice cream and broccoli. Calories = survival. Choose the one that packs in the most calories. The problem is that this decision hasn't taken into account that the world has changed. Those caves didn't have refrigerators or fast-food restaurants. Food is now (for most people) readily available, so high caloric density isn't the sole factor to consider when it comes to survival. Shoulding is a function of our rational but very young PFC. Our PFCs tell us that we should eat broccoli. Our older survival brains say, "I want ice cream."

So one of the major functions of the OFC is to make comparisons. But this goes way beyond the food itself.

The OFC sits at a crossroad in the brain where sensory, emotional, and behavioral information gets integrated. It has to sort and categorize a lot of information. Instead of trying to make a huge list of every little thing, the OFC takes what we do and how that feels in a particular context and determines a composite reward value of a behavior. This process is called *chunking*.

Think back to all of the birthday parties you went to as a kid. Your brain combines all of the sensory and emotional information it took in—the taste of the cake, the games you played, the laughter, the eye-catching decorations, the giddiness at being allowed to sing at the top of your lungs—into a single composite reward value. Birthday cake = fun! This is your brain being efficient.

So it's not only calories that count when we are deciding what to eat. Our OFC is also taking in contextual information—when we ate, whom we were with, what our mood was at the time, why we were eating (e.g., celebration or consolation)—and adds all these variables together to come up with a final answer. It literally has a formula.

Reward Values: The Rescorla-Wagner Model

Back in the 1970s, two scientists, Robert Rescorla and Allan Wagner, were very interested in how animals learn. They came up with a mathematical equation that aligned with reinforcement learning pretty darn well, but with a twist. Their model took into account our brain's ability to compare reality with expectations. The Rescorla-Wagner model is beautiful in its simplicity and delicious in its execution. It also holds that the only way to change a behavior is to change where it stands in the reward hierarchy. And this has nothing to do with willpower.

Let's start with how the OFC sets up reward hierarchies. Our brain calculates what it expects the reward value of a behavior to be in the present moment based on how rewarding it was in the past. But it builds in some wiggle room to update that reward value—and thus where it stands in the reward hierarchy relative to other behaviors—in case things have changed since the last time we did the behavior.

Here's an example. Having been to a bunch of birthday parties as a kid, I've laid down a certain reward value of chocolate cake in my mind. It has high standing in my reward hierarchy. Then a new bakery opens up in my neighborhood, and I see chocolate cake in the window on my way to work. My stomach says, "Hey, that looks good!" I go in and get a piece, assuming that it will meet my expectations. If I take a bite and my head explodes with joy—it is the most delicious cake I've ever eaten—that's my OFC telling me that I've hit the jackpot. I learn that this is a bakery that I should frequent because it has darn good cake.

How did I learn that? My OFC had a reward value benchmark in mind. And the cake could either meet, exceed, or fail to meet my OFC's expectations. If the cake simply met my expectations, my world would go on largely unchanged. I would add it to my list of places where I could get chocolate cake if I wanted some, but I wouldn't go out of my way to get it. But because the baker crushed the competition, my brain got what is called a positive prediction error. The cake was better (more positive) than predicted. A little dopamine spritz here and there in my brain's reward centers, and now I've learned that if I want cake, I should come back to this bakery. My brain now prefers this to other bakeries. It isn't a conscious thing. My brain has learned to associate this bakery with cake. So the next time I walk by, seeing cake in the window or remembering the last time I ate cake from here triggers an urge to go in and get more.

What happens in my brain if I ate the cake, and instead of its registering as heaven in my mouth, it sucked? If better than expected produced a positive prediction error, then worse than expected would produce a negative prediction error. And if I got food poisoning from eating there, my brain would tell me to avoid that bakery like the plague.

This is one of the, if not the most, important ways in which your brain works when it comes to learning how to set habits—not just food, any habit.

Let's bring positive and negative prediction errors together with how we form habits. The sequence is important.

First, we learn a behavior through positive or negative reinforcement. Taking the birthday example, we learn that cake tastes good and associate it with good feelings. Next, our OFC catalogues where it stands relative to other behaviors, and it gets inserted into our brain's reward hierarchy. We learn to prefer cake over broccoli. We repeat it a few times, which locks in the reward value and sets it up as a habit so we don't have to pay attention to the details. Now we automatically pick eating cake over less rewarding behaviors. Cake beats broccoli. Cake beats boredom. Cake beats feeling bad. In this last instance, cake doesn't even need to taste that good. It just has to taste better than bad feels. And when we're really on autopilot, we eat simply because it is there: see cake, eat cake.

We go through life stuck in these habit patterns until something shakes us out of autopilot. Again, the only way to change a behavior is to change its position in the reward hierarchy. This is where positive and negative prediction errors come in. If something is better than expected, we find ourselves seeking it out and doing it more. If the behavior is worse than expected, we won't do it as much. This can happen somewhat randomly, such as when we get food poisoning and can no longer stomach cake (at least for a while). Or this can happen on purpose. On purpose has nothing to do with reasoning or willpower. *Should* is not part of the equation. On purpose is based on one simple and critical ingredient: awareness. We'll get into how awareness helped Jacqui, Jack, Rob, and others as we go through the book.

For now, there is one other thing you need to know about your brain.

EXPLORE VS. EXPLOIT

Before you can decide if and when to eat a food, you have to locate some first. This was pretty much a full-time gig for our hunting and gathering predecessors. Think of food choices from their standpoint. They didn't have refrigerators or food delivery services, so they had to constantly search for good sources of food. They might follow a migrating herd of animals, hunting their dinners as they went. Or when they found a place with lots of berries, they might decide to camp out there for a while until they had consumed all of the good eats. And then they'd move on, looking for more to gather. In neuroscience circles, this is called the explore vs. exploit trade-off.

Our ancestors needed to be able to switch effectively between exploring new territory to find new sources of high-quality food and stopping long enough to eat some before moving on. If they moved on too quickly, they missed the opportunity to get food that was right in front of them, yet if they didn't leave when the food source was used up, they risked starving or losing the opportunity to find an even better spot where there was more or better food. Balancing this trade-off was essential for survival.

Today, our brains *still* engage in the explore vs. exploit trade-off. Think of the last time you went to your favorite restaurant. Did you order the same thing as before, or did you try something new? Sticking with your favorite menu item ensures that you have a good meal. But how do you know that it is really your favorite if you haven't tried everything on the menu? Maybe you are missing something even better.

In a world that is constantly changing, we have to be able to adapt to new circumstances. This helps us with the trade-off between sticking with our favorite restaurants and trying the new one that just opened down the street. This fits right in with how the OFC works. Remember, our brains are trying to figure out and go with the best survival behavior possible. The OFC decides whether to explore new territory or stick with a good thing.

When we exploit a resource, we maximize our rewards right now. We see a good thing. We eat a good thing. We learn that this is a good thing to eat right now and a good place to find it. Information that we get when we explore can also be used later to maximize rewards in the long term. In an uncertain and ever-changing environment, where these reward values are unknown and changing over time, we have to be flexible, alternating between exploitation and exploration. Flexibility is key. Too much exploration leads to the problem of always looking for something better and never being satisfied with what is right in front of us, whereas too much exploitation gets us stuck in habits.

Dopamine, that neurotransmitter that seems to show up everywhere from learning how to survive to getting stuck in habits and addictions, plays a major role in the explore/exploit trade-off. Just as driving to a new city to try a new restaurant uses up gas in our car, exploring new territory requires energy. That's why starting a new job can be so exhausting the first couple of weeks: we're constantly exploring and learning how things work. Conversely, when we stay put, we don't need to fill the gas tank. Similar to how we learn with positive reinforcement, we get short bursts of dopamine in parts of our brain when we are exploring and learning new things. This is technically called phasic firing. When we are exploring our new workplace and find the printer or bathroom, we receive dopamine signals and remember where they are. Instead of firing in a phasic manner, dopamine fires more regularly—*tonic tone* is the term—in places like the prefrontal cortex as a way to toggle our actions between explore and exploit. Increased tonic dopamine firing is thought to promote exploration, while the opposite moves us toward staying put and exploiting. This is how a single neurotransmitter can serve several different functions based on where and how it fires in the brain.

One thing that affects our willingness to explore new territory as opposed to sticking where we are is the amount of information available to us. Continuing with the restaurant metaphor, if we've got a favorite and a new one opens up down the street, we can either go to the new one and randomly try a new dish or simply wait for others to tell us how good the restaurant is. Neuroscientific theories suggest that there are two distinct explore strategies for resolving the "Should I try the new restaurant?" dilemma. One is called directed exploration, and the other is called random exploration. Both have their advantages.

Think of it this way. You're walking down the street and come across a new restaurant that just opened. You could take the directed exploration route. In this case, you go home and wait for online reviews to show up (hoping that they are trustworthy).

The benefit of directed exploration is that with more information, we are more likely to get an optimal result. Yet this can take time and energy, and the result depends on the quality of the information (e.g., reviews from a professional food critic as opposed to Yelp reviews from random strangers). More information isn't always better. Just ask the internet.

Or you could just walk in the door and try it out. Walking in and trying something for yourself is more of the random exploration route. Random exploration takes less time and energy but is less likely to guarantee a good outcome.

Our brains try to help us survive by exploring our options until we find good ones and then sticking with them until they are gone. We develop a shorthand for toggling that trade-off (stay or go), but it works only if we keep paying attention and making sure that whatever strategy we're employing is working as well as it did in the past. Consider a farmer with vast tracts of land that are yielding good harvests year after year, so she keeps doing what she's been doing: failing to notice when the nutrients in the soil are used up, indicating that she should let that land go fallow for a few years while exploring options for planting elsewhere. In our modern-day minds, this mindset can play out in a number of ways. Eating an extra piece of our favorite pizza or consoling ourselves with ice cream when we had a fight with our best friend may not have had any negative consequences when we were kids, but using these strategies constantly in adult life might make us feel like we're a bit stuck.

Let's connect the dots between how our brains work and how these theories play out in real life. Through positive reinforcement, Jack learned early in life that Corn Nuts tasted good. He now is in the habit of eating them automatically. Jacqui and Rob (and to a lesser degree, Jack) learned to eat as coping strategies for depression and anxiety through negative reinforcement. Though Tracy had the first-world eating problem of pounding carrots when stressed, her story also pointed out how even substituting something healthy as a snack or treat just makes the hungry ghost hungrier. Jacqui's and Rob's stories highlight how our OFCs set up preferences for bliss-point foods over healthy foods. Their stories also show how numbing our feelings or stuffing them down with food can set these behaviors higher on the reward hierarchy than being with uncomfortable emotions. And once our brains find strategies that seem to work—especially if we can't find a better offer—we lock those in through our exploit mode, setting them up as habits that feel almost impossible to change. That's one thing that Jack, Jacqui, and Rob all shared: they'd tried shoulding and willing themselves to change, and all failed (multiple times). They didn't know how their brains worked. Critically, they didn't know that the solution was right in front of and behind their eyes at the same time. They needed to learn how to use awareness to tap into the power of their OFC. But first they (and we) needed to see why willpower was failing them in the first place.

CHAPTER 3

Why Diets (and Measuring) Don't Work

The answer to our problem seems simple. We should just go back to eating when, what, and how we did before our planning brains and our emotions and the food industrial complex flummoxed our survival instincts. To paraphrase the author and journalist Michael Pollan, we shouldn't eat anything our great-grandmothers would not have recognized as food—and not too much of it.

This seems pretty straightforward. Follow these tips, and you'll live a healthy life without tipping the scale literally or proverbially. These rules help us meet our nutrient needs while at the same time keeping our brains from being tricked into eating more than we need. But following these rules is ultimately not that straightforward, especially when our emotions get involved.

Eat this and not that is not that simple. We've seen how our brains get it wrong when it comes to responding to our emotions and how companies can engineer products to hack and even bypass our survival signals. Interestingly, the weight-loss industry can be traced back over a hundred years to fad diets. Some historic notables included the lemonade diet (1941), where six times a day for ten days you drank only a concoction of lemon juice, maple syrup, water, and cayenne pepper in order to detox from junk food, drugs, and alcohol. Or there was the cabbage soup diet from the 1950s, which consisted of consuming nothing but soup for seven days. Perhaps the most iconic company in the transformation of dieting into a full-blown industry is Weight Watchers (now called WW International).

Weight Watchers was founded in 1963 by Jean Nidetch, a housewife and mother living in Queens, New York. If you remember the trivia I mentioned earlier, that happens to be the same year that Lay's came up with their "betcha can't eat just one" slogan. A few years earlier, Jean, weighing 214 pounds, had entered a ten-week weight-loss program run by the New York City Board of Health. With the help of a strict diet, she lost 20 pounds, but stalled out there. She enlisted friends and started a support group. Voilà, Weight Watchers was born. Over the next half century, the industry has largely stuck to the same "calories in, calories out" formula: eat less, exercise more. Weight Watchers groups are famous for their weekly weigh-ins as a way to help hold people accountable. A number of my patients who have been in the program have described this as "humiliating" and "fat-shaming." Diets can also create and later trigger eating disorders for at-risk individuals.

While the diet industry is built on good intentions, its focus on willpower to lose weight has one fatal flaw: that's not how our brains work. In this chapter, we'll look at why it's so hard for us to follow traditional (or not-so-traditional) diets designed to keep us healthy.

THE WILLPOWER MYTH

There is a famous skit I love from the 1970s television comedy *The Bob Newhart Show*. The scene opens with a woman walking into the office of psychologist Robert "Bob" Hartley. (Bob Newhart plays the therapist.) She asks for help with her fear of being buried alive in a box. Bob agrees to help her. They go back and forth about how long it will take for her to be cured (five minutes), how much he charges (five dollars), and how if she doesn't need the full time, he keeps the full fee because he doesn't make change. She asks if she should take notes. He reassures her that the treatment is pretty simple—most people can remember it.

Then he leans over his desk toward her. "Stop it!" he yells.

"Sorry?" she says, clearly confused.

"Stop IT!" he yells again, a little more drawn out this time.

"Stop it?" she asks, trying to understand. She can't believe that this is all she needs. Ironically, the skit runs for just over five minutes. It is worth every penny that you didn't have to pay to watch it on YouTube.

Newhart's skit still rings true today. We think we are in control of our behaviors—mental and physical—and simply need to get control over ourselves to be better at following through with the plan. We think that if we can just build up our mental strength, we'll be able to resist the pull of whatever temptation is calling to us. But our brains know otherwise. Willpower is more myth than muscle.

You already know this, likely from your own experience. Think back to all the times when your willpower failed. I cringe when I think of all the times that I lost my temper when on a call with a customer support person for one thing or another. Every time I get impatient, raise my voice, or lose control, I feel terrible afterward. It's not their fault. In fact, they (generally) are trying to help as best they can. (I apologize to all you customer support people out there. I'm going to try harder next time. I think I just need a little more willpower.)

Each of us has a guilty pleasure—an excess, a vice—or even a pesky habit that we think we can control on our best days and spend time beating ourselves up over on our not-so-best days when we fail. We try to deny ourselves, but odds are, we won't succeed.

THE ABSTINENCE VIOLATION EFFECT (AKA THE F*CK-ITS)

What happens when we can't have something? Of course we want it even more. Just like Jacqui and Rob, if you force yourself not to have ice cream, cupcakes, or chocolate, like a lost lover, the forbidden treat gets stuck in your head. You see it everywhere. You dream about it. And like the famous "don't think about the white bear" experiment in psychology, the more you try to force yourself not to think about it, the more it sticks in your head. What you resist persists. As we'll explore more in depth later in the book in the craving monster chapter, this resistance and persistence loop takes a huge amount of time and energy. The floodwaters keep building up until the dam eventually bursts. In addiction psychiatry, that dam burst is so common that it has been named the abstinence violation effect (AVE). The AVE was first described in the 1980s by two addiction researchers, Alan Marlatt and Judith Gordon at the University of Washington.

In their studies on alcoholism, Marlatt and Gordon saw a pattern: When someone who has been sober for a while trips up, they don't just get back up and keep on walking, they fall down a well. They don't just have a sip of alcohol, they get drunk and return full-on to their drinking habit. If someone relapses to cocaine, they don't just do a bump at a party, they go on a bender and quickly slip into their old ways. Smoke a cigarette a couple of decades after quitting? Back to a pack a day in no time.

My patients have a concise definition of the abstinence violation effect. They call it the "f*ck-its." As in, *I screwed up, I've lost control. I might as well keep on going. F*ck it.*

Jacqui put it perfectly: "I would obsess about food all the time. And then if I had a sh*t day, binge thoughts would start to build up and would take up so much space and energy. When you're in that all-or-nothing mentality, you're just going to go for it. When I broke a food rule, I would just say f*ck it, and basically go into the all-you-can-eat buffet mode and eat all the things I had denied myself. Let's just say I wouldn't binge on broccoli."

Some of us think that mastering our desires is a matter of practice. *If only I can practice denying myself, I'll get better at denying myself.* But research is calling into question the notion that you can do the equivalent of mental push-ups to build that critical muscle of self-control. Studies have shown that only a lucky few are genetically endowed with willpower. Other studies have specifically shown that willpower is indeed more of a myth than a usable mental muscle. For example, studies that tested willpower as a real entity found that people who exerted more self-control were not actually more successful in accomplishing their goals. Ready for this? The more effort they put in, the more depleted and exhausted they felt. It turns out that buckling down, gritting your teeth, or forcing yourself to "just do it" might be counterproductive, at best helping out in the short term (or at least making you feel like you are doing something), but setting you up for failure in the long term when it really counts.

Let's take the example of a willpower-based caloric restriction diet—one that follows the "calories in, calories out" formula (we'll call it CICO for short). These significantly reduce the number of calories you eat in a given day by as much as 40 percent. According to CICO, this should result in rapid weight loss. However, when we restrict our caloric intake, we're fighting our survival nature, so our body goes into starvation mode, decreasing our metabolism to hold on to every calorie that it can. From an evolutionary perspective, when food was scarce, our ancient ancestors had to conserve energy. As the neuroscientist Sandra Aamodt put it in her book *Why Diets Make Us Fat* and summed up in her TED talk, "Over the course of human history, starvation has been a much bigger problem than overeating . . . Even after you've kept the weight off for as long as seven years, your brain keeps trying to make you gain it back. If that weight loss had been due to a long famine, that would be a sensible response. In our modern world of drive-thru burgers, it's not working out so well."

No wonder it feels so hard to be in control when trying to diet! No wonder countless people have felt like they failed—whether it was on Weight Watchers or another program—when they stepped on the scale each week in front of the group. The formula seemed sound. They knew the formula. They, not the formula, were the reason things weren't working. Or so they thought . . .

Before we move on, let's sum up what the research shows:

FOUR PROBLEMS RELATED TO WILLPOWER

1. What you can't have, you want more of. (Denial increases desire.)
2. What you resist persists. (Don't think of a white bear.)
3. Failure → backsliding. (The abstinence violation effect. F*ck it.)
4. Willpower is not even part of habit change strategies. (The OFC focuses on how rewarding or unrewarding a behavior is.)

If you've tried to follow the latest diet trend and failed, it's not your fault. This is not because you don't have enough willpower. It is your survival brain at its fittest: giving you short-term solutions that feel rewarding but don't solve problems in the long run.

But that's not the only problem with typical diets. Let's look at how our contemporary obsession with measuring undermines our ability to break food habit loops.

THE ILLUSION OF CONTROL

"I have a confession."

This was how my Valentine's Day dinner began this year.

My wife and I had just sat down to a wonderful meal that we had cooked together. We had skipped the crowds, the loud restaurants, the jockeying for reservations. Besides, we are a good team in the kitchen, so a night in is a good night for us. I love the ritual of chopping fresh vegetables and cooking up something tasty, and she as my sous-chef is way more than support. We get to spend time together, connecting about our day.

As I looked into my wife's eyes, I couldn't see anything deeply disturbing, pent up over the year waiting to be sprung on this special night. Nothing looked to be lurking like "I've been having an affair." Or "I want a divorce."

I raised my eyebrows, waiting.

"I've been tracking," she said matter-of-factly. Ah, so that was her big secret. For many years, Mahri had been tracking her food intake and exercise (MyFitnessPal was her most recent vice). Whether she used a food tracker or not, she stayed pretty much within a pretty narrow weight range. Everyone's weight fluctuates a certain amount throughout the day, and she was no exception to this rule.

Over the years, we had circled around food tracking, including how notoriously inaccurate these types of tracking apps are. Yet she couldn't stop doing it. She had deleted MyFitnessPal from her phone many times, only to reinstall and start using it again a few days later.

Feeling guilty that she kept tracking, she'd use the app in secret. This wasn't exactly cocaine or heroin, but it had continuously caused problems for her, including her looking to the app instead of listening to her body when it came to what or how much she should eat.

Having finally spilled the beans, admitting her guilty non-pleasure, my wife went on to say how she was just going to try it for a week to see how well things went. How well *what things* went? I inquired. This forced her to articulate what was simmering under the surface. She paused.

"It all comes down to one thing," she said slowly. "Control." Another pause. "The illusion of control."

Control. Of course. Measuring and tracking give us the feeling of being in control. Quantified results reduce ambiguity and uncertainty. Measuring can *feel* good. Until it doesn't . . . I'm sure you've seen, known, or even been that person who walks in circles before bedtime, trying to complete your step count for the day. My wife is a member of this circle-walking club. "Only two hundred steps left to go. Give me five minutes, and then I'll get in bed!"

Uncertainty Sucks

Our survival brains don't like uncertainty. The more uncertainty we encounter, the less we feel like we are in control of what is happening to us. Uncertainty, for our survival brains, spells potential danger. If we hear a rustling in the bushes and we are uncertain what is making that noise, it is helpful to (carefully) go see what that is. Our fight-or-flight mode kicks in until we gather the information that lets us know that we should fight or flee because it is a lion looking for lunch, or if our alert system can stand down because it was only a family member goofing around (thanks!). Think of it this way: information is food for our brain. Your stomach rumbles when it is empty, prompting you to eat. Your brain rumbles in a similar manner, urging you to seek out information until it has enough that it is satisfied.

The more uncertainty there is—especially when it comes to looking into the future—the more anxiety-making it can be. The further into the future we look, the more uncertainty stares us back in the face, daring us to try to guess what our lives are going to look like a month, a year, or ten years down the road. Uncertainty triggers us to search for ways to feel in control.

Planning can make our days, business trips, and vacations go much more smoothly. Overplanning as a way to feel in control can act as an avoidance mechanism, helping us avoid the inherent lack of control in any situation by keeping us busy in the same way that procrastination enables us to avoid feelings of anxiety. So planning can go hand in hand with tracking: they both can make us feel more in control of ourselves and our lives.

Whether we are overplanning or excessively tracking our food intake and steps, when the underlying issue that triggered these behaviors becomes unbearable, like a car engine that is overheating, often our brains simply shut down and go into survival mode. This is like our phones when their batteries are dangerously low—they shut down everything but the essentials. Essentials come in the form of habits, because they take minimal energy. Ironically, this is where our old eating habits spring back to life.

THE CERTAINTY CRAVING

When testing a new treatment that I've developed to see if it is effective, I measure the changes from before someone started (baseline) to sometime later (a specified end point). I can even compare it to another treatment to see how well it stacks up. We often call these "horse race" studies because we want to see which treatment "wins"—basically, which one is better than the other.

Let's do a little horse race of our own. Horse number one is certainty. Horse number two is uncertainty. I'll tell you what they're racing for in a moment.

If you ask me the question "Is measuring the amount of food you eat each day a good technique for eating healthfully?" and I respond, "I can't give you an exact answer. All I can say is, it depends."

On a 0 to 10 scale, how satisfying was that response?

0 = very unsatisfying—I want to rip this page out of the book.

10 = very satisfying—I completely understand how science works.

Now here's a second scenario. Same question: Is measuring the amount of food you eat each day a good technique for eating healthfully?

Answer: Yes, it will absolutely help you reach your goal.

From 0 to 10, how satisfying was that answer?

Now which one was more satisfying? "It depends" or "absolutely"?

"Absolutely," right? Right! Absolutely! This little experiment highlights an important feature of our brain: it is designed to crave certainty. Certainty says yes, we can predict the future, so you should steer in X or Y direction because you know how things will turn out if you do. Whether it is true or not, the promise of certainty gets our brains galloping. Suppose you've been offered the opportunity to sign up for one of two possible diets. The description of the first reads: "About 20 percent of people who have used this have lost weight and kept it off for six months," while the blurb for the second goes as follows: "Six weeks and you'll have a Hollywood body! Guaranteed!" Which would you be more likely to sign up for? Yes, certainty wins the race. Every. Time.

Our brains spend a lot of time and energy trying to reduce uncertainty. One way is to reassure ourselves by getting the same information over and over until we feel sure X will result in Y. How certain are you that the sun will rise in the east tomorrow? Pretty certain, right? Do you have to measure it? Nope. Why? You've already seen it for yourself. Over and over and over. You don't even think about it. You *know* it is going to happen. That feeling of certainty. How does it feel? It feels pretty good, doesn't it?

In science, we repeat experiments over and over until we are certain of a result. We talk about this in terms of signal-to-noise ratio. The more we see a signal emerge from the noise, the more likely we are to feel pretty good that we can predict what will happen the next time we repeat the experiment. If by some strange twist of physics the sun rose in the east only 66 percent of the time and someone asked us where it will rise tomorrow, we wouldn't feel solid about our answer, because we couldn't be certain. The less certain we are, the more we get an unpleasant urge or itch to measure something again. It's baked into our brain: ambivalence and certainty activate different brain networks.

Remember that rustling in the bushes? If we know with 100 percent certainty that it has the distinct sound signature of a lion—or alternatively, of our family member—we know exactly what we need to do. That good feeling of certainty says, "Hey, we've got enough information here, no need to waste time measuring again. You can save your time and energy for other things."

TRACKING OUR CHOICES

Feeling out of control of our external circumstances—our family, our work situation, the environment around us—can make us look for things that we have more control over. Feeling out of control of ourselves—our moods, feelings, thoughts—can lead to us to search for ways that we can control ourselves. We all have to eat, so eating and exercise can become a natural target for trying to gain control.

This is where food tracking can sneak in and solidify its (largely unjustified) reputation as our savior. Tracking and measuring what we eat offers a plethora of information that promises to alleviate that unpleasant feeling of uncertainty. How much uncertainty is there when you read a nutritional label on a box or can of food? Not much. You know exactly what the ingredients are in descending order of amount. You know how much and what type of fat there is. You know how much sugar there is—even how much of it is added, as opposed to naturally occurring in the ingredients. You get the idea. If you eat this food item, you can be pretty certain you know what you're eating.

Tracking food (calories in) or tracking our steps (calories out) can make us feel like we are in control. We are the ones deciding to buy the low-carb tortillas. We are the ones who are doing the walking. It's up to us to take that ten-thousandth step, not someone else. For many, the societal pressure on them to look a certain way or to weigh a certain amount starts them down the path of trying to control their eating. For others, the promise of being healthy is that reward. And for still others—though I wonder if there is some overlap—the feeling of not having control over one's life prompts a search for something stable, something reliable, something certain that they do have control over.[1]

---

1 I haven't done a formal survey with my clinic patients, but many of them who were at a very unhealthy weight have a history of sexual trauma. (The biggest study to date documenting this correlation is the adverse childhood experiences, or ACE, study.) Others describe how they had to fend off constant and often aggressive advances at school and work and in public. The uncertainty of not knowing when or how to deal

Certainty tells our brain it doesn't need to hunt for more information. Similar to the explore vs. exploit trade-off, it says, "Stop exploring, stop searching, you've got all that you need."

Again, I'm not going to go into all of the nuances of eating disorders in this book. There are many good books dedicated to anorexia nervosa and bulimia nervosa.[2] But I do want to point out how no matter where anyone is on an eating disorder spectrum, the feeling of control can be so rewarding that it can override their own basic physiology (e.g., hunger cues) to the point where it becomes hazardous for their health. Anorexia nervosa has been reported to have the highest mortality rate of any psychiatric disorder in young females. Even healthy eating can become so obsessive that it makes its way into disordered territory. We call this behavior orthorexia, from the Greek *orthos*, meaning "straight" or "right," and *orexis*, meaning "appetite." This concept has caught fire over the past few decades thanks to the internet, which dishes up a steady stream of nutritional advice.

MEASURING IS A CRUTCH (THAT PROMISES CONTROL)

How did our ancestors measure things? There were no scales or watches. The length of a day was measured by when the sun rose and set. The size of a haul of berries could be compared with the previous

---

with these situations had led them to eating as a coping mechanism, and inadvertently learning that gaining a lot of weight gave them some control over their situation. I vividly remember one patient describing how after several sexual assaults in college and during her early twenties, she got men to stop looking at her by gaining over 200 pounds. Overweight, overlooked. As a footnote to this footnote, trauma isn't a footnote: we'll get more into this later in the book.

2 Again, see https://www.nationaleatingdisorders.org.

day's. Hunger could be measured by how loud stomachs were rumbling.

Today we've taken it up a notch (or a hundred) with our measuring. We have atomic clocks that split seconds into 9.2 billion clicks of a cesium 133 atom (9,192,631,770, to be precise), while the world's most sensitive scale can measure the mass of a single protein molecule (the unit is called a zeptogram, weighing in at roughly a billion trillionth of a gram, 10^{-21} g).

In less than a decade, technological advances have provided wearable mobile sensors and smartphone applications that track what and how much we eat, how many steps we take and whether we take those steps walking or running, how long (and supposedly how well) we sleep, how low our blood sugar is, how high our blood pressure is, and how we're feeling. In 2017, an estimated 2 billion people worldwide used digital devices to track their health. That's about 25 percent of the world's population. Let that sink in. A quarter of the world was (and likely still is) using a digital device to track their health in some way. You might even say that as a society, we've become obsessed with measurement.

You can probably make a long list of things that you have done, do, or could do to measure and track your health, including calories, steps, weight, body composition, biological markers. Heck, on the low-tech side of things, reading labels on food packages helps track nutritional intake. More tracking = more data = more better.

I'm guessing that we all sense that tracking isn't the magic bullet for losing weight, stopping our automatic snacking, or otherwise changing our relationship to food. Why is that? There are several things you need to know about your brain that will help you here. Once you understand them, you might see some new ways to change your relationship to measuring and tracking not just food but your life.

Addicted to Measuring

Our brains will do all sorts of tricks for treats. One of them is called completion bias. Completion bias is when our brain seeks the satisfaction of completing a task. This is how that works. We look at our Fitbit and notice we've taken 9,954 steps today. We see that our fitness circle on our Apple Watch isn't closed. What does our brain do? It gets restless. Our dopamine starts firing, urging us into action. A craving for completion feels pretty similar to a craving for food. We get up and walk. We hit 10,000 steps. We close the ring. Our tracker gives us a congratulatory note. Our watch buzzes and a fireworks display goes off. Trigger: noticing that we're almost at our goal. Behavior: just do it! Reward: a dopamine treat (and not much else). Yum.

In fact, most of the time we don't know exactly when we're going to cross that 10,000-step finish line. The surprise element is a bonus for our brain: it adds more dopamine spritzing to make learning extra sticky when it comes to reinforcing unpredictable but positive behaviors. This is called intermittent reinforcement, because we are basically getting random rewards: we don't know when the fireworks will go off. That's why slot machines are set up the way they are: we don't know when we're going to win. That keeps us coming back for more and more and more.

But wait, isn't this the same process leading to how habits and even addictions form? Yes, these types of random rewards are the most addictive known in science.

The simple definition of addiction that I learned in residency is this: continued use despite adverse consequences. I've written about addiction in other books, so I will jump right to the point. We can get addicted to anything, including behaviors that start innocently enough as health promoting but when taken to an extreme, suck the life right out of us. As you'll see shortly, measuring fits right in here.

The Measuring Paradox

I begin Measuring Mindfulness, my semester-long class at Brown University, by having my students list all of the things they measure in a day. They list everything from how long it takes them to get ready in the morning to watching the speedometer on their car to see how fast they are going. Then I write this on the board: "When a measure becomes a target, it ceases to be a good measure."

This is commonly referred to as Goodhart's law. Charles Goodhart, a British economist, wrote in 1975 that "any observed statistical regularity will tend to collapse once pressure is placed upon it for control purposes." This has been simplified to what I wrote on the board.

Our tendency to become overly focused on measuring our food and exercise is a perfect example of Goodhart's law in action. We get myopically focused on a goal or a target—x number of calories or y number of steps. We substitute a target for a goal, and in the process, we get disconnected from ourselves. We don't listen to our bodies. We're so busy counting calories or steps, we ignore our body's reaction to taking all those steps. We start staring at numbers and get excited when we hit them. When we're really obsessed with tracking, we can even be pulled into eating packaged food simply because it is easier to track! When we count calories, it gives us the feeling of control.

In a *Guardian* article entitled "A Step Too Far? How Fitness Trackers Can Take Over Our Lives," James Tapper interviewed a gentleman who had become obsessed with tracking his step count. Following the popular idea that 10,000 steps is good for our physical health, Martin Lewis had taken things to a new level. He has averaged close to 25,000 steps a day over the past few years. As he put it, "if I do just 10,000 steps, I'm never happy . . . It's an obsession."

Dr. Josie Perry, a sports psychologist whom Tapper also interviewed for the article, talked about a study she had done with athletes who had been injured. She described one of her participants: "She went for her first run back and it was a beautiful morning, running by the river, and she loved every second. She got back, uploaded her time to [fitness network] Strava, and she could see that her brother had run a bit further, and a friend had run a bit faster. And she said she felt like a failure, all that joy wiped out."

Notice where the joy comes from: we create the itch and then feel good when we scratch it. This external reward system and illusion of control takes our focus away from our bodies. We ignore internal cues like hunger and fullness. We don't pay attention to what foods feel truly satisfying as opposed to those that make us ache for more. And we ignore the tiredness, pain, and other signs that we've overworked our bodies. Instead, we're focusing on that feeling of being in control.

Just like eating because we crave a food instead of being hungry, we ignore our internal signals that say, "You've been exercising every day for a month straight. Forget the streak! Let's take a day off." Craving the reward of goal completion, we trust the metrics and the numbers over our own experience and bodily wisdom. The more we focus on weight or calories or steps, the less connected we are with our bodies. The measure becomes the target, making us miss the goal.

And that's only the body side of the equation. As Martin Lewis or anyone who can't not step on their scale each morning points out, tracking and meeting goals can quickly become an obsession. On top of this, measuring anything about ourselves gives our minds the material by which to judge ourselves. Rarely do we tell ourselves: "Good job, you've met your goal!" Much more commonly—especially when social media reminds us of how well everyone else is doing—we blame and shame ourselves for not being better. Tempted by the tasty treat of having control, we get stuck in cycles that give us the f*ck-its, making us want to indulge in our forbidden treats even more.

The kicker is that when we fail to reach our goals, we judge ourselves and feel bad, which of course leads to more emotional eating. When we worship the idols of calorie counting and other metrics, we make things worse, instead of looking to measures that are free and trustworthy, such as the wisdom of our own bodies.

The more obstacles we place between our survival brains and our food choices, the worse choices we make. We'll see what happens when we lose the connection between our brains and our bodies in chapter 11.

THE 21-DAY CHALLENGE

PART 1
MAPPING YOUR HABIT LOOPS: DAYS 1–5

Changing eating habits is hard. For some people, it is or will feel like the hardest thing they do in their life. And for others, it feels impossible. *No way. I can't do this. I've failed so many times that I'm not going to even try anymore.* Yes, trying to use a system that is set up to fail will fail. Every. Time.

If you've seen the *Mission: Impossible* movies—or even watched the original television series—they all have a common theme: what we're about to ask you to do seems impossible. It's your choice. You can back out now if you want (but it's a movie about good guys doing impossible things, so we know you won't). It's just like the famous line that you can likely repeat off the top of your head: "Your mission, should you choose to accept it . . ."

I wouldn't ask you to try something that was impossible. But I *would* invite you to step out of that old story line of "I can't do this" and into the new story line of "Oh, wow, I just learned a bunch about how my brain works. Maybe I can put this knowledge to good use." When I'm working with patients or people in our programs, when I'm about to invite them to try something new, I try to lighten the mood a little. Knowing that they can do what I'm about to ask them to do, I smile and say, "Your mission, should you choose to accept it, is . . ."

What I'm about to invite you to do in the rest of the book is dependent on two things: curiosity and kindness. We all have these traits, and I will help you cultivate and grow them as you go through the chapters. I'm not asking you to do anything impossible.

So your mission, should you choose to accept it, is threefold: Be curious and kind to yourself as you go through the rest of the book. Challenge yourself to step out of any old habitual ways of thinking or approaching habit change that have made this journey seem impossible. Carefully read each chapter and do the suggested practices. I'm going to suggest that you take at least three weeks to read one chapter a day, so that you can fully digest it and—I'm going to repeat this because it is so important—do the suggested practices. This is possible.

This is a book, so I can't stop you from reading all of the chapters in one sitting. Some people find it helpful to read through to the end to get a sense of what to expect. Then they go back and take the time to reread each chapter, one day at a time, and yes, do the suggested practices. So ask yourself what will be most helpful for you to be able to digest the concepts and put them into practice. It is only through experience that you develop wisdom. If going one day at a time seems like it is working, great. If one of the days seems like it needs a few days or a week (or longer) to really get the practice, give yourself permission to take the time you need. And as you go, keep checking to see if you are getting into a habit of wanting things to be different faster. Constantly check for expectations and see how much you can let those go. Instead, focus on the mission: changing your relationship to eating and building and supporting a different relationship with yourself. Mission possible.

CHAPTER 4

Day 1: Welcome to Your 21-Day Challenge

My lightbulb moment, which happened in my whiteboard session in my clinic back in 2014, was the realization that my patients—and by extension all of us that struggle with unhealthy eating patterns—needed to find a way to interrupt their habit loops by relearning how to pay attention to their bodies and minds. Here we'll put observation into action. To learn, we have to pair information with experience. That's the only way that we can develop the wisdom that will advance us in our lives. Mapping out the rocks and roots on a path helps you see them as you start to move forward on your journey so that you don't slip, trip, or get lost.

A note before we begin: There is a very common exchange that I have with people who have signed up for the Eat Right Now program. They ask how long it will take for them to lose weight or stop nighttime snacking. In response, I ask how long they've been in the program. They reply, "A couple of weeks." I ask, "How long have you had this habit?" They pause and then generally give a range between thirty and fifty years (I'm not exaggerating). One person reported that their eating pattern had been going on for a full *seventy* years. I let them hear what they've just said sink in: *I've been doing this for XX years. I've been in the program two weeks.* And then they hear that voice in their head asking: *Why isn't this working faster?* Often they have to hear what impatience sounds like from their own mouths to be able to take a step back and name it.

If your mind does the same thing, I'm asking you to have a little patience with yourself. I'm asking you to bring a lot of kindness to yourself, and I will give some tips on how to do this shortly. Remember, no matter what your brain has told you, these habits are not your fault. If you haven't completely transformed your eating habits by Day 11, don't panic. Give yourself some time. This 21-Day Challenge is about a reset of the system, not wiping the hard drive completely. With this 21-Day Challenge, I will show you how to find and even enjoy a lifetime of a good relationship to eating, but it may take time to reprogram long-standing habits. However, don't worry: if you've had your eating habits for forty years, it won't take forty years to unlearn them. Our brains have to adapt quickly in the world, so they were set up to learn quickly. But these techniques are meant to last.

You might be asking, "Twenty-one days to change a habit . . . haven't I heard that somewhere before?" You probably have. Maybe you read it in a wellness article online or heard someone quoting such an article. If you search the internet, you'll see "21 days to change a habit" plastered all over the place. This is the danger of searching the internet for scientific facts. Twenty-one days is more fantasy than reality. Here are the facts: Maxwell Maltz, a plastic surgeon, wrote a book called *Psycho-Cybernetics* back in 1960. In it, he observed that it took about 21 days for his patients to get used to their new and different-looking face after a nose job. He took a leap and added that it took people who had an amputation about the same amount of time to recover from losing that limb. He wrote his book—which was focused on changing one's self-image—and decades later, the internet took it from there.

Voilà! Twenty-one days to change just about anything, including a habit. I found it on the internet, so it must be true.

There aren't actually very many studies, and even fewer *good* studies, on how long it takes to break an unhelpful or form a helpful habit. It depends on the habit. It depends on the person's genes. It depends on the person's environment. Add in social determinants, which you can think of as social habits, and you get a big complex messy equation that is really hard to scientifically study. We don't have control over what genes we inherited. Often we don't have control over our social environment. For example, it is much easier said than done for someone without the financial means to move out of a food desert or to sign up for the delivery of organic produce that they will magically have time to cook.

But we do have some control over our own minds. And when it comes to food habits, my own lab's research has found that you can change these relatively quickly. I won't promise anything in terms of speed or results, such as "if you just follow my plan, you will . . ." You've already learned a whole lot about how your mind works, so I will promise this: you will learn how to work with your mind.

So why did I pick 21 days? When developing digital therapeutics, I've found that between three and four weeks is a good length of time to deliver core content in a program. With that length of time, we can balance concept and experience: you can get bite-size pieces of information and try them out at a regular cadence. Too much information at once and you become daunted and even overwhelmed. For example, how appetizing is a 634-day challenge? No thanks. So with a tongue-in-cheek reference to the internet meme, I found that 21 days was a good length to deliver what you need to know to actually change your relationship to eating.

Through qualitative research and observation of years of running eating groups—I think of these groups more as group trainings than support groups—I have also found that there is a specific process for changing our relationship to eating that can be broken down into three parts:

Part 1. Mapping our habitual eating patterns and loops

Part 2. Changing the reward value of eating behaviors in our brains

Part 3. Finding more rewarding behaviors

These different parts also serve as a useful guide, providing signposts along the journey of change. You can think of the 21 days as breaking these parts down into practical and actionable steps, each one moving you toward a new relationship with food, eating, and yourself.

This process doesn't require an IQ of 200, fancy letters after your name, a special skill, or a gene that only some people are lucky enough to have inherited. You won't have to go out and buy some expensive gadget—or even an app. What you will need is a willingness to cultivate one critical thing: awareness. Fortunately, we all have the capacity to find this in abundance. And we can boost our ability to be aware by freeing up any energy that we habitually spend judging, berating, or doubting ourselves. We free this energy up by learning to be kind to ourselves during this journey. Being kind to ourselves has a *huge* role in helping us break unhelpful eating habits and free ourselves from the habit of beating ourselves up when we feel like we've failed "the program." We'll explore the role of self-kindness/self-compassion as a critical factor in the path shortly, but for now, remember this: for change to happen, kindness is key for awareness to help us learn. One can't function without the other. So think of awareness and kindness like a peanut butter and jelly sandwich—one provides the protein-packed punch while the other sweetens every bite.

At times you might not feel like you are good at paying attention or at being kind to yourself. It may feel frustrating, or even unnatural. Don't worry, you'll learn how to cultivate and grow both of these. And if you are up to the challenge, you'll learn how to tap into your brain to help you thrive.

RIGHT NOW: SET A GOAL

Day 1: Set a goal. Any worthwhile journey needs a destination. Let's decide where you're headed. Where do you want to go? Take a few minutes to really ask yourself what your intention is. Goals can feel quite different based on why you are doing them. So ask yourself: *Why is this important to me? Is it driven by external factors (e.g., wanting to fit a certain societal standard) or internal ones (e.g., caring for myself)?* Why is it important to you to make a change? What do you want to be doing that you aren't doing now because of your struggle with eating? Deep down, what is it truly worth for you to embark on this journey?

Once you've changed your food habits, what would you like to see happen? Let's call it a challenge goal. Here are some of the challenge goals that my patients have set for themselves:

- Enjoy healthy foods.
- Eat when I'm hungry and stop when I'm full.
- Be healthy no matter how much I weigh or what size my body is.
- Quit the clean-plate club (that is, stop eating past fullness just because the food is still on the plate).
- Stop mindlessly snacking.
- Stop compulsively eating.
- Take care of my emotions (and myself) without food.

Eat mostly plants not too much

- Eat with intention instead of being driven by compulsion and/or impulse.

What is your challenge goal? Write it down. See if you can hold it as an aspirational goal. By this I mean an aim or intention that you hold lightly, like you would hold a baby bird, your hands cupped in support. This feels very different than grasping or holding on, tightening your grip in the hope that something will happen (or won't fly away). When you're feeling lost or aggravated or defeated, come back to this goal to remind yourself why you're taking this challenge in the first place. Check to see if you are habitually holding on to or forcing something, and remind yourself that this is an aspiration. Take a deep breath and remind yourself of your intention or aspiration, as a way to help you open back up to the journey itself.

If you find that you have a whole list of goals, you are not alone. I'd suggest picking one or two to focus on first. Then, once you've gotten the core concepts down and have made progress with these, you can circle back and apply them to other goals. Too many at once becomes a mouthful—increasing the odds of choking and not being able to properly chew or digest or get nourishment.

Get a notebook or pull out your journal. Write down your goal(s).

You are now in the judgment-free zone. Underneath your goal, make a list of all the different ways you tried to move toward your goal in the past. Next to each one, rate how much effort it took (0 = effortless; 10 = way too much). Now next to that, rate how pleasant or unpleasant the effort was (0 = torture—this should be banned; 10 = extremely pleasant—this should be bottled and sold as a miracle cure). Later in the book, we'll look at how much effort it takes to control your eating when you are working with your brain.

CHAPTER 5

Day 2: Set Your Baseline

How did Jacqui set up her different eating habits? Early in life, Jacqui's OFC learns that if she restricted her eating, she could move in the direction of her goal: rail-thin Gwyneth Paltrow. It's rewarding to restrict. On top of this, when Jacqui feels sad, her brain unhelpfully suggests food will distract her from her feelings. Her OFC learns that numbing feels better than feeling bad, and Jacqui ends up juggling restricting and bingeing. This juggling gets harder the more often she shifts from restricted eating patterns to frequent bingeing. Jacqui's brain turns this into a routine: habit steps in and urges Jacqui to keep it up, day in and day out, to the point where she entirely loses touch with herself. This pattern becomes the baseline of her day-to-day existence.

Jacqui built the foundation for her adult baseline when she began using food rules around the age of twelve. She got her start from her mom. "I watched my mom and her food rules. She would often be on a fad diet of some kind. Then she would binge and eat nonstop. Bad foods were the ones that I thought would make me fat. Salad and cottage cheese were the good ones. And also eating in smaller and smaller amounts was also good."

Jacqui's story is the story of anyone who has eaten their emotions, restricted, binged, yo-yo dieted, or judged themselves for how they looked or ate. Anyone who has felt less than, weak, or lazy or has been poked or prodded literally or just visually shamed or judged as they were walking down the street can relate to this story. Jacqui's "failures" highlight how little society knows about how our brains and bodies work.

Ironically, Jacqui told me that she started using our Eat Right Now program because she wanted "to be really skinny." Over a lifetime, she had tied herself up in knots about being a size 0. Size 0 makes sense only if you've been indoctrinated by a culture that talks in terms of women being seen and not heard and generally not taking up space.[1] Jacqui, like so many other women, was obsessed with not taking up space in the world. Each time she "failed" a diet and felt something was wrong with her, she only pulled those knots tighter. It got to the point where she felt that she'd need to be on one diet or another the rest of her life.

I'm happy to report Jacqui's story has a happy ending—more accurately, an ongoing journey that brings her true happiness as she deepens her wisdom and relates to herself differently ("heaps of self-compassion"). You'll see later in the book how she has learned how her body and mind operate and how to work with them. More important, her story is a story of hope. She is no different from you or anyone else in the sense that she could awaken to her inherent capacities of awareness and kindness and put them to use in the tools that she learned. She began by clearly seeing where she was. She had to identify what her baseline eating, coping, and intervention patterns were.

---

1 Women being invisible may apply even more to overweight women. Historically, with rare exceptions, fat women have not been depicted in television or media (this is slowly changing). The message that this sends is that they aren't worth telling stories about, that their lives have less meaning, and so on.

And you, too, can join her on this journey into freedom from whatever cycles you've fallen into.

RIGHT NOW: SET YOUR BASELINE

Before we can solve the problem, we must first identify it. As I explained in chapter 3, when scientists do experiments, we establish a baseline so we can assess how the subject changes in response to different stimuli. That's what I'd like you to do now. Write your own version of Jacqui's story. Don't skip ahead and dissect what has gone wrong in the past or use it as a way to judge yourself for every "misstep" you've taken through life. Just give the highlights of your history with eating over the course of your life.

Here are some specific questions to help guide the exercise. What are some of your earliest memories of food? What was your favorite food as a child? Did it have associations with specific moments, like summer vacations or birthday parties? What was the emotional feeling around food? Was there always lots of it? Did one of your parents struggle with overeating? Did you experience fat-shaming (or thin-shaming) as a child? Did your weight fluctuate during adolescence? At some point, did you decide that you disliked the way you looked? Did you have to follow a special diet because you had allergies or you wanted to perform well in sports? Were there points in your life in which your relationship to food changed? Did you change your eating patterns after milestone markers in your life (e.g., dating, marriage, childbirth, raising children)? What habits do you have today related to eating?

CHAPTER 6

Day 3: Map Your Food Habit Loops

You got a whole lot of information at the beginning of this book about how your mind works and how habits form. From a pragmatic perspective, those concepts can be distilled into three things: the **why**, **what**, and **how** of eating.

The **why** is the urge or craving that gets triggered and drives us to eat. "Why am I going for a snack right now?" *Because I'm craving that snack.* Eating when we are truly hungry is really different from eating when we are stressed, bored, or just consuming out of habit.

The **what** is the type of food we eat. "Am I about to reach for something sweet?" Eating food high in sugar or simple carbohydrates affects our brains differently than eating more nutritious foods—no matter how the food tastes.

The **how** is the manner in which we eat. Quickly shoveling down a sandwich at lunch or mindlessly eating potato chips while watching a television show or surfing the internet instead of sitting down to a proper meal affects our perception of how full we are.

The less we pay attention to these factors—the why, what, and how—the more likely we are to subconsciously develop unhealthy and completely habitual eating patterns.

That was my working hypothesis of what my patient Jack was struggling with.

His was the story of so many people: his brain's survival wires had been crossed with his emotional wires. Eating was not just about getting energy on board to run the brain and body systems. It was about mood, boredom, an overindulgence in food that had meaning for him, and more. Whether it was Corn Nuts, pasta, ice cream, or bagels, he was on a "see food" diet, as the overused joke goes. He saw the food, and urged on by a craving, he would automatically eat it, regardless of whether he was hungry.

At Jack's first visit, after getting his full medical history and making sure I wasn't missing anything of a physical nature, I broke it down with him. I talked about how eating habits get formed through reinforcement learning.

I pulled out a piece of blank paper and wrote TRIGGER ⇒ BEHAVIOR ⇒ RESULT/REWARD on it.

Then I mapped out Jack's habit loop.

Trigger: See Corn Nuts sitting in dish.
Behavior: Mindlessly eat Corn Nuts.
Result/Reward: Satisfy that urge.

It can be hard to notice the result of an automatic eating behavior because we're not paying attention. This is an important point. It's worth bookmarking. We'll revisit it in more detail in chapter 8.

Together, Jack and I mapped out a couple of his other eating habit loops. For example, his love of pasta triggered him to overeat it at meals. His bagel habit was driven a lot by context—he would eat one in the store, and then two more on the way home, not because he was hungry but because they tasted good. And depression triggered his "feel better with food" eating habit. Then we discussed how the reward-based learning process was keeping him hooked. He was ticking the boxes of emotional eating—eating both because of happy food associations and sad moods—as well as habitual eating. And as a sign of the eating being a bit beyond his control, even when he'd overeat to the point where he felt unwell, he would go back and do it again and again.

Jack looked relieved. I had just helped him understand something more important and seemingly infinitely more complex than particle physics: how his mind worked. Getting to the heart of the matter is surprisingly simple, yet really powerful. Already, at our first visit, he was beginning to see how his thoughts and emotions were colliding. He was realizing how his eating behaviors were strong forces, and the results of his eating were actually driving more and more of these cycles.

As we finished our video visit, I gave Jack one simple mission as homework to do before our next session: map out your food habit loops. I had him start writing down his triggers (the why), his eating behaviors (the what), and the results he was getting from how he was eating. It was important for him to be able to link what we had mapped together to his day-to-day life over the next few weeks.

Here's another example of what this mapping looks like. One of our Eat Right Now users posted their mapping process on our community board:

I understand why I go to food to avoid or cover up or distract from uncomfortable feelings such as anger, sadness, or restlessness. Who wants to feel those things?

Trigger: Uncomfortable feeling.

Behavior: Eat something that temporarily diminishes the feeling.

Result/Reward: Still have to deal with the unpleasant feelings, plus the sugar headache! I can clearly see how I got caught in this habit loop, trying to escape difficult feelings with food, but that ultimately it doesn't work.

Notice how this person is already getting wise to the fact that the habit isn't very rewarding. This is the secret sauce. You'll get more on this in part 2. Let's look at another mapping success story.

Rob, who had been referred to me for help with anxiety, quickly grasped the habit loop mapping exercise at our first visit. We started by mapping out a couple of his panic habit loops. Then I sent Rob home to map out any other habit loops related to anxiety. By the next visit, when he walked in, he already looked less anxious.

Before he even sat down, he gleefully exclaimed, "Hey, Doc, I lost fourteen pounds!"

Confused, I quickly scanned my memory from our last visit. I didn't remember talking about weight loss. I had bookmarked that for after he had a handle on his anxiety. That was mission number one, the one he had been given.

He told me how his awareness exercises had gone. He had been doing his mind-mapping homework, yet had found over and over that anxiety triggered him to eat. As he ate, he noticed that eating wasn't helping his anxiety. In fact, knowing that he had a bunch of health issues related to his weight was making him more anxious. Trigger: anxiety. Behavior: eating. Result: more anxiety.

This is often the case with this habit-mapping exercise. Some people go their entire lives not knowing how their minds work. It's like they're bumbling around in a dark room, stubbing their toes on objects. They can't seem to remember where those objects are so they can stop tripping themselves up. Mapping out these habit loops is like flipping on the light switch. It is a lot easier to navigate the territory when you can see where all of the objects are. This was the case for Rob. He had spent about thirty years being anxious, not knowing why he was anxious, trying everything, and not being able to fix it. After just a few minutes of mind-mapping, Rob had found the light switch.

Just by mapping. That's it. No willpower. Just mapping.

I don't want you to get the impression that mapping is some type of miracle. It might seem simple. It is. It might even seem oversimplified. It isn't. Just the act of naming your habit loops is incredibly powerful.

AVOIDING THE WHY TRAP

Once you start mapping your habit loops, you may be tempted to dig deeper. You may want to ask yourself why exactly you are turning to food to feed an emotional need or why you can't "just say no" to a three P.M. candy bar every day. Remembering all of the movies and television shows where the patient lies on the couch or sits across from the therapist—week after week, year after year—recalling their childhood, you might be thinking, *But shouldn't we be taking more of my emotional life into account? Shouldn't I get to the bottom of why I can't resist the siren song of Cheetos?* The short answer is no. And this is good news. To break a habit loop, you don't need to unearth childhood trauma.[1] You just need to begin by identifying the habit loop itself. To

---

1 Though this is more nuanced than a yes/no. I will talk later about how to separate and work with habits set up as a result of trauma and how to incorporate what you learn here.

be clear, understanding how our childhood history contributes to our habits, our sense of self, and propensities we have as adults can be helpful, but sometimes it does not lead to behavior change. And people who don't want to delve into their past don't need to "go there" when learning to work with habit loops.

Three elements—trigger, behavior, reward—are all that are needed to reinforce a behavior. Those Rescorla-Wagner formulas that calculate reward value and precisely determine how habits change do not include "childhood" as a variable. (Again, this is nuanced. More on it later.)

Many of my patients get stuck in trying to solve, fix, or avoid the trigger. Yes, our history is important—after all, it has significantly shaped who we are today, for better or for worse—but the why simply triggers a habitual behavior. It sets the wheel in motion, but it isn't what drives it.

Mapping habit loops around eating might not seem like a deep dive into your psyche, so until you've collected enough of your own data and learned some of the techniques for emotion regulation that appear later in the book, this is as deep as you need to go when it comes to changing these habits. Really. If you are learning where this or that path goes in the jungle, you don't need to be a botanist with the ability to name each species of tree that you walk by. You just need to be able to recognize where you are. "Oh, that's the tree with the twisted trunk." "That's where I turn left to get to the stream." Your mind is the same way. You don't need to know which neurotransmitters are firing and where they are firing in order to have a thought.

Learning that dopamine is involved in learning *can* give you a dopamine rush, but you don't need to know this to learn. Knowing that dopamine rushes can feel a certain way (excited) and can steer you in a certain direction (restless cravings) will help you keep an eye out for when your brain is about to drag you down a path that you've been down before and don't necessarily want to go down again. That's helpful. That's what keeps you going down the right path.

I'll try to make sure you are getting the information you need to know. Later, we'll explore how you can use all of this learning to trust yourself more.

So instead of going down a "why is this happening?" rabbit hole, start by mapping your mind when it is engaged in a habit. What is the trigger? What is the behavior? What is the result?

RIGHT NOW: MAP YOUR EATING HABIT LOOPS

See if you can start mapping your eating habits throughout your day. Go to www.mapmyhabit.com (it will redirect you to my drjud.com website), where you will find a printable PDF of the habit mapper that you can download and start filling out. Or if you don't have time to map out each one in real time, at bedtime you can reflect back on your day and fill it out retrospectively. Go back and map out each time you ate. What triggered it? What was the eating behavior (e.g., mindless snacking, stress/emotional eating, overeating, etc.)? What was the result (e.g., briefly relieved, bloated, lethargic, disappointed, ashamed, etc.)? Triggers can be as simple as "I was bored" or "I survived the day" or as complicated as the lingering grief of losing a loved one or relationship.

I'm going to suggest that you take as much time as you need to get this mind-mapping process down before continuing. Some of you might need only a day to start seeing the why (trigger), the what, and the how of your eating (behavior). You might find it easy to begin mapping your triggers, behaviors, and results as you go. Or some habit loops will be obvious to you, while others will be buried beneath the surface, only to poke out their heads when you are ready to see them. Knowing a little bit about human nature and how we want to get to solutions as quickly as possible, I'm going to add this comment so you can come back to it later: IF YOU RUSHED AHEAD AND BINGE-READ THE BOOK, bookmark this section so you can come back to it when you finish the book but feel like you didn't get what you were looking for.

Change isn't an intellectual exercise. Wisdom comes only from direct experience. Don't rush the mind-mapping process.

CHAPTER 7

Day 4: Your Body's Wisdom

One of the biggest challenges we face when breaking habit loops is that we suck at listening to ourselves. In his short story "A Painful Case," James Joyce wrote that his main character, Mr. Duffy, "lived at a little distance from his body." Joyce published this story back in 1914, but I can't think of a better way to describe the modern condition. We seem to live apart from our bodies, to treat them like fleshy robots whose only purpose is to haul around our brains.

This keeps us stuck in old ruts and, more important, makes it really difficult to listen to our bodies and learn from what they are trying to tell us.

Our body is an information superhighway that sends all sorts of signals right to our brain. Think of all the different ways your body lets you know what is happening in both the world around you and the world within you. The five senses allow us to navigate through time and space. We have olfactory neurons that are activated by odors in the air. Critical for our sense of smell, these neurons are so important that they are the only ones that get direct passage to the brain (through the cribriform plate). We have specialized taste buds—gustatory cells, if you want to get fancy about it—on our tongue, in our cheeks, even in our esophagus. These interact with chemicals and elements in food and

74

drink that give us the five elements of taste perception: salty, sour, bitter, sweet, and umami (a loanword from Japanese that can be translated as "pleasant savory taste"). Our bodies need to sense oxygen, carbon dioxide, and concentrations of other chemicals in our blood. Our organs each have special ways of monitoring our inner milieu, ranging from full bladders to empty stomachs.

Almost all of these different types of receptors function in a very similar manner to reinforcement learning. They provide feedback. If your carbon dioxide levels are too high in your blood, part of your brain stem—the ventrolateral medulla of the medulla oblongata, to be specific—sends a feedback signal that tells your brain to speed things up a bit, and you start to breathe more rapidly and/or deeply. If you eat something that is too hot or spicy, you might also breathe rapidly, this time because of a feedback signal of "fire in the mouth." If your bladder is full, that uncomfortable feeling gives you feedback: time to go to the bathroom.

And yet we constantly ignore the body's signals. We've gotten in the habit of overriding the messages and signals it sends us. It's 11:30 P.M. and you're sitting on the couch watching the end of an episode of your favorite TV show. Netflix or Amazon automatically queues up the next one, and your OFC has to decide, "How shall I deal with this?" Your body says, "You're yawning, your eyelids are heavy, you just spilled your tea. How many ways do I have to tell you to turn the TV off and go to bed?" That would be the right move for your survival brain. However, what actually happens is that when we are in low energy mode, we can't access that logical part of our brain. So habit mode flips on and we hear the voice that says, "You stayed up late last night, and look, you're still alive. One more episode. Go for it."

Rob, the one who had experienced anxiety and panic attacks since the fifth grade, explained, "The first forty years of my life, I was doing everything I could to get out of my body, because of either such extreme terror, discomfort, or self-hatred . . . just hating my body, so I was doing everything I could to avoid it." Here's a commentary on how powerful feedback is: Rob intentionally had no mirrors in his apartment so he wouldn't have to look at himself.

Rob's lack of a mirror wasn't a solution. Instead, it is an example of a short-term fix that helps us temporarily avoid the bigger issue of guilt, shame, and/or self-hatred that can be really toxic. For instance, we can feel guilty for things that happened to us when we were children, teenagers, or young adults, even though we had no control over them. This can then feed cycles of shame about who we are. And these guilt/shame cycles can get really solidified the more they feed each other. Similar to my patient who learned that gaining weight avoided unwanted advances from men, or like Jacqui and Rob, we can learn to eat to soothe ourselves. Yet also like Jacqui and Rob and so many others, this can then lead to us feeling more shame about what we look like and who we are, and guilt when we can't stop these eating patterns or lose weight. Our perceptions of ourselves get unfairly wrapped up in what we look like (and what society wants us to look like). So we start distancing ourselves from ourselves. We try to disown our bodies in any way that we can. We lose touch with our bodies and ourselves.

Someone from our Eat Right Now community wrote that her body was unfamiliar and unknown to her, and that she had never felt at home in her body. Others described feeling out of control and disconnected, not trusting their bodies to give them meaningful signals.

As you learned in the first section of the book, we're wired to approach things and experiences that feel pleasant and avoid ones that are painful. For example, if you accidentally touch a hot stove, you pull your hand away without even thinking. In fact, our bodies are so exquisitely designed to keep us safe that the "ouch, that's hot!" signal doesn't even have to get to our brain for our muscles to contract and pull our hand away from the stove. Our sensory neurons in our fingers fire off a signal that gets relayed in the spinal cord to our motor neurons in our arm, and voilà, we've moved before we even know what happened. Our brain comes in afterward and assesses the situation, concluding that the stove was indeed hot.

We frequently look outside ourselves for information about what is going on in our bodies. Have you ever checked the weather online or on your phone to confirm that it is indeed raining before you look out your window? We do the same thing when it comes to determining what is best for our bodies. We check our apps, looking for them to tell us if we should be hungry. We get caught up in trying to follow food plans dictated by "experts" or the cultural zeitgeist, which just creates more distance between us and our bodies. We double down on this or that fad diet or trend and then beat ourselves up for not being able to stick to it. Here's an example of what this looks like and how far it can go.

ANNE'S STORY

Anne was in her mid-fifties when she came to my eating group at the medical school. She was really good at describing her experiences with food. She had a way of articulating what everyone was experiencing, to the point that at the end of a story, not only was everyone in the room nodding but seemingly at the point of jumping out of their seats. Like one of those feel-good movies where someone (okay, let's be honest—it's almost always a man) has just given a rousing speech and brought the audience to their feet, jumping and shouting.

At one session, Anne told the story of how she had lived decades of her life in what she described as jail—the one she'd built and in which she'd locked herself up. In *food* jail.

Anne's tale began in childhood. Her mother was a reporter for *Time* and *Life* magazine and a gourmet cook. Perfectionism was the name of the game, and Anne's mom was the coach *and* referee. She wanted Anne to be her best growing up, going as far as making Anne rewrite school papers that had received a B grade. Mind you, these revisions were only for Mom—the teacher wasn't going to see them, having moved on to other subjects. Mom wanted Anne to be perfect before she took the next step.

Wanting to be like her mom, Anne learned perfectionism as a way to try to be in control of her life. In her mid-twenties she started gaining weight. Voracious for knowledge, she started reading book after book on how to control her eating.

She created a list of food rules. Her list consisted of the typical "good" guys and "bad" guys: eat this and not that. Follow the rules and you'll be fine. "I had a list of seventy-four foods at one point," she told me. "No oil, no salt, no sugar, no fast food, and you have to make everything at home."

She micromanaged each morsel she put in her mouth, carefully counting out her seven almonds at exactly 11:00 A.M., weighing her kale salad, scrupulously avoiding sugar . . . until 4:00 P.M., when she'd lose whatever control she had. At first, not being allowed to have junk food in the house, she'd eat mayonnaise out of the jar with a spoon (sometimes with rolled-up turkey slices). Later, when she had her own money, she would bust open boxes of cereal and pull out bags of pasta ("it had to be white-flour pasta to do the trick") from where she'd hidden them and "eat as quickly and ALWAYS as distracted as possible." As you can imagine, failure like that left type A Anne feeling out of control and deeply ashamed.

Anne had spent decades distanced from her body. She focused all of her energy on trying to find experts to give her the right advice, the right rules to follow. She had stacks and stacks of books on nutrition and weight loss in her basement, but none of them helped her. Each new book she bought was just brain candy for her—something that had that sweet pull of promise but left her unsatisfied and craving more. Each diet, guideline, and rule she tried to follow only distanced her more and more from herself. The further away you get from your body, the harder it is to hear its signals. The longer this goes on, the harder it is to discern those signals and the less you remember what those signals are telling you.

We can get in the habit of spending a lot of time away from ourselves by distracting or in some way distancing ourselves from ourselves. If we do this a lot, it can be really hard to know what our body is telling us when we feel certain sensations. If we feel something unfamiliar, it is hard to know what that means. Am I hungry or just stressed? And the more time we spend away from our bodies, ignoring their signals, the more we set up this way of not relating to ourselves as a habit. If we are going to get our eating in order, we have to listen to the body we have when it tells us what it needs.

RIGHT NOW: NOTICE HOW YOU IGNORE YOUR BODY'S SIGNALS

For one entire day, see if you can notice all the ways you ignore the signals your body sends to your brain. Did you ignore your bladder, your stomach, or your body in some other way? Drink a third cup of coffee even though you were already feeling jittery? Force yourself to stay at your computer even though your body is saying it's time to get up and stretch? Fall asleep in a chair rather than go to bed?

You can do this using the habit mapper or a blank piece of paper. Don't focus so much on the trigger, because when we've ignored a signal for a while, the trigger is not as relevant. Instead, focus on the behavior and the result/consequence. For each example, how did your body feel when you ignored a body signal?

The more detailed you can be, the more you can start to revitalize and strengthen your awareness skills. Building your awareness with this exercise will also serve a second function: relearning how to listen to your body's signals. You might even take a second day and repeat this exercise. As you notice what you are ignoring, zoom in on what those body signals feel like so that you can recognize them more easily. And if you're feeling like you are on a roll, see what happens when you listen to them, instead of ignoring them.

CHAPTER 8

Day 5: Identifying Your Urges—Hunger or Something Else?

CRAVINGS

Pop quiz: What is the substance most commonly craved in North American and European countries? If you answered chocolate (which includes chocolate-containing foods), you are correct. You might remember the elements that make food more craveable—they usually have that magic bliss point mix of salt, sugar, and fat that signals to our bodies what we have in our mouths is packed full of calories.

A food craving is not to be confused with general feelings of hunger. Hunger focuses on getting calories in and goes away when you eat something. Craving is centered around the desire for something in particular. "My stomach is rumbling, so I think I should eat something" is very different from "I must have chocolate now!"

Food craving has been measured in a bunch of different ways. Simple analogue scales ask people to rate their craving on a scale from 0 to 10. Fancier measures separate out state vs. trait craving: this moment (state) and what usually happens (trait). For example, the scale most commonly used in the scientific community is the Food Cravings Questionnaires (FCQs). The FCQ-Trait measures the frequency and intensity of food cravings *in general*. It includes items such as:

- I find myself preoccupied with food.
- If I give in to a food craving, I lose all control.
- Food cravings invariably make me think of ways to get what I want to eat.
- If I am craving something, I am consumed by thoughts of eating.

Notice how this last item even highlights how often we use food analogies, images, and similes to describe our own mental states— thoughts of eating it *consume* me.

The FCQ-State measures the intensity of food craving right now, *in the moment.*

For example, using the response categories of "strongly disagree" to "strongly agree," it has items such as:

- I have an intense desire to eat [one or more specific foods].
- I'm craving [one or more specific foods].
- I have an urge for [one or more specific foods].

As you can see from the items in the FCQ, *intense desire, craving,* and *urge* are pretty vague. Yet we all seem to know when we have an urge/craving—notice how the FCQ mirrors real life in the sense that it uses the terms *urge* and *craving* (and even *desire*) interchangeably. These are different words that describe the same experience. From a brain perspective, cues or triggers cause the release of dopamine (and likely of other neurochemicals such as endorphins) in the prefrontal cortex and the ventral striatum as we anticipate the reward that will come when we eat a certain food. The ventral striatum includes the nucleus accumbens, a core area involved in the brain's reward system. Dopamine fires first when something unanticipated happens. That's how reinforcement learning helps us remember where food is. Once we remember where to find food, that dopamine firing shifts from reminding us where it is to urging us to go get it. That's where the restless itchy urge of a craving comes from. A thought of chocolate pops into our head, followed by a craving to eat it. The thought is just a thought. Once we've learned that we like chocolate (or whatever our object of desire is), dopamine gets us off the couch and into the kitchen. It says, "You know you like it. What are you waiting for? Go get it!"

Notice how there's a big difference between liking and wanting. These processes have been separated out in our brains for a long time now. The pleasantness, or how much we like a food, has been linked to "hedonic hot spots" in the nucleus accumbens, and likely involves endorphins and endocannabinoids. These are brain chemicals that bind to opioid and cannabinoid receptors—the same receptors that bind heroin and marijuana. Endocannabinoids are part of our body's feedback system, helping maintain homeostasis between our different systems. Discovered in the 1990s, endocannabinoids help regulate everything from appetite and digestion to pain sensations to mood to sleep. Perhaps you've heard of or had a "runner's high," that blissed-out feeling after a really good run or a long bout of intense exercise where you truly feel at one with the universe. Researchers thought this was due to endorphin release. But more recent studies have found that you can likely thank your endocannabinoid system for that toke without smoke—these neurotransmitters don't show up on marijuana drug tests. Dopamine is more involved in wanting, not liking. The go-get-it drive of dopamine motivates us into action.

LIKING VS. WANTING

Right now take a moment to explore the difference between liking and wanting for yourself.

Start with something simple. Think of a shirt or a sweater in your closet that you like. Notice the pleasant feeling you experience when you think of it.

Now think of a type of food that you like. Does it automatically trigger an urge to eat it now? Or can you simply stay with the feeling of liking it?

My guess is that thinking of the food item you like can trigger an urge or a want. Why doesn't whatever item of clothing that's hanging in your closet do the same thing? Well, you already have it—you own it. If you want to explore liking vs. wanting a little more, you can think of a clothing item that you've seen someone wearing or in a catalogue that you really liked but don't have. Can you feel that itchy urge of wanting now?

That wanting quality of cravings can be tricky. It can be difficult to notice what cravings feel like. This is especially true if we, like Mr. Duffy, live a short distance from our bodies. Remember Jack and his Corn Nuts, eating handfuls at a time? When I asked him why he kept eating scoop after scoop, he responded, "It is momentarily satisfying," though the way he responded made me wonder if the satisfaction came from eating the snack or scratching the itch of his urge to automatically eat them when he saw them. Perhaps sensing my curiosity or wondering himself how this lined up with his previous descriptions of mindless eating, Jack continued: "There definitely is a disconnect between my brain and my body. I spend a lot of time in my brain. I'm not attuned to my body."

Jack is a good example of what we can do in moments where we are triggered to eat. We can bring awareness to these moments. Hunger signals originate in your stomach. So bring your awareness there. Ask a simple question: "Am I hungry?" If you are pretty disconnected from your stomach or still struggling with the food/mood wiring mix-up, instead of trying to force yourself to not eat, go ahead and eat the food—but pay careful attention as you do. Does that food bounce into an empty stomach, reminding you how long it's been since you last ate? Or does it go quietly into an already relatively full—or at least not empty—chamber?

Don't think about it. *Feel* about it. Feel into your body.

That's what Jack did as part of his mission. He started paying attention to his grazing. At his first follow-up visit, two weeks after our initial meeting, Jack told me about a recent car trip. He and his wife were driving back from a vacation they had taken. His wife had put almonds in a container for them to snack on along the way. He likes almonds. He kept checking in with himself to see if he was hungry or was just having an automated urge. Did he actually want them? He saw almonds, and instead of automatically eating them, he kept checking to see if he was hungry. After about two hours, he noticed that he was hungry. So he ate a few, but just a few.

He said, "It takes effort to explore how my body is feeling . . . I'm trying to rebuild a connection."

When a participant in our Eat Right Now program was struggling to feel cravings in her body, she reported to me: "My cravings seem to originate in my thoughts. Negative thoughts, *thinking* about food, any thoughts. But no bodily sensations." Notice how this person highlighted thinking about food. That's what our brains do best: think. But our brains don't have any sensory neurons. That's why neurosurgeons can do brain surgery on an awake, unanesthetized patient. Our brains cannot feel hunger. They interpret the signal our stomach sends as the sensation of hunger, but our brains don't grumble or churn.

Until we stop living a short distance from ourselves, move back in, and regain that bodily awareness, it can be challenging to feel in our bodies what a craving feels like.

Another reason that we might not recognize cravings is because of negative reinforcement. Cravings are unpleasant. They are designed that way. That dopamine firing makes our lives miserable until we carry out the desired action. Because we know how cravings feel—uncomfortable—the negative reinforcement process in our brain kicks in. Unpleasant urge? Make it go away. So we prefer to indulge the urge as quickly as possible. The more we do this, the more we learn to do this. We get better and faster at scratching the itch of craving, keeping candy in our desk drawer instead of going to the break room.

And of course we all know what happens when we try to ignore or resist our cravings: what we resist persists. In fact, cravings don't just persist—they grow. Like an itch that gets itchier and itchier until we scratch it, cravings can make us feel like our head will explode if we don't satisfy them. Jacqui calls this the craving monster. If we fight or try to ignore the craving monster, it gets bigger and louder until we finally give in.

THE TRAP OF LOW FAT: HOW LOW-FAT FOODS CREATE CRAVINGS

Have you noticed how low-fat foods keep us craving and coming back for more? This is because the fat in full-fat foods helps our bodies register fullness. Since low-fat foods have been engineered to take the fat out, we don't feel full even though we are eating calories.

Interestingly, the low-fat food movement can be traced back to 1977, when the Senate Select Committee on Nutrition and Human

Needs issued a report suggesting that Americans eat less fat and more complex carbohydrates to prevent diabetes, heart disease, and stroke. This sounded scientific and rational at the time. It sounded especially good to the food industry. Why? Well, if you remove the fat, you have to replace it with something. That something happened to be sugar. And thanks to governmental corn subsidies, sugar, in the form of high-fructose corn syrup, became dirt cheap. Whether reduced calorie, light, low-fat, or nonfat, all of these types of alternatives to the regular food have been shown to have higher amounts of sugar. Whether because with these altered foods we consciously give ourselves license to eat more ("it's low fat!") or because these foods don't provide our bodies with the natural mix of fat, protein, fiber, and carbohydrates to signal fullness, sugar sure can keep most of us craving.

THE HUNGER TEST

If you struggle with your ability to tell whether you are truly hungry or are simply having a craving, you are not alone. It is really important to recalibrate and reintegrate your body and mind. Here's the process that I developed after my aha moment with my clinic group—the women who struggle with binge eating. After whiteboarding and getting real-time feedback about the key concepts with my clinic patients, I formalized what we now call the hunger test.

The hunger test is specifically designed to rewire those tangled connections between your body and brain. It will help you interpret your signals so you can discern an emotion-based craving from actual hunger or just habit.

Assuming you don't know if you are hungry, stressed, or something else, the hunger test starts with a simple question: "Hungry for a snack?"

Our primary drive to eat comes from hunger. This is called homeostatic hunger, that familiar feeling when your belly is empty and you may experience a lack of energy, difficulty concentrating, irritability, and even dizziness.

Secondary drivers of eating are learned. We also eat when we're emotional—that mood/food relationship where we're basically eating our feelings. As I mentioned earlier, this is called hedonic hunger.

There are a million examples of what hedonic hunger looks like. The odds are that we've all encountered that mood/food relationship in one way or another. For example, the mother of one of my clinic patients recently moved in with her, and it was stressing the patient out "a little" (a lot). She found herself turning to sweets—cookies in particular—to soothe her stress. Rob's go-to for alleviating anxiety was fast food.

It is not easy for a person experiencing the desire to eat to tell the difference between homeostatic and hedonic hunger.

So the first step is to help you figure out if that urge to eat is coming from hunger, emotions, or habit.

Step 1. Check all that apply:

○ Irritable or easily frustrated
○ Stomach empty
○ Overwhelmed
○ Dizzy or light-headed
○ Headache
○ Moody
○ Tense
○ Difficulty concentrating
○ Stomach growling, rumbling, or gurgling
○ Boredom

○ Avoiding something
○ Restless
○ Tiredness
○ Other

Notice how some of these are specific to hunger. For example, stomach gurgling is relatively specific to homeostatic hunger. Yet difficulty concentrating can be a result of our stomach's being empty, but stress can also make it difficult to concentrate.

Here's the list again, with the overlap between the different categories:

	STRESS/ EMOTION	HABIT	HUNGER
Boredom		x	
Avoiding something	x	x	
Restless	x		
Tense	x		
Overwhelmed	x		
Difficulty concentrating	x		x
Moody	x		x
Headache	x		x
Irritable or easily frustrated	x		x
Stomach growling, rumbling, or gurgling			x

	STRESS/ EMOTION	HABIT	HUNGER
Dizzy or light-headed			x
Stomach empty			x

Because there is a lot of overlap between the different items on our checklist, we needed a way to tell whether the urge to eat was caused by one category or another. For example, if we feel irritable, that could be a sign that we're stressed/anxious or hungry. How can you weight— in other words, give more emphasis to—the different categories? The simplest way to do this is to note when you last ate. If you had just eaten, your stomach is full, *and* you're irritable, you can cross hunger off your list of what might be causing that irritability in that moment.

So the next step is to check to see how recently (and how much) you ate.

Step 2. How many hours ago did you eat? (0 to 5+)

Step 3. Look back at the list in step 1 and add up all of the items for each column. Whichever column has the highest score can be an indicator—or at least help you recognize—what is the most likely cause of the urge. If two categories have similar scores, use step 2 as a tiebreaker: if you just ate, the stress/emotion category wins; if you haven't eaten in a while, the hunger category gets that tiebreaker point. Four to five hours is a good cutoff to start with, but this can be different for each of us.

When we built the Eat Right Now app, rewiring our brain-body signals seemed foundational, so we built the hunger test right into the app and had people start using it on Day 1 (we named it the stress test in the app). We came up with an algorithm that would compute a composite score based on their answers, automatically weighing the different categories based on how recently people had eaten. The idea was to help people develop their awareness, while at the same time learning more quickly and accurately what their triggers were for eating. Awareness is to habits as yeast is to bread: it is an essential ingredient for change to happen. The hunger test was a simple way for people to start baking awareness into their lives. Here are some real-life responses from people using it:

> I did the stress [hunger] test today, and it really worked. In the past I've gotten burned out by diets because I felt like I had to pay attention to food so much, that after six or eight months, I'd be exhausted. I think the stress test helped my attention stay on my body and situation, and not really on food/healthy choices, etc. I followed the ERN advice, and in the end, was actually hungry for healthy food. That's a good day!

> After so many years of calorie-restriction dieting, I run the risk of confusing real hunger pangs and anxiety-driven craving. The stress test helps me think about how long it's been since I've eaten and whether or not I am in fact hungry. Today, for example, I felt like I was fighting a craving, but the hunger test helped me realize that it really had been 4 hours since I had lunch and I probably was actually hungry.

In parts 2 and 3 of the book, you'll learn tools and exercises to help you work with your urges.

RIGHT NOW: USE THE HUNGER TEST

Over the course of the day, start using the hunger test when you feel the urge to eat outside of mealtimes. Follow steps 1 to 3 above to determine whether your urge comes from hunger or something else. If you are a habitual overachiever and really want to go for it, use the hunger test every time you have an urge to eat. It doesn't take very long, and the more you practice it, the more quickly you will recalibrate and/or get better at recognizing your hedonic and homeostatic hunger signals.

PART 2
INTERRUPTING YOUR HABIT LOOPS WITH AWARENESS: DAYS 6–16

In part 1 of the 21-Day Challenge, we focused on the why, what, and how of eating. Why am I reaching for food? What type of food am I reaching for? And how am I eating it? Am I hungry, stressed, bored, lonely, or all of the above? We also focused on bringing light into that dark room of habit by having you map out your eating habit loops. All of these critically depend on one thing: awareness. Of course, being kind to ourselves through the process helps us be open to learning and change and repurpose any energy we waste in habitual self-judgment or doubt. In part 2, we're going to use awareness to supercharge the process of change itself.

It might seem strange for someone who wants to quit smoking to go to their doctor, only to be told to keep smoking. In medical school, I learned the five A's for helping my patients quit: Ask, Advise, Assess, Assist, Arrange. It is still the standard today. We were supposed to urge our patients to quit, prescribe anti-smoking medication (as appropriate), and schedule a follow-up within the first week of their theoretical quit date. The problem is that this doesn't work very well. When I started researching why, I realized there was a sixth A that may be as—if not more—important than the other A's: Awareness.

From a neuroscience perspective, the only way to break a bad habit is to pay attention to how rewarding—or unrewarding—it is (remember Rescorla and Wagner's positive and negative prediction errors?). So, in a seemingly heretical way, I started telling my patients to keep smoking, but to pay attention when they did so. What?! My doctor is telling me to smoke? My lab did a randomized controlled clinical trial and found that teaching people to pay attention to what cigarettes tasted and smelled like (and also how to use mindfulness to ride out cravings) was five times more effective than the gold-standard treatment. One person in our program summed it up in a sentence: "Today all of the cigarettes I smoked were disgusting." That's right, if we follow the neuroscience and go right to the source—the OFC and reward value—we can break all sorts of unhealthy habits (smoking, eating, worrying, procrastinating—the list goes on) and build new healthier ones at the same time.

Part 1 was setting the stage for change. In part 2, we are going to make change happen. If we try to force change, we fight against our brains, because our brains don't like change. To our brains, when something is different, it signals the potential for danger. Think again of our ancestors out on the savanna searching for food. If they venture into unknown territory, they can't be certain there aren't tigers hiding in the bushes waiting to eat them, so they have to stay on high alert as they explore, mapping out the territory carefully until they are convinced that this isn't tiger territory. That's why thousands of years later we still get nervous doing new things. It isn't that they are necessarily dangerous—but our survival brains don't know this. We start with caution and have to learn for ourselves that whatever we are trying out won't harm us. Over time, the behavior becomes familiar, even comfortable. That's where the term *comfort zone* comes from: comfort =

safety to our survival brain. The goal is to make paying attention to your eating part of your comfort zone.

And as a preview of part 3, if you're up for it, another broader goal is to make change itself more comfortable. When you venture out of your comfort cave, instead of going right into the panic zone, can you start getting familiar and comfortable with change itself? You can instead move into your growth zone and learn to stay there more, as you see that learning and growing don't have to be scary; instead, growth can be intrinsically rewarding itself.

In part 1, we focused a lot on identifying the what—what you eat. In part 2, we'll deepen our exploration of the whys and hows of what you eat. I might even suggest that you go ahead and eat those forbidden foods, the same way I suggested that my patients go ahead and smoke. I'll introduce you to tools you can use to help train your mind to attend to the present moment, instead of slipping into an automatic or default mode, so you can make wise food choices that are in line with what your body and brain actually need. Then I'll show you how to use your ability to pay attention, to eat more mindfully, so you can learn which foods are satisfying and which suck.

Now pay careful attention to this next sentence. If you don't pay attention, it will be really, really hard to change your habits. If you pay attention, your habits will change for good. And this might be easier than you think.

CHAPTER 9

Day 6: The Power of Paying Attention

Has this ever happened to you? You're listening to a true-crime podcast as you clear the dinner dishes. Will your kids ever learn to finish their meals? They've left half their dinner on their plates. You follow all the twists and turns of the cold case the host is trying to solve, and when you look down, you see that your kids' plates are empty. You've eaten their leftovers like a human vacuum.

I'll bet you're familiar with the smack-your-head feeling that arises from situations like this. They all could have been avoided if you'd only been paying attention.

I'm sure you've been admonished by dozens of people throughout your life for letting your attention wander—whether it was a teacher who caught you staring out the window as he tried to explain fractions or your spouse as you were driving down a particularly windy road. Or maybe those dozens of people are those judgmental voices in your head (more on this later). "Pay attention!" is a phrase that we've heard so often, we tend not to pay attention to it. Ironic, no?

However, the science is pretty clear on how we have to pay attention to learn new concepts and skills, make empathetic connections with others, and even change addictive habits. And you've probably done the experiment countless times yourself. It's much easier to understand what someone is trying to explain to you if you're paying attention.

This is one of those wonderful and rare instances where conventional wisdom dovetails with scientific research *and* with spirituality. Even if you're not a practicing Buddhist or your idea of Zen is ten minutes of quiet time in the bathtub, you're likely aware that there are deep spiritual practices that hinge on the ability to attend to the world around you and the vast universe of your own internal state.

In this chapter, we're going to look at how awareness will help you change the way you eat. We'll focus on tuning in to the third element of your habit loop, the result/reward value of the behavior (in layperson's terms, "What am I getting from this?"). When we know how rewarding a food is (or isn't), we can determine its value to us relative to other foods and make a decision about which food to eat.

In part 3, you'll learn how to train yourself to choose different (that is to say, healthier) rewards, but for now let's zoom in on how exactly our brain makes decisions about what to eat.

The only way we can change our habits is if the orbitofrontal cortex (OFC) employs attention to help accurately assess the reward value of a food choice.

HOW PAYING ATTENTION CAN CHANGE REWARD VALUES

One of the OFC's most important duties is to determine reward hierarchies. As we go through life sampling different foods, our brains learn how tasty each one is and we develop preferences, so when we are offered two foods we've eaten before, we can choose the one with the greater reward value. It's the old "tasty ice cream trumps poor broccoli" situation.

We can't expect to pay attention to everything at once. Remember the "set and forget" function of the brain—the bit that helps us develop habits so that we can save our energy to learn new things? Habit tells us, "This worked before, so don't think about it, just keep doing it." This is where paying attention is helpful if we are looking to break out of our old routines.

If we pay attention as we eat, the OFC notes the options available. If a food tastes really good, the OFC determines that this food should be on our approved list. If the food tastes bad or makes you feel sick, the OFC will blacklist those foods. As we'll see in a bit, this also goes for the amount of food we eat—that is to say, if we habitually overeat but don't pay attention to what our bodies are telling us about the results ("Urrgh, this doesn't feel so good"), we'll keep doing it.

The positive and negative prediction errors we discussed earlier are critical in helping our OFC update reward values in our brain. If you pay attention and experience (see/taste/feel) that something is better than expected, you get a positive prediction error and that behavior gets reinforced. If given a choice, you will definitely choose this option over other options lower on the list.

If you pay attention and experience that something is worse than expected—that cigarette tastes awful; that bag of super salty potato chips gave me a headache—you get a negative prediction error in your brain and that behavior doesn't get reinforced. You are less excited to repeat it in the future. None of this happens without awareness. If you don't pay attention, you can't get a positive *or* a negative prediction error. You just keep the old habit going.

Notice how this has nothing to do with willpower. Awareness is everything when it comes to behavior change. Let that sink in. *Awareness is everything when it comes to behavior change.*

Practically speaking, for most unhelpful behaviors, the more we pay attention, the more disenchanted we get. They appear less and less magical because we're seeing and feeling clearly that they aren't as rewarding as we remember. It's important, so I'll say it one more time: Habit change is dependent upon and propelled by paying attention. When the OFC has real information gleaned from your paying attention, the OFC will opt for what's most beneficial. When the OFC sees clearly that the old ways aren't working anymore, it pushes them aside to clear brain space for something better. Let's see how this works in real life.

My Sticky Situation with Gummy Worms

My personal food weakness was my relationship with gummy worms. I used to be totally and helplessly addicted to them. They had charmed me with their colors, sweetness, and yes, gummy mouthfeel. (What is it about that type of chewing that really gets us? Whatever it is, I was hooked.) My gummy worm affair wasn't pretty. I bought bag after bag of these rainbow-hued semitranslucent snacks that could double as fishing lures and gorged on them.

I had been smitten since sometime in graduate school. As soon as I thought of them, I had to have them. The siren song would usually start after dinner, and if I tried to tune it out, my desire would only increase in intensity throughout the evening. Like all the other engineered food-like items, gummy worms are designed for wanting. I would eat a couple and then want more. I would try to resist for a while and then would eventually cave and eat the whole bag. I'd rationalize it to myself this way: *Well, at least it's over. You feel crappy now (and will in the morning), but at least they're out of the house.*

Because I had eaten gummy worms for so long, they had established a reward value in my brain. They had moved in and to the top of my "when I want something sweet, I want THIS" list. This had become habit.

And then one day I made a change. I had been practicing mindfulness—learning to be aware and paying attention to my inner and outer world—for a couple of years and decided to turn my attention to my gummy worm habit. One night, instead of getting it over with—eating the whole bag, feeling crappy the next morning (and guilty that I couldn't control myself), but not having to think about it until the next time they were in the house—I started paying attention as I ate them. I noticed that they weren't that great. The sweetness was a bit off: it was sickly sweet, nothing like the complexity of good dark chocolate or honey. And the texture really was kind of like chewing on rubber—not as satisfying as crunching through something or even as good as chomping on a piece of gum. In fact, when I really became aware of these elements, they didn't add up to whatever it was before that had gotten me hooked on them. You can't fool the brain when it is paying attention.

My brain gave a solid negative prediction error: not as good as expected. And that began the end of the affair. My brain had taken notice. Each time I ate them and really paid attention, I would wonder what I'd ever seen in them. I became less and less enchanted. Over time, I lost all interest in them.

I've been paying attention ever since. I've taught myself to pay attention before, during, and after I eat. When I'm hungry in the morning, I can check in and quickly get a sense of just how hungry I am so I can prepare the right amount of food to satisfy that hunger. I also know that if I eat too much, I'm not as sharp and have lower energy. To be clear, this isn't some intellectual calculation of how much I *should* eat; this has all come from checking in with my body and listening to it. I feel sluggish and lethargic. That negative prediction error (overeating doesn't feel good) has helped me stop when I'm full. Being too full is uncomfortable, especially when compared with stopping before that point. And I'm not driven anymore to eat too much. When I map out my eating habit loops and pay attention to the results, I've been able to learn what works and what doesn't when it comes to finding my own sweet spot for mental and physical health.

I want to highlight an eating habit loop in particular that a number of people struggle with: food insecurity. By this, I'm not talking about societal, population-wide levels of food insecurity that result from global supply chain issues and affect millions and millions of people every day. This is an actual and really pressing issue that I am absolutely no expert in. When we zoom in on these population-level issues and become aware of how they affect the individual, we can see the immediate results of our survival brains at work: feel hungry, need food, don't know if I will get more later, eat as much as possible now. As an example, I have always been fortunate enough to have access to food. Despite knowing intellectually that I will be able to access food later, I used to have a habit of eating more than I actually needed at a meal or snack. This had come from times when I had run out of juice way before I could eat again, and my body had let me know through negative reinforcement that I should try to find ways to avoid this in the future. When I mapped this out, it looked like this:

Trigger: Experience fear that I would run out of energy before my next meal and physically and mentally crash.
Behavior: Eat past being full. Try to load up on extra calories.
Result: Avoid crashing.

When I started examining this (and continue to do so, as this habit is still actively showing up for me), I started experimenting with not loading up on the extra calories and found out that generally, I'm just fine. (I can also keep snacks around as a backup.) The fear was loud, while my body was quietly saying, "Hey, this doesn't feel so good. Can you try something else?" I see this survival mechanism power struggle a lot in my patients and Eat Right Now members. Fear is loud. Change is also scary. Together they can drown out the voice of wisdom that comes from our bodies. When we pay attention and listen to all of the voices, it's easier to figure out the wise decision to make, or at least try on for size. When we pay attention, our OFCs move the "eat because I'm afraid I'll be hungry later" choice down in the reward hierarchy through that negative prediction error process.

Once you learn how your brain works, you can start working with it instead of fighting against it. The more habitual the behavior, the less likely your OFC is to notice. So in the next chapters, I'm going to show you how to bring your awareness to the fore to help your OFC discover the unwanted habitual eating behaviors in your brain so you can shake up that reward hierarchy. You'll even see from some of my studies that we can map that change in reward value, and it happens surprisingly fast. As you'll see from Jacqui, Rob, Anne, Jack, and others, once that hierarchy shifts, there is no going back.

Someone in my eating group joked with me that I should have warned her about her favorite foods no longer being top of her list. So I guess I should warn you as well: when you really pay attention, you may fall out of love with certain foods you once couldn't get enough of. As was true with gummy worms for me, those food affairs might end. This tends to happen most with processed foods—our wise bodies know what is best for them and give us feedback signals to that effect, with everything from taste to how we feel after eating. But don't worry, you won't suddenly stop loving things that really taste good. (Just compare eating ice cream with a bunch of ingredients that you can't pronounce to that which is made with just a few natural ingredients.) You might simply eat less of them, while at the same time enjoy them more. That's the power of paying attention.

RIGHT NOW: PRACTICE PAYING ATTENTION

Before you start your day, set your phone or online calendar for a minimum of five reminders during the day. These don't have to be around mealtime or snack time, just random times during the day. Pick a buzz phrase or single word that invites you to stop and drop into awareness for a moment. If you are old school and prefer paper as your go-to technology, put Post-it Notes on places around your house you regularly visit—your refrigerator, your bathroom mirror, the closet, etc. Each time you encounter a reminder, stop whatever it is you are doing (unless it's driving!) and ask yourself, "What am I aware of right now?" Are you dialed into what you are doing, or are you on cruise control? Can you feel any sensations in your body or are you living in your head?

Don't be discouraged if at each of the five points during the day, that reminder is what pulled you off autopilot in that moment. You'll get better with practice. Just take a moment to see how it feels to be present and aware of what is happening in your mind and your body (what thoughts, emotions, and/or bodily sensations are present). How does it feel to be aware, as opposed to being on autopilot?

CHAPTER 10

Day 7: Mindful Eating

WELCOME TO THE SECRET RAISIN SOCIETY

Hopefully, you're getting a sense of the power of paying attention. But what exactly does that look like when you are in the act of eating? Perhaps you have heard of mindful or intuitive eating. In the past several decades, there has been a huge rise in articles, books, and now apps that talk about how to bring paying attention together with eating. For example, the book *Intuitive Eating* that Evelyn Tribole and Elyse Resch originally published in 1995 has ten core principles that fit beautifully with what we now know about the neuroscience of eating, and many—if not all—highlight the importance of bringing awareness (and kindness) to ourselves so we can listen to the wisdom of our bodies.

My own introduction to mindful eating came when I learned about Mindfulness-Based Stress Reduction (MBSR).

Jon Kabat-Zinn came up with the idea of MBSR back in the 1970s. He wanted to meld meditation and yoga practices with Western medicine, so he designed an eight-week program and started teaching it at the University of Massachusetts Medical Center. Over the next several decades, Jon became a rock star in the mindfulness world, and the Center for Mindfulness at UMass was the center stage for training instructors and advancing mindfulness research. I first met him at a summer research institute in 2006, when I asked his thoughts about adapting MBSR for addictions.

I was an assistant professor at Yale's medical school when I was asked to become director of research at the UMass Center for Mindfulness and jumped at the chance. Not only would I get a chance to lead a research portfolio studying MBSR's effects, but I'd get a chance to deepen my mindfulness teaching.

The MBSR program is perhaps most famous for a seemingly small thing: a raisin. The raisin exercise is a rite of passage. Upon finishing the eight-week MBSR program, graduates confess to each other what they really thought of "the raisin exercise" and what they did with their raisin. When they hear that someone is about to sign up for the MBSR program, they say, "Oh, wait for the raisin!" and "Hope you like raisins."

Most MBSR classes are conducted in a circle. Groups of ten to forty people sit in chairs in this formation so that they can see one another. The instructor sits in a chair within the circle to indicate he or she is part of the group.

The raisin-eating rite happens in the first class. Instructors take a bowl and walk around the inside of the circle. They say something to the effect of "I'm going to place an object in your hand. Just let it sit there until everyone has one." They walk from chair to chair and use a spoon to—as hygienically as possible—place a single raisin in each person's upturned palm.

When I've been the instructor leading the raisin exercise, I'll admit I do try to stoke the mystery and suspense.

Once everyone has their raisin, the instructor sets the stage for what's next. Aiming to instill in the group what Zen practitioners refer to as the beginner's mind—a state of infinite possibility and no expectations—the instructor suggests that people imagine that they don't know what this object is. They've never seen it before, and their job is to explore it from every angle. I've gone as far as suggesting group members imagine that they are a Martian news reporter having just landed on Earth. Their job is to write a story about this small object so that Martians can read all about it in the next edition of their *Red Planet Daily News*.

You're likely already able to picture what happens next. (Here's a great example of your brain making predictions about the future based on past experience. Our brains are really good at filling in the blanks.)

As you might expect, the members of the group go through a long period of observing what the raisin looks like, exploring what it feels like, investigating all of the nooks and crannies with their fingers, noticing the different colors, holding it up to the light to see if it is translucent. Generally they do this in silence, taking notes in their head so that they can report back to the group (or to their editor in the newsroom on Mars) at the end.

After they've seen the raisin/object as they've never seen it before, the group goes on to the next sense: hearing. This might not compute to you. You might be thinking, *What the heck does a raisin sound like? They seem awfully quiet to me.* Well, if you hold a raisin up to your ear, especially if you roll it between your fingers, this seemingly silent object makes all sorts of sounds when squished.

Then it's on to smelling. What does a raisin really smell like? I've heard answers that range from "dirt" to "very sweet."

And finally tasting? Not so fast.

We have people bring the raisin right up to their mouth, and then just as they're about to insert it, we have them stop. Stop and note what your mouth is doing. Like good dogs in a Pavlovian experiment, people notice that they're salivating. Sometimes quite a bit. More brain predicting the future! With the expectation that raisins go in mouths to be eaten—because that's how it has happened in the past—our bodies go into motion, preparing for the inevitable. We ask students to stop and notice this reaction.

Finally they get to eat the darn thing. The instruction is to eat it slowly, letting it sit on the tongue for a while, then taking a single bite to notice exactly what is happening before taking the next few mindful bites before swallowing. But for some, it is already too much. They've held back for what seems like forever. They release all of that pent-up expectation and gobble it down.

At the end of the exercise, the instructor debriefs the group, asking with a smile: "What did you notice?" Here the expectation is that people will have noticed something about the raisin that they hadn't noticed before. And invariably the group reports the newness that they just discovered about raisins. You'd be surprised at the different things people notice.

And when a few weeks later a friend tells them that they're thinking of taking a MBSR course, they start to smile . . .

Okay, nice story, but so what? Who cares about the secret raisin society?

I'll put you out of your misery: of course, the raisin rite is a perfect example of mindful eating.

Let's zoom in on what mindfulness is all about: awareness and curiosity. It doesn't take a neuroscientist to predict that eating something slowly is going to help us pay attention and become more aware of what it actually tastes like. Mindful eating is about aware eating. When we pay attention while eating—eating with awareness—we notice how food looks, smells, feels, and tastes. We can enjoy it more. And it is a lot harder to shovel in a mouthful of raisins, Corn Nuts, gummy worms, almonds, peanuts, or whatever when we're taking half an hour to do it. We break that chain of automaticity. We step out of the habit loop by paying attention.

And it doesn't take special rarefied conditions—a sandy beach, candles, incense, or any of the other stereotypes of meditation—to eat mindfully. It certainly helps to have a quiet place free of distractions (books, smartphones, televisions, etc.) to pay attention while eating a snack or a meal. But once you get the hang of it, you can eat mindfully just about anywhere. (Please don't try it while driving.)

But this is only half the story . . .

HOW MINDFUL ARE YOU WHEN YOU EAT?

Have you noticed that when you start eating a meal or a snack, you pay the most attention to the first bite or two and then your brain quickly loses interest and focuses on other things? Why is that? Once again, this is your brain being efficient. It tunes in when you first start eating to make sure your food isn't spoiled or rotten. Once your brain gives the "all good here" signal, you can stop paying attention to the food and go back to the conversation you were having, the book you were reading, the show you were watching, or the work you were doing and not give your food another thought.

A few years ago, Celia Framson and her colleagues at the University of Washington developed a useful tool for evaluating how mindful we are when we eat. It is called the Mindful Eating Questionnaire and is a bit different than being preoccupied with food when we're restricting our eating or on a diet—other questionnaires have been developed to measure these types of things. The full version includes 28 questions. Many questionnaires ask very similar questions in slightly different ways, so I'm including ten of the most relevant ones so you can use this abbreviated version to set your baseline.

MINDFUL EATING QUESTIONNAIRE

On a scale of 1 (never/rarely) to 4 (usually/always), how would you answer the following questions?

1. I snack without noticing that I am eating.
2. When I'm feeling stressed at work, I'll go find something to eat.
3. I notice when I am eating from a dish of candy just because it is there.
4. When I'm sad, I eat to feel better.
5. I think about things I need to do while I am eating.
6. If there are leftovers that I like, I take a second helping even though I'm full.
7. I stop eating when I'm full even when eating something I love.
8. I recognize when I am eating and not hungry.
9. I notice when the food I eat affects my emotional state.
10. I taste every bite of food I eat.

How did you score? If you were high on numbers 1 through 5 and low on numbers 6 through 10, you are not alone. The last question is a bit much for anyone. Who really tastes every single bite of food they eat? But you get the idea. What these questions really highlight is how often we are distracted, eating due to external instead of internal cues and due to emotions instead of hunger. Mindless eating is much more the rule than the exception to the rule. Remember, set and forget is our default. We learn how to eat and set the mechanics of fork meets mouth as a habit. We learn what foods we like and set our preferences as habits.

While not as old as our evolutionary mechanisms for setting up habits, the concept of mindfulness is rooted in Buddhist psychology and dates back thousands of years. Originating roughly 2,500 years ago in Southeast Asia in a language that is now dead (Pali) at a time before paper was even invented, the term *mindfulness* undoubtedly morphed as it moved through time and space, first in oral form, then through translators and cultural traditions to the point where it is now bandied around on social media in the West.

Jon Kabat-Zinn's definition of mindfulness could be tweeted as follows: "Paying attention, in the present moment, on purpose, and non-judgmentally."

Countless books have been written on what mindfulness is and how to practice it in every shape and form. The list of ailments and conditions that these books address cover the entire life span, from birth to death. While the science behind mindfulness is still in its infancy—my lab got in at the beginning, and that was only twenty years ago—more and more is being discovered about how well it works and for what, as well as what happens in our brain when we're being mindful. If you're really interested in that last neuroscience bit, here's a shameless plug: I wrote *The Craving Mind* to explain how we can get caught up in craving and addiction ranging from substances to social media to our own thinking patterns, and how mindfulness might help. Yet you don't need to read that book because it distills down to this: pay attention and your brain will take care of the rest.

The pragmatic point is that often mindfulness gets mythologized into some rarefied state that only gurus and monks can attain. That is not the case. We all have the ability to be curiously aware at any moment. It's more a matter of waking up to what's happening right now and then remembering how much better it feels to be aware than unaware.

MINDFUL EATING IN THE REAL WORLD

About a year ago, someone posted this question on our eating program's online community:

> I work as a live-in caregiver. I work ten- to fourteen-hour shifts, so I've been struggling with mindfulness. If I really pay attention to my meal, it can take upwards of half an hour to finish it. I feel like I really just don't have the time to spend so long on meals/snacks.

Another person asked, "I only have about twenty-five minutes to eat lunch. How do I take each bite mindfully?"

Someone else pointed out: "I'm finding it difficult to do the mindfulness work when I only have a fifteen-minute break to make and eat my lunch."

Having the time to sit down and meditate on a daily basis can be a luxury. Walking or eating slowly can be seen as a privilege. Many people work multiple jobs and juggle family, school, work, and so on. My mom raised four kids by herself while working full time and going to school at night. Try to picture her sitting down for even five minutes with a single raisin. Not going to happen.

Ready for the second half of the story?

Somewhere in the secret society's history, the raisin exercise became the poster child for mindful eating. In other words, people think that mindful eating is *slow* eating. But I would argue that we shouldn't hold our eating to the standard of the raisin rite. After all, how often are you able to dedicate half an hour to a single morsel of food? But some people hold themselves to that high bar. The fear is that if they aren't eating slowly, they aren't—or can't be—eating mindfully. "Mindfulness = doing things slowly" can become a rule our brains try to follow and then use to judge ourselves when we don't.

I get it. If you look at monks in their temples or meditators on retreat, they all seem to be moving at half speed. So our brains, ever extrapolating and predicting, assume that doing things at half, or even quarter, speed is the only way mindfulness works. Well, just because a monk is walking slowly or someone is taking thirty minutes to eat a raisin doesn't mean *that* is how mindfulness works.

Regardless of our personal situation and time constraints, we all have the ability to be aware. We can all be curious. And it doesn't have to be in the form of getting to know a raisin for ten minutes before eating it. We can be aware at any moment, no matter how fast we—or our mouths—are moving.

So when someone says they have only fifteen minutes to eat, I say, "Great, you have fifteen minutes to pay attention while you eat." If they seem squeamish about breaking the "mindfulness is chewing slowly" rule, I help them bust that myth by sharing my own not-secret: As a relatively busy guy, I have to juggle a bunch of things on a daily basis. I don't build a lunch hour into my schedule and often have meetings booked the entire day. So sometimes—gasp!—I eat while I'm in a meeting.

You might be thinking, *He didn't just admit that. He's the mindfulness guy. He's writing a book about eating mindfully. He didn't just say that he eats while doing other things. Stop reading the book. Don't believe anything he says.*

Yes, I did. I'm trying to point out that we have to work with whatever life we've been given. I could schedule a lunch hour. I could eat meals really slowly, but that's not how I roll. My wife jokes that I have two speeds: fast and off. Either I'm moving quickly or I'm in bed, asleep.

However, fast doesn't mean rushed or mindless. Moving quickly just means not moving slowly. Yes, we can move quickly and be aware that we are moving quickly. Athletes are a good example of mindfulness in movement. They have to keep their eyes on balls that are often moving at great velocities. Running backs can't slow-roll their way into the end zone. If you're playing softball or baseball, you can't politely ask the pitcher to slow it down so you observe the ball coming toward you.

We can be eating quickly and aware at the same time. We can also pay attention to why we are about to eat. This takes only a moment. We check in with our urge, asking, "Why am I reaching for food right now? Am I hungry, or is it something else [boredom, stress, anxiety, loneliness, etc.]?" We can question ourselves, as the hunger test teaches us to do. The better we get at this, the faster we can gauge why we're reaching.

Paying attention is just about remembering to put our phone, book, or other distractions away while we eat. If we're in the middle of a meeting, this might not be possible. And that's okay. We can pay attention to the results of what and how much we eat. That's just as important, if not more so, than how quickly we eat or if we're forced to eat while doing something else.

If you drink alcohol before or during meals, you might have noticed that you overeat when you do this. Alcohol is a double whammy: it makes it harder for us to pay attention when we're eating, and also makes the PFC go offline, reducing whatever self-control we think we might have. So to state the obvious: applying mindfulness when drinking is a challenge to say the least.

Mindful Eating in Social Situations

A very active thread on our online community was started by someone posting this simple scenario:

> Suppose you're eating dinner with your family or having lunch
> with business colleagues. The conversation is interesting and fast-
> moving, and you're an important part of it. How do you eat mindfully

in this circumstance? It seems like I'm disconnecting from the group if I try to turn inward and focus mindfully on each mouthful. Not sure how to thread the needle here.

Someone else replied:

> The social situations at a table work better for me because I am talking and listening. I don't talk while chewing or with my mouth full. So I take smaller bites, chew, swallow, put my fork down, etc. I am careful to cut things properly and lift them to my mouth so I don't end up with sauce or whatever on my dress. All of it is much more mindful, although not-by-the-book mindful.

This response is especially insightful. It highlights the stereotype of what "by the book" mindfulness is. It also points out a paradox: eating in social situations can be an opportunity to practice paying attention, one bite at a time. Many folks agreed that this can be challenging and that this challenge can be taken as a mission (should they choose to accept it). We form any habit in short moments, over many times. Taking a short moment—even one bite—helps to develop the habit of paying attention when we eat, even in "suboptimal" conditions.

Here's an example from someone in our program:

> I decided to get a snack because I was tired. Even thinking about the reason for that craving is so much more than what normally happens automatically. But much better, I enjoyed four M&M's—yes, four. And I was fine. I never, never, never ever was able to leave an open bag of M&M's in my drawer in my complete life before. That is so amazing.

I asked Tracy to describe what mindful eating is like for her. She realized she had started eating mindfully over a decade before formally learning mindfulness. She described how one of her favorite treats in middle school was a pumpkin truffle from Godiva chocolates, which was available only once a year. She'd use her allowance to buy a box of five. These cinnamon-sprinkled milk-chocolate-with-pumpkin-pie-filling treats were "glorious," especially because she knew she had only five of them to enjoy before they were gone for another year. She'd eat them slowly, with her eyes closed, each one "a flood of delight and joy." Ten years later when she did her first mindful eating exercise, she realized that she knew how to do this already. "Nobody had to teach me!" This gave her a lot of hope that learning mindfulness wasn't actually about learning, but instead just remembering—for example, remembering that delicious things can be savored.

THREE MYTHS ABOUT MINDFUL EATING

1. Mindful eating is slow eating.
2. Mindful eating can be done only in isolation.
3. Mindful eating turns eating into a chore, robbing food of pleasure.

So your mission, should you choose to accept it, is to see if you can start getting in the habit of eating mindfully. Play with the experience of simply paying attention and being curious while you eat. Even if you eat only a few bites this way, it's a very good start.

In the next chapters, we'll dive deeper into the waters of awareness to see how you can use it to tap your brain's strengths to break unhelpful habits and establish healthier ones.

RIGHT NOW: THE RAISIN RITUAL

I'm not going to make you eat a raisin, but I am going to suggest that you perform your own version of the raisin exercise at home. Pick a food you eat fairly regularly. It can be a piece of bread, an avocado slice, a bit of banana, or a walnut. Try to select a food that doesn't have a lot of ingredients—no Doritos or Twinkies, please—so you can really home in on the experience of eating it without getting distracted by trying to figure out what it is you're tasting. Sit by yourself in a quiet place and really experience eating this food.

What does the food look like? Describe its color, size, and texture.

What does it smell like? Does it smell the way you think it will taste?

If you can pinch it between your fingers, what consistency do you feel? If you can't, what is the surface like? Rough, smooth, pitted?

Yes, you can even try listening to it.

Before you put it in your mouth, ask yourself, "What am I expecting this to taste like?"

Then, of course, put it on your tongue, take a bite, and explore the taste. Was it what you expected?

And what is it like when you pay attention as you continue to eat it?

If you are even mildly inspired after doing this ritual, I'd suggest transferring the practice to snacks and meals. Remember, you don't have to eat slowly. That's not the point. Start to explore what and how much you eat when you let your senses and your body be your guide.

CHAPTER 11

Day 8: Reconnect with Your Body

Let's rewind a bit and go back to the moment where you decided to start eating in the first place—whether it was a single raisin or an all-you-can-eat buffet.

Even with the tool of the hunger test in chapter 8, some people may find it hard to say with confidence, "Yes, I am actually hungry. I have a genuine biological need for food," because we have gotten so divorced from our body's signals. Fortunately, our brains are terrifically flexible, or in scientific terms, they have a high degree of neuroplasticity. We can retrain our brains to pay attention to our bodies.

Our brains have real estate devoted to paying attention to not only sensation and temperature but also emotions, what's known as *interoceptive awareness*, and it seems to involve the insula (from the Latin word for *island*). The insular cortex is thought to be involved in sensing homeostatic emotions such as hunger and thirst. It is also involved in sensing emotions—our own and others'. For example, the insula has been shown to be hyperactive in people with anxiety disorders. Yet often we don't utilize our insula enough.

THE BODY SCAN

Satya Narayana Goenka, more popularly known as S. N. Goenka, was an Indian businessman who lived in Burma in the 1960s. Troubled by debilitating headaches, he learned to meditate and found it so helpful that he eventually dedicated his life to teaching Vipassanā meditation (the documentary *Doing Time, Doing Vipassana* highlights how he even taught meditation in India's toughest prison to a thousand inmates and staff). Before his death in 2013, he had established meditation centers across the world.

Goenka helped popularize a meditation that he called the body sweep, in which one scans the body from head to toe as a way to anchor one's awareness in the present moment. This technique can help us develop insight into our bodies: what the underlying physical sensations are and how we relate to them. At the end of the 1970s, Jon Kabat-Zinn incorporated this meditation—renamed the body scan—as a foundational practice in his MBSR course.

The body sweep/scan can be a helpful way to start reinhabiting your own body. It is remarkably simple and remarkably powerful.

BODY SCAN EXERCISE

If you find it too distracting to read the exercise below, you can do a simple internet search and find many recordings of it, in many languages. I've also posted a recording that you can listen to on my website (https://drjud.com/mindfulness-exercises/).

Sit or lie down in a comfortable, quiet spot. Allow your eyes to close gently. Take a few moments to notice the movement of your breath.

When you're ready, bring your attention to the physical sensations in your body, especially to the sensations of touch or pressure, where your body makes contact with the chair or the floor. On each out breath, allow yourself to let go of any tension that you might be holding in your body.

The intention of the practice is, as best you can, to bring awareness to any sensations you feel as you focus your attention on each part of your body. If you find your mind wandering, gently bring it back to awareness of your body.

Take a moment and thank yourself for making the effort to be here right now. Notice what this feels like in your body.

Now bring your awareness to the physical sensations in your abdomen, becoming aware of the sensations there as you breathe in and breathe out.

Having connected with the sensations in the abdomen, invite the focus of your awareness to shift to the toes of your left foot. See if you can bring a childlike fascination to the sensations, as if you're exploring them for the first time. Focus on each of the toes of the left foot in turn, bringing a gentle curiosity to the quality of sensations you find, noting what they feel like: a sense of tingling, warmth, pressure, pulsing, or no particular sensation. If there are areas you can't feel, keep your focus there, noticing whatever you can about that area.

When you are ready, let go of awareness of the toes, and invite your awareness to notice the sensations on the bottom of your left foot. Bring a gentle, curious awareness to the sole of the foot, feeling all the sensations there. Now invite your attention to the top of the foot, then to the ankle. Now move it up to the calf, the knee. Detect and note as best you can all the sensations in these areas. You might think of your awareness as a spotlight, moving slowly through your body, bringing into awareness any sensations you encounter along the way.

Again, if there are areas where it is difficult to detect sensations, just feel as much as you can. If you notice you are judging yourself for how well or not well you are doing, notice that thought, and bring your awareness back to your body. If you notice that you are judging yourself for how your body looks or feels, same thing: notice it and see how much you can stay in a judgment-free zone.

Now invite your attention to the left thigh. Notice the sensations there. Maybe you feel the pressure of your leg against the chair or the floor.

Throughout this exercise, your mind will inevitably wander away from your body from time to time. That is entirely normal. It is what minds do. When you notice your mind has wandered, gently acknowledge it, noticing where the mind has gone off to, and then return your attention to your body.

Now invite your attention down to the right foot, and to the right toes. Continue to bring awareness, and gentle curiosity, to the physical sensations, allowing whatever sensations are here to just be here as they are. Notice now what you feel in the bottom of your right foot, in the top of the foot, and the ankle, whether that be pulsing, pressure, tingling, warmth, coolness, or anything else.

Next, invite your awareness up to your calf and notice the sensations there. Now to your knee. If you feel any pain or discomfort in any of these areas, just be aware of it. As best you can, let the sensations be as they are. Now gently guide your awareness into your right thigh. Notice the sensations.

Then move on to your hips and waist. Feel your weight on the chair or the floor, and all the sensations. Become fascinated—what are the sensations that make up your experience right now?

Move your focus slowly up to your abdomen. What does it feel like? Notice it rising and falling with each breath. You can start with your skin, becoming aware of the sensations there, and then move your attention inside your abdomen, to your internal organs.

Now invite your awareness into your rib cage. Just feel as many sensations as you can. Now move up to your chest and your shoulders. You might note pulsing when you notice your heart beating, or movement when you notice your ribs expand and contract when you breathe. See if you can bring a childlike fascination to the sensations, as if you're exploring them for the first time.

If you notice your thoughts wandering, or if you become distracted by a sound or feel restless, note this as "thinking," "sound," or "restlessness" and gently guide your attention back to the sensations in your body.

Guide your attention now to the fingers of your left hand. Feel each finger and the places where they contact the chair or your body. What happens when you pay attention to your whole hand all at once, just resting in awareness of it? Now move up into your wrist and forearm. Notice all the sensations here, then in your elbow, upper arm, and your shoulder. Notice any tension, tightness.

Gently invite your attention to the fingers of your right hand, feeling each of them separately. Notice any tingling or urges to move them. Now guide your attention into the palm of your hand and the wrist, the forearm, and elbow. Now focus on your upper arm and shoulder.

Let your attention now come into your neck. Notice if there is tightness or tension, pressure, heat, or whatever sensation is predominant. Now bring your focus up the back of your head. See if you can feel the hair on your head. Bring awareness to your left ear, then over to the right ear.

Now guide your attention to your chin. Focus on the sensations in your face. What do your teeth feel like? What does your tongue feel like? Be curious. Consider your cheeks, your nose. See if you can feel the temperature of your breath and if that changes when you breathe in and out.

Pay attention to your eyes and the muscles around your eyes. What do they feel like? Now move on to your eyebrows and forehead. Be curious. Bring that childlike fascination to each sensation that you feel. Now bring awareness to the very top of your head.

After you have "scanned" the whole body in this way, spend a few moments resting in awareness of the body as a whole. Notice how it doesn't take much effort to simply rest in awareness of whatever sensations are arising.

Finally, very slowly and gently, while still maintaining an awareness of your body, when you are ready, open your eyes and allow your awareness to expand to include the room.

Paying attention to what the sensations in your body feel like will help you become aware of and feel emotions and body sensations more clearly, so you can learn exactly what these are and how they might be driving behaviors. This can also help tune your brain so it is better able to notice subtle sensations in your body and understand what these signals are saying to you. It boosts your ability to use the hunger test because it becomes easier to discern the difference between hunger and loneliness or boredom. Don't worry if it feels like your body is a foreign place right now. As you practice, you'll get more and more attuned to, and in tune with, it. That's why it's called mindfulness *practice* and not mindfulness perfect.

The body scan can be a great practice to do as you go to sleep. This is especially true if as your head hits the pillow, your mind says "my turn!" and starts racing with all of the regret, worry, or planning it didn't seem to have time for earlier in the day. Doing the body scan helps steer you away from those thought patterns, so you can get to sleep more quickly and wake up refreshed.

If you do the body scan regularly, you might also notice that the results of your hunger test will be easier to understand. You will become more expert in interpreting your body's signals on the fly.

DROPPING INTO THE BODY

One of my favorite stories about how paying attention helped someone listen to her body's signals came from Anne. She had just gotten off a phone call with her sister that had left her furious. In a huff, she had been driving and happened to notice a McDonald's. As she put it, "the thought popped up . . . go there now!" Someone once described eating in fast-food restaurants as "going for a shame burger." Anne was aiming for an anger burger, extra burnt. The drive-thru line was long, so she had to park and go inside to order. As she walked across the parking lot, she thought, *I'm going to get this, this, this, this, and this.*

Suddenly she had a moment of clarity. She noticed her brain was telling her what to do with no regard for what her body wanted or needed. She thought, *This is messed up. You're mad at her, so you're going to punish yourself. You're going to stuff yourself until you're sick because you're angry with her. She wins. Is this what you want?* She took another moment and went even deeper, asking herself, "What are you trying to stuff down and not feel? How does it feel in your body right now? Not good. How do you want to feel? Good. Okay."

She explained the realization she had in that moment: "When you drop into your body, your mind is sort of quiet. It's like it's kind of watching. 'What's she going to say?'" She described what happened next. "The feeling. The wanting—wanting to shove it down—left. I just remember: I don't want any food. I'm just mad. I'm just really mad and I'm tired of picking up the pieces, but I don't want to eat. I'm not hungry. I'm just mad. Letting go was actually easier than hanging on."

When she took that moment to drop into her body, it helped her notice she wasn't really hungry.

She turned around and went back to her car. Anne emphasized the importance of that moment. "I sat in the car and it was instant: I didn't want anything. I just didn't want it. And then I just drove away. I went home."

This was a great example of how quickly things can change when we pay attention to our body. We experience a moment of awareness about how we're acting out an old habit that isn't going to fix whatever it is—the anger and the hurt that Anne was feeling, in this case—and we are able to listen to our body instead of following through on the impulse.

Toward the end of our conversation, Anne reflected on how she was the only person she knew who *lost* 10 pounds during the pandemic. She pointed to a blackboard on the wall next to her kitchen table. It was full of grocery lists and other writings. She told me how for a long time now, she had written *Trust* on it. It was her little reminder—her mantra—to remember to trust that she had eaten enough. She explained, "It's almost a physical thing where you sigh and you want to push away from the table. You're like, 'I'm done.' If you pay enough attention, your body will tell you what's going on."

Your body has so much wisdom to offer if you just let your attention show you where it is stored.

RIGHT NOW: TRY A BODY SCAN

Try doing a body scan today. See if you can even begin practicing it on a regular basis. As I suggested before, a good place to start is at night as you first go to sleep, so that it doesn't feel like yet another thing on your to-do list that overwhelms you or makes you feel bad that you didn't get to. Even if you make it only to your knee before you fall asleep, all is well. Compare what you feel like before you start and afterward. If you fall asleep, you can chalk it up as "restful." Learning to listen to your body is an excellent way to begin the process of breaking long-established food habit loops. Over time, you might notice that you are more attuned to your body's signals and better able to interpret them. That's not to say you won't have cravings triggered by stress or emotions, but you should be better able to distinguish them from homeostatic hunger. In the next chapter, we'll look at what to do when those cravings do manage to sneak up on you.

CHAPTER 12

Day 9: Get to Know Your Pleasure Plateaus

CHOCOLATE: A SCIENCE EXPERIMENT

Imagine you are driving down the highway when you see a billboard that reads EAT YOUR FAVORITE CHOCOLATE. ALL YOU WANT. GET PAID!

You do a double take. What's the catch? Is this a market research project where a candy company is recruiting chumps to help them dial in the bliss point for some new chocolate bar so they can get us to spend our hard-earned money to buy even more chocolate?

But this ad is not the work of an evil corporation out to increase its profits. It is the brainchild of Dr. Dana Small, a graduate student at Northwestern University at the time, who cooked up this scientific experiment to measure our pleasure.

Dr. Small is now a leader in the field of food research. A professor of psychiatry and psychology and director of the Modern Diet and Physiology Research Center at Yale University, Dr. Small has published hundreds of papers related to how our brain integrates sensory and metabolic signals and how these affect food choices. To measure how smell, taste, and other sensory input affect brain signals, she's had to invent all sorts of crazy contraptions to deliver food, liquids, and even smells to people's mouths and noses.

Dr. Small wanted her subjects to eat their *favorite* chocolate, so she let them choose. She did a pilot test with fifteen people. They ranked twenty kinds of chocolate from most to least pleasant. Lindt bitter-sweet (50% cocoa) and Lindt milk chocolate were consistently ranked highest. However—and this might fit with your experience—people who liked the bittersweet didn't like the milk chocolate, and vice versa. To keep things simple, when it came time to scan their brains, Dana gave people a choice between those two highest scorers.

Dana then set up a scale to measure how much her subjects liked the chocolate. They would be put in the PET scanner and fed chocolate, one piece at a time, while their brain was being scanned. After each bite they would be asked to rate, on a scale of -10 to +10, how much they would like another piece: -10 was scored as "Awful—eating more would make me sick," and +10 was scored as "I really want another piece."

Imagine taking your first bite of your favorite chocolate. How would you rate it? Probably 10 out of 10, "I really want another piece." Not surprisingly, this is what her study participants reported. And then she continued. Another piece. Rating. Another piece. Rating. And another piece.

It was innocent enough at first. But Dana kept feeding her subjects until they were way past their bliss point. She wasn't force-feeding them excessive amounts against their will. They had all signed consent forms and knew what they were getting into. Yet, it's surprising how quickly one can go from "I really want another piece" to "Awful—eating more would make me sick." For some, this happened after as few as sixteen squares. For others, it took up to seventy-four.

How could pleasant-tasting chocolate be awful at the same time? Well, our brains have to tell the difference between when something tastes good and when something feels good. We are set up to know the difference between good and too much. These function very differently for survival. Pleasant and unpleasant let us know whether food has calories (and even how many) or is poison. Hunger pangs let us know when we are hungry and when we've had enough to eat. Liking is very different from wanting. We can like something, and depending on the circumstances—for example, just having eaten seventy-three squares of chocolate—either want it or not want it in that moment.

Dana Small wanted to capture the difference between liking chocolate and wanting—or not wanting—more. She focused on the wanting—how the chocolate made people feel. What did her subjects' brains reveal? As the reward value of the chocolate decreased, blood flow in the OFC increased. One way to interpret this is that the OFC was noting how a good thing can become too much.

Even more interesting was that the posterior cingulate cortex (PCC for short) was firing off the most at both ends of the spectrum: wanting more and wanting this experiment to end. This brain region is a hub of a neural matrix called the default mode network. It gets activated when people who are addicted to certain substances and behaviors are shown cues (think of them as brain triggers) that remind them of these habits—cocaine, cigarettes, gambling, you name it.

PLEASURE PLATEAUS

Dana mapped out what I call the pleasure plateau:

Let's see how the pleasure plateau plays out in real life. When you are hungry for a meal, you sit down and your body says, "Feed me." You start eating, and if the food is edible (and hopefully tasty), it will register in your brain as a safe source of calories. Then your

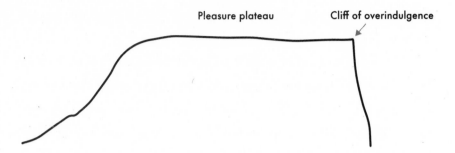

FIGURE 1. *Pleasure plateau.*

brain checks in with your stomach to see if it has more room. You're headed up the hill, driven by both liking and wanting. That is, until you have eaten enough. You've reached the top of the pleasure plateau.

When you hit the plateau, the liking goes down a little. The food doesn't suddenly taste terrible; it's just not as pleasant as before. And the wanting goes down a lot. That's your brain's signal to slow down. Without awareness, you keep eating and building momentum. You don't notice the guardrail up ahead. You don't see the warning signs that say this is the end of the road. Suddenly you shoot right off the cliff. We all know what it feels like to eat too much, whether we are participating in a holiday meal or just not paying attention when we're in a rush. When we've crashed at the bottom and the dust settles, our stomachs let us know how much we've overindulged through signals of feeling bloated and sick, having indigestion.

Now let's add dessert into the picture.

Once you've finished your meal, if you have a habit of eating dessert—or simply feel like something sweet—you might have a craving for, say, chocolate. Since that itch of an urge isn't really about hunger, you have a much smaller hill to climb—one that is more about satiation or contentment than about fullness. So you hit the plateau more quickly, which also makes it easier to speed off the cliff of overindulgence.

Whether you eat mindlessly, have the habit of overeating, or are a member of the clean-plate club, all of these make it really easy to drive off that cliff. When you crash, you pull yourself out of the wreckage and feel horrible—mentally and physically. It doesn't feel good to overeat. It doesn't feel good to overindulge in sweets. Our bodies know this. They are wise and have the natural systems to help us stop, yet we override them over and over and over. We go off the cliff many, many times before we start paying attention to exactly how it feels to go off the cliff—and then we become disenchanted with continuing to crash our car.

Tracy told me about her experience with the pleasure plateau and ice cream. "It was a matter of really learning over time how many bites do I really enjoy? At some point my mouth will get so cold, I stop tasting it after a while. At the end, it's not enjoyable anymore."

Another member of our program reported, "I really examined each mouthful and was able to leave food on my plate and walk away feeling satisfied!!!"

Cultivating awareness helps us see when we've had enough. We naturally start to take our foot off the gas, so we coast to a stop without even needing to put on the brakes. Anne shared her experience with how eating mindfully helped her find her pleasure plateau and stop eating when her body did not want more. She explained how she'd recently eaten a reasonable portion of healthy food for lunch. She ate without looking at a magazine or reading on her phone. She gave herself permission to have a second bowl if she wanted it. She paid attention and enjoyed how everything tasted, but when it stopped tasting good to her, she stopped eating. Then she marveled that four hours later she still wasn't hungry, even though all she'd eaten was a single portion. Her pleasure plateau let her know when her body had had enough.

RIGHT NOW: FIND YOUR PLEASURE PLATEAU

It's simple (but not necessarily easy). To locate your pleasure plateau with your favorite foods or the quantity you eat at meals, you'll need to pay attention with each bite. Ask yourself, "Is this more pleasurable, the same, or less pleasurable than the last bite?" No need to make or take notes beyond this bite vs. the last bite. Awareness won't make your favorite food suddenly unpleasant, but if you can notice that as you eat, it is becoming less pleasant, that's a sign that you might have reached your pleasure plateau and future bites will decrease in their reward value.

Map out your own pleasure plateau, bringing awareness to each bite. You can pull out a piece of paper and draw a Y axis denoting *pleasure* and an X axis with *number of bites* on it. You can measure and then make a mark of an X for each bite. See where and how quickly you top off. Two potato chips? One piece of dark chocolate? You might be surprised.

You might start at a time when you're not ravenously hungry—for example, with a dessert or one of your favorite snacks—as a way to get the hang of it. When we're starving, it can be pretty hard to pay attention.

Then you can build this awareness exercise into eating meals, focusing on pleasantness, wanting, and fullness. Use your mouth as your main guide here, and give your stomach fifteen minutes to catch up so that it can let you know when you've hit "enough!" Satiety signals are processed about twenty minutes after your first bite, so it takes approximately that long from the time you start eating for your brain to register fullness—though you can certainly reach satiety sooner. You don't have to wait a full twenty minutes from that last bite, but you do have to give your body a bit of time to process what and how much you've eaten.

When you get started, you might go off the cliff a couple of times. That's fine. As long as you pay close attention to what that feels like, you'll learn from the experience. You'll see the signs earlier the next time. With practice, it will get easier and easier to coast to a stop.

CHAPTER 13

Day 10: The Craving Tool (Part 1)

If you've already played with the pleasure plateau a bit, you might have noticed what seems to be a problem: your plateau seems pretty high. If you've had a history of restrictive eating—"oh, I can't eat X at all, I'll go off the rails"—it might seem like you'd never hit that plateau or that there aren't even any rails to let you know where that cliff is.

This is not a problem with you or your brain. This is more of a reflection of the limits of restrictive dieting. The "head first, body not even second" approach isn't a brain-based approach. As such, it shows its brittleness when pressure tested. When stressed (or pressured by another strong emotion), we can easily lose control and the abstinence violation effect kicks in, accelerating our speed as we go off the cliff. Here we need to reconnect the wires between brain and body.

It turns out that this recalibration process has a long but largely ignored history.

PAYING ATTENTION TO GRATIFICATION

As we were developing tools for Eat Right Now, I came across an article entitled "Overeating and Mindfulness in Ancient India" by my friend, the Buddhist monk and scholar Bhikkhu Anālayo, who was in residence at a Buddhist studies center in Western Massachusetts. I had been meditating for about twenty years at this point and was always interested in geeking out about how Buddhist concepts translated into pragmatic tools. Anālayo was very much on the same page. The core teachings in Buddhism—no matter what tradition or lineage—are about ending suffering in all shapes and forms. I had asked Anālayo if there were examples of struggles with eating in the Buddhist texts. The good scholar that he was, he did some research, which resulted in the article.

In the paper, Anālayo wrote about the story of a king by the name of Pasenadi who struggled with overeating. Being a wise king, he came to the Buddha for advice. The Buddha said that "people who are constantly mindful know their measure with the food they've gotten." Anālayo points out the Buddha's choice of the word *measure* likely refers to eating enough, but not too much. That sounded a lot like a pleasure plateau to me. The king sees the wisdom of this suggestion and pays someone in his court to memorize the teaching and recite it to him before every meal. By being constantly reminded to pay attention while he is eating, the king is able to stop overeating and gradually loses weight.

In addition to what Anālayo pointed out, the Buddhist texts talk a lot about three dimensions of experience (eating and otherwise): gratification, disadvantage, and release. For example: "I set out seeking the gratification in the world. Whatever gratification there is in the world I have found. I have clearly seen with wisdom just how far the gratification in the world extends."

Think of gratification of a desire as indulging an urge, scratching an itch, or quenching a thirst for something. Interpretation: the

Buddha became enlightened—as in no more suffering—not by forcing himself to stop doing things that brought him pleasure. There are many stories about how as a prince, he had indulged himself in all sorts of worldly pleasures—food, drink, sex, and so on. That hadn't worked, so he had tried the opposite extreme, becoming an ascetic, denying himself these pleasures by abstaining from sex, starving himself, and so on. Yes, he, too, tried the restriction diet—applying it way beyond food. This hadn't worked, either.

Instead, he tried a radically different approach. He paid attention. He *really* paid attention to the process of indulging his cravings and denying himself worldly pleasures. He basically asked himself, "What am I getting from this?" Through this exploration, he saw indulging his desires was not rewarding in itself. And that led him to be less excited about continuing to do it. In fact, he became disenchanted with it. Why do this if it doesn't feel good?

He also discovered that the gratification of his desires was fleeting—and paradoxically created only more desire. This is important, so don't skip over it. Gratifying that urge to eat a piece of cake can feel really good in the moment, but it may not have a high reward value—the pleasure of the cake is fleeting, and it will make you desire even more of it. It's like we have an insatiable itch that we just have to scratch. So we scratch. It feels good to scratch it, but then a few moments later, it itches *even more,* on and on, in a cycle that the Buddhists call *saṃsāra* (endless cycles of suffering). He was even more disenchanted when he saw this process clearly.

The Buddha figured out how to release himself from this wretched and endless cycle of suffering, simply by paying attention and mapping it out. The parallel to what modern science has found with breaking habit loops is almost too perfect. Awareness helps us learn the results (reward value) of our behavior. If we pay attention and tune in to our body's signals, we clearly see the cause (scratch the itch) and the effect (itch keeps itching). This leads us to become even more disenchanted with the old ways, and to see something else.

We release ourselves from this endless habit loop only if we try something else. We try not scratching the itch, and the rash clears up. We are free. But doesn't that not scratching feel pretty uncomfortable? You bet. But what feels worse? Having an itch for a little while or having an itch for a long time? It is hard for our brains to see past the immediate itch. How can we leverage the immediate gratification to stop scratching? And might we use it to recalibrate the system at the same time so that we can find our actual pleasure plateaus?

A reward value sets the pleasure plateau in terms of both what we eat and how much we eat. Eating until we are full leads to contentment. Overeating might have some qualities of satisfaction in our minds, but also brings discontent in our bodies and minds. A piece of chocolate can be rewarding—seventy-two pieces, not so much. According to the ancient teachings, we have to explore gratification to its end. The only way to calibrate the system—find that actual contentment point—is through positive and negative prediction errors. When it comes to overindulgence, it is all about that negative prediction error: knowing from our own experience that eating too much doesn't feel as good as our brains expect it to.

We created a tool to test this in real life. The idea is to bring awareness to overindulgence so that we can see where the cliff is and also find our actual plateaus. Once we do this, we no longer have to slam on the brakes when we see that we are right at the cliff's edge and are going way too fast; coasting to a stop on top of the plateau becomes much easier.

THE CRAVING TOOL (PART 1)

The craving tool works like this:

Notice when you have a craving for a food.

If you decide to indulge the craving, go for it. But pay attention—*really* pay attention—to what it feels like as you do so. Check in with your body, emotions, and thoughts. Basically, eat whatever type or amount of food you'd usually eat when the craving comes on, but do it as an expanded mindful eating exercise where you add in paying attention to how it makes you feel.

Afterward, ask yourself one crucial question: "What am I getting from this?" This links up the cause (what or how much you ate) with its effects on your body and mind. Your brain might have some immediate answers—usually in some form of judgment like "you shouldn't have" or "this is bad"—but your body knows best. Seek wisdom by listening to what your body has to say.

If you like a more step-by-step process, below is a description of how to break this down to more easily quantify your results.

THE CRAVING TOOL

- Pay attention to why you want to eat right now (hunger, emotions, boredom, etc.).
- Pay attention to what you are about to eat. What is it made up of? What does it look and smell like?
- Pay attention as you eat each bite (smell, taste, texture, temperature, etc.).
- Keep paying attention until you finish eating.

After you've eaten, ask yourself the following questions:

1. How much did you eat? (Circle the answer in your head.)

Way too much

Too much

Right amount

Too little

None

2. Check in with your body. How do you physically feel right now?

Awful! -10 -5 0 +5 +10 Awesome!

3. Check in with your emotions. How do you feel right now?

Awful! -10 -5 0 +5 +10 Awesome!

4. Check in with your thoughts. What type of thoughts are you noticing right now?

Awful! -10 -5 0 +5 +10 Awesome!

Now add up your results. A positive score suggests that you are enchanted with whatever you did, and a negative score suggests that you are well on the road to disenchantment land. Remember, reward-based learning is based on how rewarding a behavior is. If you can clearly see the results of the behavior, your brain can add up just how rewarding or unrewarding what you just did is. Adding it up like this can help make this prediction error calculation clearer for your brain.

You might be shaking your head in doubt right now. I ate the food and it satisfied my craving. I indulged and I feel fine. I feel better than fine because cravings don't feel good and now the craving is gone and I'm satisfied. Yes, scratching itches can feel good and satisfying in the moment. Later they start to itch more. And you have to scratch them again. Also, the "gut bomb" effect may not have taken hold yet, so give it a minute or five or fifteen if you answered "too much" or "way too much" to the question of how much did you eat.

There is more to this equation.

As you probably know, our brains are so tied up in language—how we describe to ourselves what just happened actually affects how we experience what just happened—that the words that we use to ask ourselves questions shape our experience.

My lab tested a number of different questions to figure out the best way to get that composite score of people's experience after they did the exercise. We had people check in with their thoughts, emotions, and bodily sensations after they ate, and then compared how satisfied they felt with how content they felt. On the surface, *satisfied* and *content* might seem like the same thing. But they aren't.

Check this for yourself. After indulging a craving, how satisfied do you feel? How content do you feel? For some, the answer is the same. But for many, there is a critical difference. That's what my lab found. Asking whether people were satisfied missed the mark of whether someone was zeroing in on disenchantment. Asking whether they were content hit the bull's-eye. *Satisfying a craving is different from feeling content afterward.* We can feel momentarily satisfied by scratching an itch when we have poison ivy, but not content because the underlying cause of the itch is still there. Scratching the itch is different than not having the itch.

Being temporarily satisfied with something doesn't necessarily make us content and can make us miss the fact that we might be unconsciously keeping ourselves in a cycle of suffering. Being discontent helps us become disenchanted with the cycle, which motivates us to step out of it. Notice how this is a natural motivator. We don't have to force ourselves. We want to change because we're not happy with the way things are. More evidence that we don't need willpower.

You can simplify part 1 of the craving tool to these two questions:

1. **What am I getting from this? (Notice your thoughts, emotions, and bodily sensations.)**

2. **How content do I feel? (Ask this now and again in five and fifteen minutes.)**

Each time you do part 1 of the craving tool, you help your brain determine the new reward value for each old (or new) eating behavior that you use it with. As you'll see soon, each data point helps move you toward a tipping point where the behavior shifts. That shift signals a new/recalibrated pleasure plateau. And as was true with my gummy worm obsession, if you really find no satisfaction in the "thing" (I wouldn't count gummy worms or Doritos as food beyond the fact that they are very efficient calorie delivery vehicles) that you're eating, that plateau might be flat. Flat is the potato chip industry's worst nightmare. Flat means "I betcha can't get me to eat even one."

You can even practice using the craving tool with other behaviors as well, as this is how your brain learns to change with any behavior (for example, see how content you feel after yelling at your kids or partner).

Here's another important idea. Eating with awareness doesn't magically get you to stop liking chocolate or cake or doughnuts or ice cream or whatever your indulgence of choice may be. In fact, you might like it even *more* when you notice how great it tastes. The money is in exploring gratification to its end. When we built the craving tool into the Eat Right Now app, we programmed it to ask you to rate how content you feel now. And then it asks you again five and twenty minutes later. These latter steps help if you've eaten a large amount of food quickly. Remember, it can take that long for calories to get absorbed, insulin to go up, satiety signals to fire, and fullness to register in your body. This gives your stomach, body, and brain time to let you know if it isn't keen on what just happened. If you happened not to have overindulged when doing this exercise, that's good information, too. It builds enchantment with hitting that pleasure plateau and stopping before you go off the cliff of overindulgence.

Our bodies are wise enough to know that processed or junk food doesn't feel as good as unprocessed food. Our bodies are wise enough to know that overeating doesn't feel good. Sure, we can use eating comfort food or overeating to soothe or numb ourselves, but this is anything but comfortable. We just need to see that process of cause and effect clearly. The cause—overeating—leads to an effect: not feeling good. We need solid data.

The process of disenchantment is usually gradual. If we've had a habit of eating a certain type or amount of food for a long time, what happens when we start paying attention? As happened in my experience with gummy worms, we might notice that they aren't as nice as we remembered. Yet that doesn't magically kick my gummy worm habit to the curb. Why is that?

Well, if I've been eating gummy worms for a long time, that reward value is pretty locked in. So if I pay attention enough to get a negative prediction error (worse than expected), my brain might discount that piece of data. Because I have stored a vast database of "gummy worms are good" information, a single data point to the contrary gets shoved to the side. "Oh, you must have made a mistake," my brain tells itself. It was expecting gummy worms to taste good, and in the name of stability for the system, it isn't going to suddenly change everything just because of one piece of information.

From a survival standpoint, that's a good thing. When we've seen over and over that something helps us survive, it isn't good to suddenly change course just because of one piece of new information. We'd be running for the hills every time we heard some loud ambiguous noise. We have to figure out what made the noise so we can determine if it is dangerous or our family members goofing around. Years of waiting for the light to change before safely crossing the street should not be wiped out because we made it across alive one time when there was no traffic.

I had to pay attention each time I ate gummy worms to make sure that first negative prediction error wasn't a fluke. The more information I gathered, the more likely it was accurate and trustworthy. And that outlier—meaning it was really off from what I was expecting— transformed from outlier to the norm. It became a reliable signal. I didn't need willpower for this. I simply needed to pay attention so I saw over and over that I don't really like the taste of gummy worms. That's how my disenchantment built. And it has stuck around to this day.

But that's just me and gummy worms. How quickly does this process work in general?

HOW LONG DOES THE CRAVING TOOL TAKE TO WORK?

As a science geek, I wanted to know how long it takes someone to become disenchanted with a food. In a study led by Isabelle Moseley (an undergraduate at Brown at the time) and Véronique Taylor (a postdoctoral fellow), we started with a small cohort of sixty-four women who were overweight and tracked their craving tool use as they went through the Eat Right Now program. Eight weeks later we measured changes in food craving, stress eating, and reward-based eating, and found that similar to Ashley Mason's study a few years prior that I mentioned in the introduction, all of these had dropped significantly. That was nice to see. Replication is the hallmark of science.

Then we looked at the craving tool. We could calculate changes in reward value. And we could see how quickly these changes happened. It took only ten to fifteen times of using the craving tool for that reward value to drop *below zero*. We could watch the values drop down and down—craving tool use to craving tool use—and even watch participants' behavior flip from following the urge into eating to not following it. We repeated this with a study of over a thousand people in a community sample and saw the same thing: when we pay attention, it doesn't take long for reward values to change and behavior to shift.

This is good news. If you've had a habit of overeating (for example) for years or decades, you don't need to spend years (and decades) to shift that behavior. Our brains are pretty plastic. We have to be able to adapt to our environment quickly. Our ancestors didn't have the luxury of being chased by the tiger twenty times before they realized that it was dangerous. They needed to learn quickly. We still have that capacity. The more we employ our awareness, the faster we learn.

Rob put it this way:

> I wasn't trying to change anything. I had no agenda. I wasn't on a diet, I wasn't restricting. I had tried everything at that point, and when I came to the program, I had fully surrendered. When I became introduced to curiosity [paying attention with a curious attitude], everything changed. I quickly saw that I could tolerate being alive. I could be with discomfort. I was so beat up after years of anxiety and

obesity that I don't think I had anything left in me to change anything even if I wanted to. The little bit of effort it took to remember to shift into awareness was all I could muster up. After a few weeks, even that little bit of effort was almost unnecessary. It was replaced with a calling from within to be curious because it just felt better.

Rob didn't need someone to remind him to pay attention. His suffering was painful enough to motivate him. He explored gratification to its end and became disenchanted with the process. Whether you are using the craving tool or simply asking, "What do I get from this?" you can do this on your own.

RIGHT NOW: USE THE CRAVING TOOL

See if you can use the craving tool at least once a day for the next couple of days. In particular, pull it out when you have an urge to eat something even though you aren't hungry or when you have a habit of overeating and are about to embark on that behavior. You can simply open the book and ask yourself the questions in the craving tool as you eat. At the end, pay careful attention to how content you feel.

CHAPTER 14

Day 11: Build Your Disenchantment Databank

Let's review where we are so far. In part 1, you learned how to map your eating patterns. In part 2, we've been learning how to pay attention to how rewarding—or not rewarding—your behavior is so you can interrupt that habit loop.

You've just seen how you can evaluate what it feels like to eat a particular food using the craving tool. Used regularly, the craving tool will help you establish what I call a disenchantment database—a store of memories of negative prediction errors your OFC can draw on when making a decision about what to eat. Before you can make better choices, you need to undercut the appeal of your long-held habitual behaviors.

Each time the reward value plummets, that is another entry in the disenchantment database. As the true reward value becomes clearer, the behavior moves up or down in the reward hierarchy. The real pleasure plateau becomes easier to find.

The craving tool is specifically designed to give you real-time data from your own experience. Those data points are gold. When it comes to behavior change, nothing is more valuable than your own experience. And immediate feedback is the best way to learn. We see the results of a behavior in real time, so we can't get them confused with any other cause. If the result comes later, it is hard to know what caused it because it is harder to directly connect it with behavior A, because behaviors B and C happened afterward and possibly could have caused it. The more you use the craving tool, the more data you deposit into your disenchantment bank account.

A very cool thing happens when you have enough data in your disenchantment database. Your cravings don't have the same pull as they used to. Why? When we taste, smell, and feel how crappy a cigarette is, when we recall that experience, our brain says, "Why would I do that?!" When we recall what our body and brain told us the last ten times we overate, our brain starts asking us, "Really, are you sure? Remember how this felt the last time you did it."

ALL IN GOOD TIME

Over a decade ago, in one of our studies of smoking cessation, we observed how building disenchantment can help curb cravings over time. At the end of a four-week treatment, people quit smoking, yet still reported strong cravings. They had not vanished immediately. A couple of months later, their cravings for cigarettes were significantly down. They had stopped fueling the fire of craving, yet like what happens with a fire when you stop adding wood, it took a while for the cravings to burn down on their own.

About a month into treatment, Jack asked me how long he should expect it to take for the techniques he'd been learning to work. I could tell he was hoping I'd say, "Any day now, Jack!"

He had been using the tools we'd talked about in his last two sessions: paying attention when he had the urge to eat—the why—and also bringing awareness in as he was eating to better gauge when he was full—the how. He put it this way: "I ping myself and ask, 'Are you hungry or just in the habit of consuming more food?' I have a level of awareness but need to go more into my body. I can make the determination that I'm not really hungry, but I still have the urge to go and have some more food." Talking about his clean-plate club habit, he noted: "There's a conflict. I know there's going to be the unpleasant experience [of overeating]. My brain is telling me that this is going to be delicious—a sweet reward. [His brain talking to him:] 'You don't want to put that away. You might as well finish it.' It's very seductive."

Jack was describing the classic tug-of-war between brain and body. Our brains tell us one thing, and our body signals indicate another. Which one do we listen to?

I asked Jack how long he'd had his eating habits. "I can trace them back to childhood. I remember them painfully—fifty years of these habits." He went on: "I see these habit loops, what is inspiring me to eat more. At times I eat because of anxiety or sadness, but at these times it's just a trigger to go back for more because that's what I've always done."

Fifty years is a long time to build and reinforce a habit. In our eating study, the reward values were shifting relatively quickly. We also looked at changes in food craving using the Food Cravings Questionnaire. After two months, food cravings dropped significantly, which coincided with reductions in stress eating. Fortunately, as the data seem to suggest, it doesn't take fifty years to break these habits. But it does take some repetition to build awareness.

Toward the end of the session, I gave Jack his mission: see how long it takes for your experience to win out over your brain.

I also explained that he could probably trace his frustration to a quirk of our brains called delay discounting.

DELAY DISCOUNTING

Our brains like to look ahead. We project into the future and imagine where we want to go and what behaviors will get us there. For example, for those of us in the northern hemisphere, January 1 is generally pretty cold. We're bundled up in our sweaters and sweatpants trying to stay warm. We imagine what summer will be like when we can go to the beach or simply go outside to soak up some of the sun's warmth. How many of us start projecting—societal norms, expectations, and customs play a big role here—what we want to look like when the warmth comes? We look at the vacation brochures and see the skinny people sunbathing in their skimpy swimsuits. Billboards, magazines, and social media all urge us—consciously or unconsciously—to look like the skinny people. Our brain gets on board with the idea, and we set (yet another) goal of slimming and trimming so that the swimming will go well. Spurred on by massive food intake from Thanksgiving to New Year's, January 1 is a traditional time to set that goal of eating less and going to the gym more. Our brain urges us into action. It says, "Do this now, and you'll be rewarded later."

The idea of setting a plan today that will help us out in the future makes a lot of sense. If we get good grades in high school or college, we'll get a good job. If we save money today, we'll have more for retirement. If we brush our teeth tonight, we'll be less likely to get cavities and need a root canal. If we stop smoking, we won't get cancer. If all goes well, we'll be smiling pretty (no dentures!) in the mirror (looking at our cancer-free beach bod) when we retire somewhere in the sun.

On January 2, when we are back at work, we check our long list of emails and we get stressed. All of those plans go out the window as we reach into our desk drawer for some candy.

What happened?

The scientific term for the January jump start turned February failure—if we make it all the way to February—is delay discounting. There is a lot of research on this (scientists such as Warren Bickel and others have led the charge here), but basically it goes like this: We prefer a smaller reward now over a bigger reward later. In economics they can dial this in to the penny by giving people choices between getting, say, $10 today as opposed to $11 next week. What would you prefer? For me to hand you a crisp new $10 bill now, or promise to meet you next week and add a buck on top of the ten? Most people take the cash-in-hand approach. Why? Our bookkeeping brains might calculate the difference and point out that $11 is 10 percent more than $10 and that we could never get that return on our investment if we put the $10 in the bank this week and withdrew it next week. On the other hand, our survival brains tell us, *Hey, I don't know if this guy will show up next week. Don't risk it. Take the money and run.*

Time is such a crucial element in this process that delay discounting is also called temporal discounting, time discounting, or simply time preference. We prefer the sure thing. The longer we look into the future, the less sure things are. Anything can happen between now and next week. Many more anythings can happen between now and next month or next summer.

So when given a choice, our brains stick with what has worked over and over and over—that is to say, habit. We could try to lose weight for the summer, but the summer is pretty far off. We don't know what will happen in the meantime. We might or might not make it. We *do* know what candy tastes like. We do know that it can give us some brief relief (or at least distraction) when we're stressed right now. Summer clothes six months from now? Gummy worms right now!

You might be wondering, "Why is he giving us bad news about our brains?"

Well, you have to hear the bad news sometime. Would you rather delay reading this for six months or get it over with right now? Like a quick rip of the Band-Aid, it might sting a tiny bit, but it's a whole lot better than prolonging the pain. In fact, most of the painful part is already over. You already know how delay discounting works—from your own experience. You've no doubt experienced times when that urge to indulge overtook that sensible "you shouldn't" voice in your head. So perhaps you can see this as good news, and as a twist to leverage your delay discounting brain: Doesn't it feel better to learn and change now, rather than putting it off into the future, when the habits will be even more entrenched?

For starters, seeing how delay discounting works helps you put less trust in willpower. Willpower often dangles those delayed rewards in front of us: eat less, quit smoking, save money, exercise more now, so that you will be happier in the future. But don't you want to be happy now? YES! Of course you do.

This is where you can start hacking your brain's reward system now. That's what we're already doing. That's what asking yourself "What am I getting from this?" is set up to help you do right now. And each right now puts money in the brain bank today so that it can earn interest, which can be cashed out as disinterest—disenchantment—when we need it in the future.

Tracy described how it took quite some time before she became disenchanted with overeating at holiday meals with her family. She said:

> **This past Thanksgiving was the first Thanksgiving that I didn't feel ill because I had eaten too much. That was cool to see, because as I was taking my plate and going around the table as we were serving ourselves, I just knew how the food was going to impact me. So I just took a small amount of everything I wanted to try. I had learned how much makes me**

feel satisfied and where that tipping point was of where it doesn't feel good anymore.

There are some times when you just notice something once and you're like, 'I don't want to do that again,' and then other times when it takes many trials. So this has been many trials, over time, because of how many Thanksgivings I needed to go through to notice that I'm crashing at the end. I'm in a food coma. I'm no longer enjoying social time with people that I don't see that often. And then I want to go home early and go to bed early. It took many years and many holidays and many events, just not wanting to do that anymore, not wanting to feel gross in my body.

Tracy pointed out how this wasn't about calorie tracking or will-power. It highlights the real and tangible rewards of being content right in that moment. She continued: "That has nothing to do with how much I should eat. It didn't have anything to do with measuring servings on my plate. It's really learning over time how many bites do I enjoy."

Tracy also pointed out the importance of being patient with the process. It is very easy for our brains to forget what it feels like to overeat, discounting that for the remembrance of positive things past: *It tasted soooo good. I had such a great time.* And so on. Our brain wants to get on the positive side of history, so it remembers the good things, and forgets what really happened—until it happens enough times that we can no longer ignore the truth. Repeated observations are what lead to lasting change. The more we pay attention, the more accurate the observations are, and the more quickly our brain believes them to be a solid sign that something has changed. Our reward value signals in our brain have been updated. The pleasure plateau has been recalibrated and realigned based on today's reality. That's when we know that we've filled our disenchantment databank to the point where, like a bank account, it has accrued enough value that we can start cashing it in.

We've got to fill up our database with this new information so that it crowds out the old information and clearly establishes the new reward. Only then can this change in behavior become our new habit. My gummy worm disenchantment databank is full. I don't need to eat gummy worms anymore to know that the signal is solid. Simply recalling what it was like to eat them is enough for me to say, "No thanks."

In case you glossed over it earlier, or your brain didn't want to take in the information, remember disenchantment does not make tasty food bland or chocolate unappealing. You might have started to notice that if you pay careful attention, yes, your favorite ice cream is still your favorite. As I noted, you might even like it more. But as we've seen, liking is very different than wanting. There is no problem with enjoying food that tastes good. By paying attention, we can move from the overindulgence and automatic eating—which take away from the experience—to being content now. Each time we shift these behaviors, we deposit data into our disenchantment databank, making it easier to draw upon our past experience in the future.

RIGHT NOW: BUILD THE DATABASES

Let's build those disenchantment databanks. Fortunately, you already have the tool to do this: the craving tool. If you've already used it a few times, you're on your way. Pick a food that is particularly problematic for you—in other words, what is your gummy worm equivalent? Or if overeating it is a continual struggle, focus there. See if you can use the craving tool ten to fifteen (or more) times with this behavior and track the results. You can even graph out the composite score to see how it changes over time (score on the Y axis and time on the X axis).

CHAPTER 15

Day 12: Retrospectives—Looking Back to Move Forward

No matter how well you pay attention to your body's signals, no matter how good you get at discerning whether you are hungry or in the grasp of a hungry ghost, you are going to slip up. You are a human, not a robot. Fortunately, your incredible brain processes experiences in ways that put even the world's most powerful computers to shame and allows you to learn from setbacks. Ate a full bag of chips yesterday? Not a big deal. Helped yourself to two—okay, fine, three— slices of pie at a holiday or celebratory meal? All good. Haven't quite been able to kick your midnight snack habit? Don't sweat it. As long as you put those experiences to good use, you can transform them from a feeling of failure or a source of shame into an impetus for progress.

FUEL WITH FEEDBACK

Think of your favorite athlete. As hard as they train and as much innate talent as they might have, they won't be able to achieve peak performance without the help of a coach. Even the best of the best athletes actively seek out feedback because they know that they learn from others pointing out to them what they could improve on. They welcome those feedback opportunities. If they don't listen to their coach, they don't learn.

Coaches don't just point out what their athletes do well; they also note where there is room for improvement. *You were too slow to react here. Make sure your legs are snapping out.* Good athletes will take that feedback and make adjustments next time they take the track or the field. We learn from our mistakes.

In fact, I would argue we learn more from when we stumble or fall than from when we don't trip. This is great news because if the goal is to learn, we move forward no matter how we perform on any given task. Too often, people let themselves be crippled by "one step forward, two steps back" thinking when they've slipped up. They feel defeated when they don't make uninterrupted progress forward, but that assumes that only forward progress matters. It ignores the fact that learning from mistakes is the best way to move forward.

Learning is not linear. It's more of a sawtooth. At times when we're learning from what just happened, it can look like we're moving backward, but that may just be setting us up for a leap forward. That's what insight is all about.

Mindfulness in the moment is wonderful—ideal, even—but it can be really challenging to pay attention to the results of our actions in the moment, because, well, we're in the moment. There are people clamoring for our attention, our favorite song plays in the background, a work issue keeps pushing to the forefront of our mind. We can't always step back and see exactly what we are doing. Also, the moment might feel like it is going by quickly. Or we simply might not be in the mood to pay attention. This last bit happens a lot. That's the f*ck-its in a nutshell. *This is too much. F*ck it. I'm not going to pay attention.*

Ready for this? That's *fine.* If you toss all of your carefully culti-vated mindfulness out the window now and then, it's okay. All is not lost. One of the incredible facets of our minds is our ability to revisit an experience after it is over. We may not always be able to eat mindfully, but we can recall what happened afterward when we didn't.

In fact, sometimes we can learn more by looking back on an event than we can when it is happening. To revisit our sports analogy, what might not have been obvious in the moment seems really obvious when we can watch the replay, slow it down, and watch it again.

JACK'S SLIPUP

At our fourth session, Jack told me about his dinner the previous evening. He had gotten takeout from a Mexican restaurant. Before placing his order, he checked in with himself to see what he wanted and decided to get a large salad. So far, so good. When he and his wife began eating, he started paying attention and noticing that his wanting was ebbing. He was approaching his pleasure plateau. "I was eating, recognizing that I was filling up. Fuller than I needed to be." Nice work, Jack! He told himself that he was full, but . . . he kept eating. He also noticed how he was telling himself that at least his salad was healthy, which only seemed to feed the overeating behavior.

Jack was proof that we can't just think ourselves out of these habits. His example illustrates how our brains switch their stories to stay on the winning side. First they tell us to stop. If they see that that isn't working, they say, "Well, go ahead and eat. At least it's healthy."

Paying attention to the results of our actions is critical for updating their reward value in our brain and thus changing them. If you can't pay attention to the results of actions before you do them, pay attention while you're doing them. Do they lead to painful results? If you can't pay attention while you're doing them, you can at least pay attention afterward. Did they lead to painful results? Afterward still counts.

Those painful results can show up in our bodies (as Jack put it) as feeling fuller than we need to be. They can also manifest in our minds (and bodies) as thoughts and feelings of regret. Even if you can't pay attention and draw upon your disenchantment databank before you carry out an action or find yourself lost in the action while you're doing it, you can learn an awful lot in hindsight.

As an important aside, regret is different than shame. Regret can give us a signal that something is off and needs to be changed in the future. Shame simply gets us stuck in spirals of guilt and shame—which draw the focus away from the action and suck us into beating ourselves up (more on this later).

I could see the connections forming in Jack's brain. "That's where I am! That's a nice way to look at it. It's a process."

Jack was ready to hear about retrospectives.

Retrospectives

To help him make use of and learn from his slipup, I walked Jack through the process of doing a retrospective—basically a replay of what happened. I asked, "Can you bring up that feeling of being over-full from last night now?" He nodded, indicating that he could.

"How does it feel in your body?"

He paused, feeling into his body as he recalled the experience. "I feel uncomfortable. My stomach is pressing against my organs, my skin. I feel like my stomach is extending. Fuller than it needs to be. Discomfort."

I continued, "If you had dinner in front of you now and you remembered this, would it help you with how you eat dinner tonight?"

He said, "Is the next bite going to be more satisfying than the last? The answer is, when I reach fullness, no. Those two pieces in combination will allow me to say *enough*. I'm just so into the mindset of

157

finishing. I always finish. I did think to myself, 'I don't need to finish this,' but I pushed that thought aside. It was a salad. I convinced myself that it was okay. I went into my head instead of into my body."

He finished the retrospective exercise with "How will I feel if I stop now? Which is a much more comfortable place to be?"

Our brains predict the future based on past experience. When we do a retrospective, whether a few hours later or the next day, we can slow down and get all the details of what happened. If we recall it vividly enough, simply feeling the feelings through this recollection can change the same brain patterns as when we did the behavior the first time. Our brain registers feeling X as feeling X, whether we felt it a day ago or feel it right now.

Retrospectives can be really powerful. We pay attention to the results of the action—eating or otherwise. We recall it again afterward, asking ourselves, "What did I get from this?" We lay down that memory. We can repeat this as many times as is helpful for us to learn. The more vividly we can recall the results of the action, the more we can zero in and get that negative prediction error and become disenchanted with the behavior. The more we build up that disenchantment, the more we lay down that memory. The more we lay down that memory, the more easily and readily we can recall it in the future.

Recollection does a neat thing with our memory. The next time we find ourselves in the same situation, it gets easier for us to recall what happened last time because we've grooved that brain circuit a bit. The more we recall, the more deeply we groove it. With each recollection, we build up our ability to make a better choice.

How we recall is as important, if not more important, than *what* we recall. We really have to feel what it felt like so that we re-create that feeling in the recollection. If we don't feel the bloated feeling, the indigestion, the regret, or whatever the result was, our brains won't learn. The *felt experience* of the result of the behavior is more important than the behavior itself. That's what signals to our brain whether we should repeat the action. Every time we do the replay and feel into the results, it gets easier to remember exactly how rewarding—or unrewarding—the behavior was.

Best of all, recollection costs us nothing. It is a wholesome mental snack that we can chew on anytime we need to (as long as we bring curiosity and kindness to the table instead of our old habits of judgment, guilt, or shame). Here is an example so you can see how it works in real life.

In one of the weekly live Zoom groups that I colead, one of our participants was struggling. She described how the previous day she had gotten home from work, having planned a healthy meal for dinner. She was tired from a long day at the office, so instead she made tortilla chips with cheese in her air fryer. This dish resulted in a horrible stomachache, after which she tried antacids and other medications to ease the bloating. No matter what she did, nothing helped. Her discomfort kept her up until three in the morning. She had been using the Eat Right Now program for about two and a half weeks, so she understood the concept of paying attention, but as she said, "Sometimes I'm tired. I can't do it. I just want to eat what I want." She was bummed out that she couldn't control herself.

As I'd done with Jack, I shifted the conversation away from self-control and asked her if she could still recall the results of what happened. Yes, they were pretty clear. I pointed out her experience wasn't wasted. Every time she could recall enough of the situation, she could lower the reward value—without actually having to go and repeat the action itself. Her tone and facial expression shifted from worrying that she couldn't do it to insight. She was learning, right in that moment of recollection. And that inspired her to keep going, shifting her mindset from "I screwed up" to "What can I learn from this?"

We can apply this retrospective practice to moments when we have an urge to eat when we're not hungry or even when we've gone off the cliff of overindulgence. We can also apply it even after healthy eating episodes, when we've successfully coasted to a stop on the pleasure plateau instead of bingeing or overeating. Just as our brains learn from negative prediction errors ("Urrgh, overeating feels pretty unpleasant!"), our brains also benefit from positive prediction errors ("Wow, I feel light and energized after not overeating/eating a healthy meal. I feel proud that I can do this, no guilt!").

Each step, whether we are looking at it in the moment or taking a retrospective, can move us forward—as long as we're open to learning.

RIGHT NOW: DO A RETROSPECTIVE

See if you can practice doing a retrospective right now. Pull out your journal or notebook. Recall the last time you ate your version of gummy worms or went off the cliff of overindulgence. Take a moment to focus on the taste or the amount. Now drop your awareness into your body. Can you remember how it felt afterward? Can you remember any thoughts or emotions that also came up? How did it feel twenty minutes later? Ask yourself, "What did I get from this?" Don't let your brain do the talking; simply see what your body has to say. Now put the experience in words, and as Rob did, get the details down on paper. This will help you remember it so you can more easily recall it in the future. And it will set you up for part 2 of the craving tool.

CHAPTER 16

Day 13: The Craving Tool (Part 2)

One very ordinary day in 2018 I was getting on an airplane. It was a cross-country flight, so I would be in the air during at least one of my typical mealtimes. I usually pack myself some healthy food to eat on a plane (my current go-to is a sandwich that always involves avocado), but I'd been in a hurry that morning and had boarded with no food in my carry-on. As we were preparing to leave, one of the flight attendants asked me if I wanted a snack. She held out a package of cheese crackers, those bright orange ones that are the color of traffic cones. Remembering I'd come onto the plane empty-handed, I looked at the snack in all its prepackaged bright orange glory. I'll admit, I was briefly tempted (free food!). But then I did something that changed my mind: I imagined opening them up, popping them in my mouth and crunching down on their faux flaky pastry and fake cheese paste, and then noticed my stomach turn. I hadn't eaten the snack. I had only *imagined* what it would be like to eat the snack and my stomach had reacted.

It turns out that our bodies are pretty wise. They don't need to be able to read ingredient lists to know whether something is good for us or not. We just have to listen to them.

Those ten seconds—simulating eating the crackers and being

repulsed—was what planted the seed for the craving tool. When you ask yourself "What am I getting from this?" you get a clear sense of how rewarding or unrewarding it is. With retrospectives, you look backward to learn from your previous behavior. With part 2 of the craving tool, we'll bring the past of the retrospectives together with data collected from present-moment experience using the craving tool. You will take these data points and look to the future to predict the outcome of your behavior *before* you do it, so that you can change its course.

USING THE CRAVING TOOL TO ASSESS STORED REWARD VALUE

First, notice when you have a craving for food.

Second, *imagine* eating it, in all its glory. Imagine what it looks like, what it smells like—its temperature, texture, taste, and so on. If you're struggling with the quantity of food, focus on how much you eat. Don't hold back. Go for it.

Third, imagine what the result will be. How does it feel sitting in your stomach? What does eating too fast or going past full feel like? How does it affect your mood and/or energy level? What emotions come up? Frustration? Anger? Disappointment?

Here's part 1 of the craving tool again, so you can use it to quantify your results. The only thing that I've changed is that you will now answer the questions after imagining doing the behavior, rather than after actually doing it.

THE CRAVING TOOL (PART 2)

Imagine the following:

- Pay attention to why you want to eat right now (hunger, emotions, boredom, etc.).
- Pay attention to what you are about to eat. What is it made up of? What does it look and smell like?
- Pay attention as you take each bite (smell, taste, texture, temperature, etc.).
- Keep paying attention until you finish eating.

After you've imagined eating, ask yourself the following questions:

1. How much did you eat? (Circle the answer in your head.)

Way too much

Too much

Right amount

Too little

None

2. Check in with your body. How do you physically feel right now?

Awful! -10 -5 0 +5 +10 Awesome!

3. Check in with your emotions. How do you feel right now?

Awful! -10 -5 0 +5 +10 Awesome!

4. Check in with your thoughts. What type of thoughts are you noticing right now?

Awful! -10 -5 0 +5 +10 Awesome!

Part 2

Now answer the following: How strong is your urge to eat that type or amount of food now as opposed to before the exercise?

A lot weaker -10 -5 Same as before 0 +5 +10 A lot stronger

A couple of things tend to happen after this exercise. If you haven't paid careful attention in the past to what the results of eating this type or amount of food are, you might actually crave it more. No problem—that just means you need more data. You can continue using the craving tool (part 1)—eat with awareness. You can keep repeating the process over and over as long as you need to. Keep adding that data to build that databank.

If you *have* paid careful attention and have a full databank, you might notice that you're less excited to move forward with eating than you were before you started the exercise. My cheese cracker craving tool results gave me a clear reading: I would feel better if I didn't eat the crackers than if I did.

If you haven't eaten a certain type or amount of food in a while, you might also crave it more. That's because our brains use past experience to predict future behavior. If it has been a while since you indulged in something (e.g., gummy worms), it can be hard to remember what that experience was like. Thus it can be hard to recall the reward value. That's fine, too. If this happens, you can simply reflect on the most recent time that you indulged. Recall that memory. Recall what it felt like *in your body*. Your feeling body is much stronger than your thinking brain. Your OFC listens to the evidence your body presents to it from the last time. If it is hard to retrieve that embodied memory, no worries. That simply means that your databanks need some updating. Like a CD-ROM or memory card that is too old for your computer's new operating system to access, you need to collect more data. Back to the craving tool (part 1).

To be clear, using the craving tool is not an intellectual exercise. We all know—in our heads—that eating certain types or amounts of food aren't "good" for us. We also know that simply knowing something intellectually isn't enough to have an effect. If you are thinking your way through this exercise, take note and see if you can place that off to the side. Focus on your direct embodied experience. Drop into your body. What does this feel like in my stomach? How do I feel emotionally after I do X? Remember, feeling bodies are much stronger than thinking brains. That's where the action is. In science speak, you are bringing the previous reward value of the eating behavior into your working memory.

The craving tool depends on one simple ingredient: awareness. When we pay attention to the results of eating to satisfy a craving in part 1, we can see more clearly what and how much makes us discontent. Each bit of information gets deposited in our databank until it is full enough to draw on it for part 2 of the tool. Here we bring in awareness to our present moment so that we can push the pause button on automatic eating and instead run the simulation in our brain to predict the outcome of our behavior: What will happen if I eat X amount of Y?

Interestingly, the word *mindfulness* is a modern-day translation of the ancient Pali word *sati*, which means "to remember" or "to recollect." From a brain perspective, we recollect past experience in the present moment to predict future behavior. With part 2 of the craving tool, we're imagining what it would be like to eat X amount of Y. But what our brain is really doing is remembering that eating X amount of Y makes us feel a certain way. If it is a net positive, our brain says go ahead. If it is a net negative, that disenchantment helps us not repeat the behavior because our brain has enough evidence to not repeat something that doesn't feel good. If we don't have enough data to simulate what will happen or can't remember what it was like, we simply repeat part 1 of the craving tool to collect more data.

Jacqui described how learning disenchantment was a "mind-blowing life-changer" for her. She was even more excited when she realized that she had decades of disenchantment data to draw from to plug right into part 2 of the craving tool. As she put it, "Who knew all those past unwanted experiences could be so helpful now!!" Even now, years later, she easily recalled the entire experience of her last binge. It started with a "screw it" cocktail made up of a combination of anxiety, excitement, anticipation, and shame that drove her to break out of her food restriction jail. The pleasant taste of doughnuts lasted only a few bites before it was drowned out by an urgency to keep shoveling them in to try to numb the initial stress emotions that triggered the binge. This was followed by "extremely uncomfortable feelings of bloating, heaviness, and nausea that made me feel like I couldn't move or even breathe that easily." She normally binged at night, so more negative results followed. The next morning she'd had a food hangover—all the food felt like a gut bomb, a sickly and achy feeling "with an extra portion of self-criticism for good measure." Not much fun to recall, but at least she put the memory to good use.

After learning to explore what she got from her binges, Jacqui was able to draw upon this disenchantment databank to utilize part 2 of the craving tool:

> When I felt like I was going to binge, often on my way home from teaching or caregiving, I would just park up in front of the shop or fast-food place and with full permission to go binge if I wanted to. I would replay how things would go if I binged. I would play it all out—the uneasy purchase, the brief relief—AND the bloating,

discomfort, shame, nausea, carb coma, poor sleep, food hangover, and self-criticism. Then I would drive off (often laughing to myself), feeling free and empowered beyond words!!! It was a little game I played for a while because it was so strange, new, and fun not to be a slave to cravings anymore!

So see how much you can start bringing the two parts of the craving tool together in your own life now. As was the case with Jacqui, see if you've got a lot of disenchantment data stored away such that you can jump right to the simulations. If you don't have much data, again, don't worry—it can take some time to get there. See how much data you can collect each time you eat. Also, be on the lookout for self-flagellation habit loops like judging yourself or beating yourself up for not having nailed it already. In these instances, apply the craving tool in the same way: ask yourself what you're getting from that habit, and see if you can build disenchantment with it at the same time. The more aware you are with each bite (or self-judgmental thought), the more quickly that databank will grow.

RIGHT NOW: USE PART 2 OF THE CRAVING TOOL

Use part 2 of the craving tool the next time you have an urge to eat a type of food that you struggle with or are about to eat a meal where you typically eat beyond fullness (the clean-plate club). Make a note of how strong that urge is to continue with the behavior. Next, if the urge has passed or lost its power, make a note of what that feels like: the power of disenchantment. If the urge has become more urgent, go ahead and eat, but as you do, follow the steps in part 2 of the craving tool so you can be sure to collect every morsel of data to build your databank.

CHAPTER 17

Day 14: RAIN on the Craving Monster's Parade

As we discussed in the first section of the book, some of our eating is spurred by experiencing emotion or shifting to autopilot. When our planning brain and our survival brain communicate poorly, the OFC can get overwhelmed, and emotional or habitual eating takes over. In this chapter and the one that follows, you'll learn two key tools to step out of autopilot and instead bring awareness into moments like this *before* the OFC decides to lift a fork.

Think of the next two chapters as a master class in attention. They build on the awareness that you have already been honing, and specifically use it to unmask the scariness of cravings or moments where you feel out of control. By the end of them, you'll have tools that will help you ride out cravings the moment they come up. You'll be able to apply these tools to eating as well as any habitual behavior.

I lead a weekly group supervision with Dr. Robin Boudette for people going through facilitator training for the Eat Right Now program. Robin spent twenty years of her career as a psychologist specializing in recovery from disordered eating. As a mindfulness practitioner and instructor, Robin was seeking ways to bring mindfulness into her work, and working on Eat Right Now offered the perfect opportunity to do exactly that.

When Robin and I sort through applications for each new cohort that we're about to train, the credentials—or lack thereof—people bring to the training are not nearly as important to us as their life experience and history with food.

Take Mary Beth, a substance abuse counselor and MBSR instructor in Florida. Having completed our facilitator training program, she now leads groups, mainly with people who are struggling with anxiety and habitual patterns that no longer serve them. One week, during our training session, Mary Beth told us about how her father shaped her relationship with food from the time she was very young. Her father was a New York City bridge and tunnel toll collector (before coin baskets and subsequent automated technology) who took thirteen years to complete his college degree. He valued education deeply and he wanted to pass those values down to his daughter. He even developed a reward system to encourage Mary Beth to work hard at school.

When Mary Beth came home with her report card, he would ask to take a look at it. If she got all A's, he rewarded her by taking her out for a banana split, her favorite special treat. If her grades weren't quite that good but she had demonstrated that she'd put in a lot of effort, she still got a treat, just not the prized banana split. She would get an ice cream soda. As she put it, "I always envied my brother, who always got the banana split, while I had my ice cream soda." At the end of the story, she added, "My dad must have known about reward-based learning."

Mary Beth's dad had set up a habit loop:

Trigger: A need for good grades.

Behavior: Study hard.

Result/Reward: Banana split.

As she got older, Mary Beth found herself wanting to reward herself with food whenever she accomplished something hard. Got her first summer job? Treat. Completed a college application? Treat. Broke off a difficult friendship? Treat. Treat. Treat. Her body may not have wanted a banana split, but her hungry ghost sure did.

HOW WE ACCIDENTALLY CREATE MONSTERS

Almost all of us internalize this type of habit training over the course of our lives. We reward ourselves when we're "good" and punish ourselves when we're "bad." I attempted to capture this when writing the script for an animation we use in our programs. It has us imagine seeing a child throw a temper tantrum, which quickly gets soothed by giving the child a lollipop. What happens? Children learn that screaming and throwing a tantrum might get them lollipops in the future. Then the animation suggests that we explore what happens to the tantrum if the child isn't given a sweet. The tantrum can be uncomfortable to be around for a bit, but the child eventually stops screaming. It also has us imagine what inner children we have inside ourselves, how many of them we have accidentally fed sweets to in order to make the tantrum stop, and what might happen if we learn to be with the screaming instead of habitually doing something to make it go away.

As you can imagine, I believe we need to treat our children with love and compassion. (We also need to treat ourselves in the same way.) But sadly, blindly indulging our children's every want wouldn't win awards in parenting contests. (Raise your hand if you as a parent have felt judged in public for how you've interacted with your child.) We need to also know how our children's minds work so we can avoid accidentally falling into unhelpful habits as Mary Beth's father had— using food to train them to work hard in school or scream for sugary things. Learning what our children (and we ourselves) need is a critical part of this love. When a child cries, our compassionate response is to see what they need and provide that, not simply give them something that they like.

This goes for our inner children as well. We all have the equivalent of a screaming toddler inside ourselves. Sometimes when it feels like the world decided to hand out all its annoyances and injustices to one person—you—it can seem like the only thing that will help quiet your little screamer is a lollipop or banana split. But we can love ourselves and train ourselves to choose helpful behaviors at the same time. (More on the compassion and love a bit later.)

THE CRAVING MONSTER

For our friend Jacqui, cravings were less like a sweet inner toddler having a tantrum and more like a raving craving MONSTER.

During the period of her life when Jacqui was restricting the type and amounts of food she ate so she could meet some milestone such as losing 10 pounds, she would find herself bothered by persistent thoughts like "I could have this or that" (Chinese takeout was one of her favorites). Whether it was a reward for meeting a goal, an impulse brought on by a mood, or even something seemingly random, her craving monster stirred whenever she tried to follow the rules she'd set up for herself too rigidly.

Jacqui's craving was often for Chinese takeout. Whenever she was rigidly keeping to her careful eating regimen, the thought of rewarding herself with this forbidden food would pop up in her head. Most times, she managed to resist the initial impulse. When she didn't cave, she'd think with relief, *I was able to resist this time.* But the craving monster had not vanished. It was still lurking. She knew it was going to be an ongoing battle. She had a sense that the next time would be harder. When she described her monster to me during one of our sessions, she motioned behind her head and said, "It's literally here [pointing behind her head], and it just gets bigger and bigger and bigger. It just starts to take over. It just eats away at you."

Her craving weighed heavier and heavier on her the more time passed. The feeling could go on for days or even a week. "You just battle it and battle it. You're fighting something that's getting bigger and bigger and then . . ."—she put it bluntly—"the craving monster is like, 'F*cking eat it!'"

Feeling like there was no way to win, she'd relent. Defeated, she'd dial her local Chinese restaurant and order "disgustingly vast amounts of carbs": fried potatoes AND rice AND rice noodles with curry dishes. Afterward, "There is this huge relief that it's not there anymore, even though you feel all battered and bloated, [but] at least you're not fighting that anymore."

Like screaming children, our craving monster screams, "Handle me NOW!" You can't ignore it. You can't resist it. You are not going to be able to turn your attention to anything else until you address the craving. But how to do that without feeding the beast?

RAINing on the Craving Monster

The craving monster is a formidable enemy, but it is no match for your incredibly plastic and powerful brain. Here's a tool for you that is beloved by some of the great meditation teachers of our day. It is called RAIN. It can change your brain and your life.

RAIN PRACTICE

Here's the instruction I give when people are learning how to use RAIN:

First, **RECOGNIZE** that the craving is coming on and **RELAX** into it.

Don't grit your teeth and brace for impact! Just let go and feel it come on, since you have no control over it anyway. **ALLOW** and **ACCEPT** this wave as it is. Don't try to push it away or ignore it.

Don't distract yourself or try to do something about it. This is your experience. Here it comes. It's even okay if you smile a little—really.[1]

To catch the wave of craving, you have to study it carefully, **INVESTIGATING** it as it builds. Investigation is all about being curious. You can do this by asking, "What is going on in my body right now?" Don't go looking for it. See what arises in your awareness most prominently. Let it come to you. Where does the feeling originate in your body? What does it really feel like? Is it tightness in your chest? Is it a burning feeling in your belly? Is it a restlessness that urges you to run away?

Finally, **NOTE** the experience. This keeps you here now, curious, focused, and riding the wave. Keep it simple by using short phrases or single words. This will help you stay out of thinking or figuring-out mode and will keep you in your direct experience of

---

1 Jacqui commented that it was a bit of a shocker for her to hear this the first time she tried the RAIN exercise. She put it this way: "It was a real surprise to hear that [I could smile while doing this exercise]. I did a little smile and it changed my experience in a huge way from the very first time I tried it—I didn't know I could smile at cravings!!"

what is currently happening. For example, you might note: clenching, rising, burning, heat, restlessness as the feelings come on and peak, and then vibration, tightness, tingling, lessening, relaxing, relief, expanding as they subside. If thoughts arise, simply note "thinking" and don't get caught up in trying to analyze your thoughts or switching into fix-it mode. If you get distracted or your mind shifts to something else, simply return to the investigation. Be curious and ask, "What is going on in my body right now?"

RAIN is an acronym for a practice developed decades ago by Michele McDonald, an American meditation teacher. I first learned it from the influential psychologist and meditation teacher Tara Brach. RAIN stands for Recognize, Accept, Investigate, and Non-identification. You might be asking yourself, "What does non-identification mean?" Basically, it means that we practice not being identified with our thoughts, emotions, and body sensations. But non-identification can be a bit complicated without explanation or previous experience with this concept. So when I first started using RAIN to help people in my programs work with cravings, I adapted the acronym slightly, based on "noting practice," which had been popularized by the late Mahāsi Sayādaw, a Burmese meditation teacher. (I'll explain noting practice in depth in chapter 18.)

THE POWER OF RAIN

I have seen remarkable results from people using RAIN to curb their cravings. In my first book, *The Craving Mind*, I wrote about a patient who walked into my office and declared that his head would explode if he didn't smoke. He felt like his craving for cigarettes was so strong that the pressure to smoke was going to blow his lid off. I walked him through an improvised RAIN practice using the whiteboard in my office, where I had him name out loud what that craving felt like. As he noted his body sensations—for example, tightness, heat, restlessness—I also asked him to rate how strong they were. We plotted an upward trajectory as they intensified. And at some point they topped off and then started to drop off. His eyes got really wide at that moment. I asked him what had happened.

He told me how he usually smoked at that peak moment because he couldn't tolerate the craving anymore. He'd never gone over the edge and down the back side of the mountain that he had built in his head. As we traversed the unknown territory of his craving's subsiding on its own—without the cigarette—he realized that he didn't have to light up. The cravings could go away on their own. All he had to do was watch them.

I suspected that using RAIN could help people ride out food cravings as well. I first tested it with patients in my clinic (it worked) and then did more formal research on it by embedding it in our Eat Right Now app. Remember the study led by Ashley Mason that I mentioned in the introduction? The RAIN practice helped people in the program drop their craving-related eating by 40 percent. They learned to ride out those cravings.

As one participant in the Eat Right Now program said, "I experienced some stress at work, and right afterward, I thought, *I feel bad. I think I need some dark mint chocolate to make me feel better, to reward me for this trouble.* Fortunately, I caught that trigger and potential behavior, and instead chose to do RAIN to feel into the unpleasantness. (I did intentionally decide to have a small piece of dark chocolate after dinner, though, and enjoyed it very mindfully.)"

It's worth looking at the elements of RAIN one by one.

RECOGNIZE AND RELAX. By now you should have some idea of how to recognize that what you're feeling is a craving, as opposed to homeostatic hunger. You're experiencing those telltale signs of a persistent desire for a specific food. You're irritable, maybe even a little obsessed. This first step does big work. This is a great time to do a body scan so you can recognize what you are feeling right now. Simply by recognizing that what you're feeling is a craving, you've already taken away some of its power. It's similar to the way a monster in a horror movie is less terrifying once you've seen it. Once you know what you're dealing with, you have a chance to handle it. Just as in a horror movie, you will do better if you stay calm instead of panicking. The more you can recognize what is happening, the more you can relax into this restless, *do something* energy, rather than be controlled by it.

ALLOWING/ACCEPTING. Allowing or accepting a craving to exist is crucial. Remember, what we resist really does persist. Observing the craving as it comes on helps us not get caught in judging it or ourselves. We feed our cravings not only by giving in and creating habit loops, but by actively resisting or denying them. Like an athlete who has an injury and keeps playing through the pain instead of listening to her body, denial of or resistance to a craving only makes things worse. And by resisting—*I will not eat this entire bag of cookies, I will not eat this entire bag of cookies*—we're keeping that object of desire in mind, which only increases the craving. One Eat Right Now user nailed this sentiment, saying, "When I want to eat but resist, I become obsessed and can't move on until I eat anyway."

INVESTIGATE. Cultivating a gentle interest in and curiosity about our craving helps us stay with the experience instead of leapfrogging over what's happening in our body right now and anticipating the result. The moment you start telling yourself "I'm going to RAIN the heck out of this craving and make it go away" is the moment you undermine the process and do a face-plant. I see this happen with results-oriented eager beavers all the time. Keep a keen eye out for the attitude that you bring to the process. Are you looking at your watch or the clock, gritting your teeth each second that you note, counting the moments until the craving subsides? These are also likely signs of resistance. Instead of "Oh no, here comes a craving!" we can flip the script by getting curious. "What does this feel like in my body?" That attitude of curiosity helps us turn toward our experience rather than running away from it. As you'll learn in part 3 of this book, curiosity is key.

Noting. When a craving strikes, we can note the physical sensations in our bodies from moment to moment. Simply by noticing our experience, we are already less identified with it, but the practice of naming or noting it allows us to manage them better. We'll explore noting more in the next chapter, but for now, see if you can put all of the pieces together.

RAIN Works

Jacqui managed to beat her craving monster using RAIN. After years and years of losing the battle against her cravings, Jacqui began going through the modules of the Eat Right Now app. Early on in the program, she had just come from visiting her mom—yet another "horrible" trip where the two didn't connect. She pulled her car over into a grocery store parking lot, where she would typically listen to loud music and just "binge and binge." She had recently listened to the module on RAIN and wondered if she should give it a try. She was dubious that such a simple process would have any impact on her raging craving, but as she said, "I thought, *Well, I can always just binge afterward if I want to. I'll just give it a try.*"

She sat in her car and began by simply noticing how the craving for Chinese food felt. She could already taste that magic combination of sweet and salty on her tongue.

"I gave myself permission to do RAIN and I felt like I had been tossed onto a beach after a storm. It didn't make the upset go away. I still felt really upset and hurt. I just bawled my eyes out in the car."

She allowed the craving monster to get in the car with her instead of ignoring, resisting, or fighting with it. Next, she investigated how it felt in her body, asking herself what exactly she was feeling, and then she noted the sensations—that anticipatory excitement, the eagerness to dive into the takeout containers—and named them. Before long, to her surprise, the urgency of her craving started to wane.

She described her moment of revelation: "I realized that I don't have to do that. I went into the grocery store and each time I picked something up, I asked myself, 'How am I going to feel if I eat this?' I gave myself permission to binge if I wanted to. I bought some avocados and spinach."

"Laughing like a lunatic," Jacqui left the store and drove out of the parking lot. As she put it, "It was like my first taste of freedom as an adult that I don't have to be scared of the craving. Because the craving monster is real for so many people, and once you get that thought, it's like it's not going to go away until you give it what it wants. But I was like, 'I see you [craving monster]. Yeah, you can't hurt me.' I couldn't believe I had done it. I couldn't believe that it was possible. I didn't have to go down that path.

"The fear wasn't there anymore. I dropped this fear of food."

The more Jacqui practiced RAIN when a craving hit, the more she began to lose something else. "I stopped focusing on the weight. I just trusted. It was more about trusting my body." Without the fear, she could look more closely at how food affected her. She learned that while her partner could eat rice and other carbohydrates just like any other foods, these tended to make her just want to eat more instead of feeling satisfyingly full. In case your habitual mind read this last sentence in a certain way, to be clear, this is not to demonize rice or carbs in general (food rules and food jail don't work), but to point out how important it is for each of us to discover what foods work best for our own individual selves. By exploring and listening to her body, Jacqui found that legumes and veggies without the rice worked much better for her. She relearned how to listen to her stomach's signals and eat when she was hungry—as compared to restricting, craving, and then crashing with a binge. With this, she began eating "a normal amount of food."

With this shift in focus, she lost 28 pounds over the next year.

She summed it up: "I never thought I'd have a normal relationship with food. Now I can eat a little bit of anything, and I don't feel deprived. A little bit is delicious, and I don't have any consequence. If I ate the whole thing, I would need a nap."

CRAVINGS ARE NOT TATTOOS

Whether it's a craving for a cigarette, food, our news feed, our email, or whatever, we all can benefit from knowing that cravings come and go. We don't have to indulge them or try to annihilate them. As you saw from Jacqui's story, the more we fight our cravings, the more they feed on our energy, growing stronger and sticking around longer. Like a parent meeting their screaming child's needs instead of feeding their wants, we can hold our cravings in a kind, curious awareness until they get tired and stop.

How long do cravings actually last? It depends. As my patients begin to use RAIN, I often instruct them to time their cravings so they can see for themselves. One person reported: "I try to note how long the craving lasts, and I know now from experience that it isn't that long (remarkably, having never ever thought about this before, I'm surprised it's only a minute or two)." This is generally true for most people: cravings are shorter than they expected. The record? About twelve minutes. That's the longest that anyone has reported to date. That may feel like a long time, but in the grand scheme of things freedom lasts a lifetime and is worth a few minutes of unpleasantness.

RIGHT NOW: TRY RAIN

Whenever and wherever you experience a strong craving, take a moment to pull out the RAIN practice and see if you can start riding out your cravings. It can be helpful to start with small ones at first. I've also posted a recording that you can listen to on my website (https://drjud.com/mindfulness-exercises/). Once you get the hang of it, you can play with using it for bigger and bigger cravings. Don't skip over the acceptance and curiosity bits. These are key attitudinal elements that help you step out of the old habit of trying to force things to change and into the experience where you can observe—and note—change happening by itself.

CHAPTER 18

Day 15: Noting

When I was in residency, I used to get full-blown panic attacks. I would wake up in the middle of the night with all of the symptoms: cold, clammy hands; sweating; a racing heart; shallow breathing; tunnel vision—the works. Sometimes I thought I was dying. But because I happened to be training to become a psychiatrist at the time, I knew what I was experiencing was a panic attack.

When my panicked brain started sounding the alarm (*You're dying!*), my survival brain kicked in. When we are panicked, we fall back to our old habits. That's why we do all sorts of things that we later regret, because our thinking brain has shut down. The good news is that this was a few years after I had started learning mindfulness, and a particular part of my practice kicked in: I started noting. It had become a habit.

Even before my prefrontal cortex could come online to try to figure out what was happening, I started noting all my signs and symptoms. I don't know how long my first panic attack lasted, but after the dust settled, my habit brain handed my thinking brain—which was now wide awake—what looked like a diagnostic checklist for a panic attack. I didn't see anything on the list indicating that I should get myself to the hospital's emergency room, so being a sleep-deprived resident, I went back to sleep. A few weeks later when I had my next panic attack, it was shorter, because my brain already knew what was happening and I recognized that I could use noting to ride it out. Eventually I stopped having panic attacks altogether.

Practicing noting was truly transformative for me. Even before it helped me ride out full-blown panic attacks, noting helped me stay in the present moment. By creating some distance and perspective from my thoughts and feelings, noting helped me to be more present and closer to myself. How?

I've created this separate chapter to take a deeper dive into the noting aspect of RAIN and to point out how you can sprinkle noting throughout your day even if you are not engaged in a full RAIN practice.

My meditation teacher, Joseph Goldstein, talks about how noting practice helps us observe our experience more clearly. He uses the analogy of a picture on the wall: if you put a frame around it, the frame makes the picture really stand out. Think of all the paintings and pictures you've seen at museums. Sometimes the frame is more intricate—and much bigger—than the artwork itself. The frame gives the artwork a bit of pop, drawing your attention to it. If the painting is a similar color to the wall, the frame also helps you see where the artwork ends and where the wall begins. Noting is like putting a frame around our experience. Noting pulls our thoughts and emotions from the background, drawing our attention to them and giving them that pop: "that's a thought," "that's a body sensation." By observing the thought, emotion, or body sensation, we can be with it more easily.

Each time you use noting, you're inserting that little bit of mental distance between yourself and your thoughts—putting that frame around them. Distance gives you greater perspective. Perspective gives you wiggle room to make a decision that is not automatic, habitual, or motivated by emotion. When you gain perspective, you aren't as identified with your thoughts, emotions, or body sensations. Paradoxically, with noting, these become less monstrous, less scary, and less powerful, so that you learn that you can actually get closer to them. Their proverbial bark is all bark and no bite. When you are less afraid of them, they stop snarling and start wagging their tail. That's when you can begin to befriend them (more on this in chapter 19).

This is where getting closer comes in. Often cravings and other emotions are scary or unpleasant. Our survival brain tells us to run away, fight, or subdue them. By noting, we see that we don't have to fear them. We can watch them come and go, and they will come and go—on their own. When we're no longer afraid, we don't have the urge to fight or flee. As such, we can get up close, we can get really curious and observe them as they dance across the stage of consciousness.

A good way to start the practice of noting is to pay attention to your experience in one of six categories: seeing, hearing, feeling (body sensations), smelling, tasting, and thinking. Beginning with this categorical level helps keep you from getting lost in the conceptual realm of thinking. You can try it right now. Take a moment and simply see which of your senses is most active. Are you seeing the words on the page? If you are listening to an audiobook, are you hearing my voice? Is there a strong sensation in your body? Don't go looking. See what comes to you, and note whatever is predominant. Then repeat the process to see if another sense comes forward. If your predominant experience is still the same sense, simply note it again. For example, if seeing is still at the top of the list, note *seeing* again. If your predominant sense has changed, note whatever is most present now.

Here's an example of how to use noting. Let's say you're walking down the street, listening to the sounds of your neighborhood. Then you hear someone honk their horn. You think, *I can't believe that person honked their horn*, and start wondering why they would do that. Then you remember a time when you were in a crosswalk and someone honked at you: *that jerk . . . I have every right . . . they should put their phone away and pay more attention . . . I heard texting and driving is more dangerous than drunk driving . . . I wonder if they were texting and not paying attention . . . people are so distracted these days . . . these tech companies sure are getting us addicted to our phones . . .* And then you're lost in thought about a viral social media post that a friend sent along and found either hilarious or outrageous. You just got on the thought train without even knowing that it was moving and rode it out of town. Before you realize what happened, you're disoriented. You have to look around and get your bearings. After a few moments you realize that you have drifted off in a meeting at work, in the middle of class at school, or even in conversation with friends.

Now consider the same situation with noting. You're walking down the street, listening to the sounds of your neighborhood or the city. You hear someone honk their horn. You start thinking, *I can't believe that person honked their horn.* Instead of getting lost in thought, you simply note "thinking." Then you notice that you were startled by the sound and note "feeling" as you feel adrenaline pumping through your blood vessels. Maybe you notice a fear response, so then you note "fear." The fear response brings you back to your body, so you note "feeling" a few more seconds. Things quiet down and you hear a bird, so you note "hearing." It goes like this: "thinking" [1 second], "feeling" [1 second], "fear" [1 second], "feeling" [1 second], "feeling" [1 second], "feeling" [1 second], "hearing" [1 second]. And so on. More distance, more perspective. This is the observer effect in action.

Once you get the hang of it, you can start adding some nuance to the noting. For example, as I described with the RAIN practice, you can note the specific body sensations that you are feeling from moment to moment. You can also note different categories of thoughts: future thought, past thought, planning thought. You can note specific emotions: fear, anger, anxiety, boredom.

When we note our experience, we gain the perspective that we are a person having thoughts, emotions, and body sensations, instead of being so caught up in them that we fuse with them.

Here's a bonus to noting: If you can get your planning brain (which doesn't like uncertainty) to label a thought, feeling, or body sensation, your survival brain says, "Oh, *that's* what's going on. I knew I was upset, but now I can see that more clearly. I feel a little calmer now." It no longer has the same degree of uncertainty and eases out of the mode where it will make a panic-based decision to engage in an unhelpful habit. Naming is satisfying to our brains because it gives us a measure of control. Naming an emotion in particular gives us something constructive to work with (e.g., note it) instead of racing down the street of self-sabotage or stress eating.

When I first started learning the practice of noting, the advice that I got was "note your ass off." In other words, start noting when I first wake up in the morning, see how much I can note throughout the day until I go to sleep, and repeat the process the next day. It took me a little while to get the hang of it, but that's how I was able to make it a habit. When I walked down the hall, I would note the colors, the textures, the shapes, and my body sensations as I walked. For a few moments before a meeting started or between patients in my clinic, I noted my thoughts and mind state. When I ate food, I noted. I could note anger and it would dissipate more quickly because I wasn't getting caught up in it. My food was tastier. My relationships became richer. I even noticed (and noted) that as I became more practiced at noting, I was able to be more present with my patients.

To form any new habit, you have to do it over and over. And the more rewarding the behavior is, the more likely you are to do it, so note what it feels like to do some noting as compared to being lost on autopilot. For me, noting helps me be calmer and more engaged with myself and the world, which feels better than being judgmental or reactive. You can do noting practice of short moments many times throughout the day to start to set it as a new habit for yourself. I'll repeat this so you don't miss it: short moments, many times. Before long, you'll establish noting as a new helpful habit.

When we studied participants in the Eat Right Now program who had learned how to use mindful eating, RAIN, and in particular, noting, they reported an appreciable shift in perspective. They repeatedly used the word *uncoupling*—being able to uncouple a bad day at work or a fight with a significant other from using food and eating as coping mechanisms. It was as if noting a behavior broke—or at least weakened—its power or charm.

Here are a couple of real-life examples of people using noting in our program:

> That feeling of temper tantrum showed up today, and I stayed with it as you recommended. It's funny, I initially noticed that I didn't want to stay with it or make contact because I was afraid it would last forever. Didn't realize I believed that deep down! I'm reminded of the "screaming child," where a child never screams forever. I tried noting the feelings as a way to stay in contact with my temper tantrum, and this was uncomfortable during, but what ended up happening is that (shortly after) my mind drifted away to some other topic and I found

myself eating my muesli without thinking much about the tantrum, going at a reasonable pace and tasting the food reasonably well enough. The feelings of victimization and tantrum came and went throughout the meal, but I never stopped just trying to connect with whatever came up. I felt so proud of myself at the end. Definitely a win over here!!!

I have often found certain types of work frustrating, especially working on the computer. Today I tried noting as I worked and found that my frustration subsided, and I was able to work without craving food. I also made fewer errors.

Today I had a really stressful day in London for work. My boss can be a real pig sometimes, and he was on fire today. I usually work from home, but I have to go in once a week. I had a horrible meeting with him and afterwards as I was on the tube I felt anxious, full of emotion, and tears were burning behind my eyes, making my head hurt. So I did the noting practice. Noting what I saw, what I heard, the feelings I was experiencing—anger, hurt, upset, fear. As a result when I got to the station and had half an hour to wait for my train, I got a healthy snack instead of what I wanted to do, which was to eat junk food.

I really like the noting practice. I always use it in my thrice-daily short walks at my community park to stay present and enjoy nature better. I also do it when I'm caught in the habit loops of ruminating and chatting too much in my head. I also noticed that I noted "thinking" a lot when I do my noting practice. "Hear" is next, likely because I am an auditory learner. Yeah, I think too much. Staying alone, working from home, being under government-imposed nationwide lockdown due to the COVID-19 pandemic has led me to spend too much time in my head. I need to explore this habit loop further.

TROUBLESHOOT YOUR NOTING

When people start noting, sometimes it can be confusing or feel like another item on the to-do list. Here are a few common questions and suggestions on how to work with them that can help you stay on track instead of stumble as you get started:

NOTING FEELS LIKE WORK. Yes, starting any new habit can feel like work at the beginning. This is your brain needing some time to get into the groove of things. Be patient with yourself. If you slip up and find yourself acting mindlessly, no big deal. Just pause and try again.

HOW MUCH EFFORT SHOULD IT FEEL LIKE? If it feels like effort, this can be a sign your brain is trying to be too specific with what it is noticing. In cases like this, simply bring the noting back to the categorical level. The process of noting is more important than the thing being noted. For example, if you are noticing an emotion come up in your body but can't immediately name it, note "feeling." Sometimes I'll note "thing" if there is a bodily sensation that doesn't immediately have a name and move on instead of getting stuck in the naming itself.

NOTING FEELS LIKE IT IS DISTRACTING ME FROM THE PRESENT MOMENT. Yes, noting is an extra cognitive process that our brain has to do to help us stay present. There is an irony here: we're adding in a practice that can seem to get in the way of the present moment in order to help us stay in the present moment. Noting is here to help us learn the habit of being present—we are noting what is happening in our inner and outer world in the present moment. We use noting to frame our experience. Once we can easily see what is happening instead of being identified with it, we don't need to note it. If we are already present, we can drop the noting and simply be present. If we get lost in thought, we note that—and maybe do noting for a few more seconds to help us reground ourselves—and then drop it again. It's like dancing. When we are learning a new dance move, it doesn't feel like we're dancing. Once we get the move down, we move out of our heads and into our bodies and just dance.

NOTING CAN CREATE ITS OWN HABIT LOOP. Note note note note note until the craving is gone, right? Well, sometimes. Our habit-forming brain is always looking for ways to create more habit loops. If we note because we want to make the craving go away, we're actually feeding another cycle of wanting: I want my craving to go away, so I'm going to do RAIN. Trigger—craving. Behavior—do RAIN. Expected result—craving goes away (and never comes back). Expectation habit loops are tricky. Because they are dependent upon something happening—that's what expectations are all about—we can get stuck in focusing on the end result instead of the process. RAIN can start to focus on the outcome rather than the journey. But it's all about the journey.

When people adopt noting purely as a way to change their experience, it is a marker of our tendency to resist what is happening. If you notice this in yourself, remember that noting is to help us see and feel our experience more clearly, not to push it away. Here we can note "resistance" or "wanting" if we notice that we are wanting our experience to be different in that moment, so we don't inadvertently create a noting habit loop. We can also bring in RAIN in these moments as a way to bring in the antidotes to resistance as an on-ramp to noting—acceptance and curiosity—and then keep noting.

CAN I NOTE WHILE DRIVING? I'd hope we're all practicing paying attention while driving. Driving is a great time to practice noting. Just be sure to keep it simple, noting big categories like seeing, hearing, feeling, and thinking. This helps us keep our eyes on the road (seeing), listening for trouble (hearing), checking to see if we are tense or stressed (feeling), and not getting lost in thought (thinking). All of these help us stay present and safe while driving. I particularly like the practice of noting while driving. If we're headed somewhere, we might as well be practicing being present! As an aside, I've used this practice with a lot of my patients who have the habit of being anxious or even panicking while driving, and it helps them break those cycles.

Noting practice is helpful for training our minds to be present and less identified with our thoughts, emotions, and body sensations. As part of RAIN or by itself, noting is an essential skill that can help us step out of our eating habit loops. The more we make it a habit, the more quickly we can shift direction from fighting or feeding the craving monsters to being more present with ourselves.

RIGHT NOW: DAILY ROUTINES AND NOTING

Take a moment to reflect on your daily routines. What do you do every day that is pretty much the same, such as bathing, brushing your teeth, and so on? Make a note of these. Now see if you can start building one more habit on top of each of these: noting. When you bathe, note thoughts, sounds, sights, and body sensations. When you brush your teeth, note thoughts, sounds, sights, and body sensations. See how many of these routines you can layer noting on top of. And reflect on the experience afterward. Does being present feel better than being lost on autopilot (e.g., constant overplanning, worrying, etc.)? Take a note of that as well.

CHAPTER 19

Day 16: Fire Your Committee

For more than twenty-five years, I've read, researched, performed studies, run experiments, personally explored, and thought about the wonder that is the human mind. This three-pound bundle of tissue can regulate our breathing, think critically, make decisions, and cue our body to move us from one side of a room to another to stop the cat from scratching the couch. Amazing. But that's not all. It can also process a boggling array of emotions, which are a combination of thoughts and body sensations, so technically and experientially are thought/felt. It's hard not to feel awe (another emotion!) when you stop to think about it. However, our brain can also turn its considerable critical faculties on ourselves. We can be our own harshest critic. We know our soft spots, our weaknesses, and we're not afraid to exploit them.

One way this manifests is when we judge ourselves for our food choices. How many times have you said to yourself, "You are so bad," after an extra helping of dinner? "What's wrong with you?" or "You really shouldn't have" after you've licked your dessert spoon (or the plate) clean? We've seen how we can develop the habit of eating in response to emotion, but our crafty brains don't stop there. Not only do we eat in response to emotions, but our eating behaviors actually *create* emotions—namely the dynamic duo of guilt and shame.

THE COMMITTEE INSIDE YOUR HEAD

We all have a group of pesky voices in our head giving their opinions on everything we do, like people talking at the screen when watching a movie. "She shouldn't have gone in there!" "Did you really need that third glass of wine? See what happened!" It's like having a hundred judges observing your every move ready to sentence you to shame when you fail to live up to their standards.

They give us advice or tell us what to do, and it is really hard not to listen. These voices are always with us. Some are really loud. Whether it is a single dictatorial voice or multiple voices representing our different moods, we all seem to carry these voices around with us wherever we go. You probably have a select subcommittee of these voices devoted to assessing your food choices.

Anne told me about the large and loud food committee in her head. The members would remind her what her food rules were and how they applied to different foods. Some would gently point things out; others would rationalize or justify their positions based on what the latest experts had said or what she had read in a health magazine. As Anne's committee members spoke up, she tried to negotiate with them. Eventually she came to realize that there was no rationalizing with them. As soon as they started in on her, as she put it, "I was screwed."

Jacqui's committee was just as bad:

> There are committee members who say "Eat the cake!" and
> committee members who beat me up for it afterward! They would

have a feeding frenzy whenever I did something I wasn't supposed to do. I had all of these food rules, and they would send me to food jail whenever I broke them. Then after they'd locked me up, they'd sit there and tell me how bad a person I was. It was awful. The funny thing was that by seeing that these committee members were just me telling myself things, I was actually locking myself up.

If you're wondering how this leads to unhelpful food habits, it's because when we feel ashamed or bad about something we've done, we feel the urge to do something about it. Since we can't change the past, we focus on what we can do right now. One action we can take is judging ourselves. It feels better to do something than nothing. We might even rationalize that somehow that judgment will make us change in the future, but all it accomplishes is making us feel bad.

Trigger: Shame about an unhelpful habit.
Behavior: Self-judgment.
Result: Feel like we're doing something, but that something feels bad.

And what do many people do when they feel bad? They eat. Before you know it, you're in the middle of yet another habit loop:

Trigger: Feel bad.
Behavior: More eating.
Result: More shame.

I think you can see the problem with this.

Before you can change your behavior, you need to learn to stop listening to those judgy and shaming voices in your head that are so quick to offer unwelcome feedback. Fortunately, we can leverage our awareness to help us out.

THE OBSERVER EFFECT

To get at how awareness keeps our self-talk in line, I'm going to explain a phenomenon that physicists use to describe the physical universe, and then we'll see how it applies to our emotional universe.

Here's how it works: Electrons are really small. They weigh next to nothing: $9.10938356 \times 10^{-31}$ kilograms, to be exact. It's something of a marvel that we even know how much an electron weighs, since you can't exactly ask an electron to stand on a scale or even hold still, for that matter. To even *detect* an electron, physicists shine light on it. They hit it with photons—light particles—and measure how it affects the speed and momentum of the electron. But there's a catch: by trying to observe electrons, scientists are affecting the results—in this case, changing the speed and momentum of the electrons by hitting them with photons. The mere act of observing electrons changes their physical properties.

The way the process of measuring an electron's weight changes its weight is an example of what physicists call the observer effect. Why should you care about the observer effect?

The observer effect is not limited to the quantum world. When you check the air pressure in your tires, what happens when you push the pressure gauge onto the valve? Do you hear a little hiss? That's air coming out. It is nearly impossible to measure your tire's pressure without affecting the result.

The observer effect has also been extended to the field of psychology. There are many ways to accidentally or inadvertently bias the results of a study. You've probably heard of confirmation bias—the tendency to notice and give greater credibility to evidence that fits our existing beliefs. The observer effect and confirmation bias are examples of only two of many biases that have been identified in psychology.

One way the observer effect can affect the results of a study is by watching participants while it is happening. In psychology, the observer effect is often referred to as the Hawthorne effect. Named after a series of experiments that were performed at an electric factory between 1924 and 1932 in a suburb of Chicago—Hawthorne—these experiments looked to see if different lighting conditions affected worker output. The researchers found that no matter what changes in lighting the workers were exposed to, output improved. Dimmer, brighter—it didn't matter. Here's the kicker: when the researchers were finished futzing with the lighting, production returned to normal. Now you might think, "This is obvious. I don't need a scientist to tell me that if my boss is standing over my shoulder when I'm doing something, it's going to affect my performance."

Now that you know what it is, let's explore how you can harness the observer effect yourself—in a helpful way.

Put the Observer Effect to Use

Just as when a physicist changes an atom's weight when she measures it, when we observe our thoughts, we affect the results. Identifying the voices in our head gives us the distance to see that we are not our thoughts. We are people who have thoughts, and we can decide whether to listen to them or not. That's a *huge* distinction. With this perspective, we can start to step out of our heads and break the cycle of unhelpful behavior leading to self-judgment leading to more unhelpful behavior.

I first learned about the idea of the committee in our heads from a

Western monk—a person born in the West who has taken monastic vows in an Eastern tradition (Buddhism). Ṭhānissaro Bhikkhu is the head abbot of Metta Forest Monastery in San Diego County, California. I was listening to several of his lectures in my free time, and one in particular made my ears perk up. When I heard him describe a committee in our heads, I could absolutely relate. It was one of those "of course!" moments that helped me make sense of my mind. I recognized that I had a committee of my own. There was the boss who told me what to do, the judge who evaluated everything I did as good or bad, the politician who was always looking at how my actions might be seen by others, and so on. They were always chattering, creating noise in my head and making it hard to think straight.

Naming these voices helped me sort them out; I could see them much more clearly as thoughts instead of as a jumble of commands and comments. But there was something that the monk pointed out that was pure genius: Just because we have these voices in our heads doesn't mean that we have to listen to them. By naming them, we're already shining light on their true nature—they're simply thoughts in our heads. Naming them helps us track them.

Sometimes it is helpful to literally give these committee members names (my apologies if I've used your name as an example): Judgmental Jonas, Gertrude the Guilt-Giver, Shamer Shiloh, Must-Try-Harder Madison, You-Are-Useless Eugene, Beat-Yourself-Up Bertie.

We name the committee members and then keep an eye out for when and under what circumstances they rear their heads. We can track their orbits and patterns and more easily predict when they're going to show up. More important, by tracking them, we're observing them. By observing them, we're changing our relationship to them. That's right, we're bringing the observer effect right into our heads.

When working with patients or participants in our programs, I often explain this strategy while using a visual. I take my left hand and make a fist. I take my right hand and hold on to that fist. I explain that my left hand represents our thoughts, and my right hand represents us. Then I start moving my left hand—which of course pulls the right hand with it. While moving my hands, I point out that if we are identified with our thoughts, they yank us around. They can pull us wherever they want us to go. By observing—I open my right hand and move it a few inches away from the left at this point—we don't have to be pulled. No longer attached, my left hand can move around, and my right hand can stay still. We now have distance between us and our thoughts. Distance gives us the ability to step back and gain perspective. We can simply notice thoughts as thoughts and watch them come and go. In the same way, by naming our committee members, we get that needed distance and perspective.

USING NOTING TO DISEMPOWER YOUR COMMITTEE

We have to notice that we are caught up before we can step out of that cycle of being identified with it. If we're caught in a self-judgmental habit loop, we cycle through judgment, guilt, and shame. We're so identified with what is happening that we can't see that we're stuck in the cycle. If we overindulge in a guilty pleasure at a party or after dinner, we feel—surprise!—guilty for eating. While guilt is about something we've done, shame is about who we are. The guilt of overindulgence triggers self-judgment, which results in our feeling ashamed of ourselves. By naming our committee members, we can identify "guilt," "shame," "judging," or whatever is happening in that moment. This helps us gain perspective so that we can disengage from the cycle and reengage with whatever is happening in that moment in our lives. Instead of getting stuck in our heads for hours, we can shut down the head games our committee members are playing and move on with our evening.

NAME IT TO FRAME IT

Dr. Dan Siegel, psychiatrist and author of *Aware* (among other books), coined the phrase "Name it to tame it" to describe this practice of naming your committee members in order to shrink their power over you. Committee members don't really have any power; they can only try to influence you to do their bidding. Noting or labeling these committee members helps you manage them.

When we bring in awareness, we can see these committee members for what they are—voices in our heads that might be giving us bad advice and making us feel guilty if we don't follow it. Naming the voices gives us the distance to see that we are not our thoughts. As I mentioned earlier, we are people who have thoughts, and we can decide whether to listen to them or not. We can also see how unhelpful these thoughts are and become disenchanted with them. That's how we step out of our heads so that we can live our lives without being yanked around by our thoughts.

COMMON COMMITTEE MEMBERS

It can be tricky at first to identify your committee members. Most of them have been in residence for as long as we can remember. If you can't tell which unhelpful voice is speaking to you and making you feel bad, you can just say "Unhelpful committee member" until you learn to distinguish them. A few common culprits:

SHAME

SELF-DOUBT

DISGUST

CONTEMPT

INFERIOR

DESPAIR

NOT WORTHY

BROKEN

USELESS

A FAILURE

Simply calling out your committee by name will diminish their power. They haven't helped run the business of your life. In fact, they've caused waste, fraud, and sometimes abuse.

Someone tagged me in a Twitter post once, writing: "This is the committee that has been with me for so many years. Hard to ignore at times."

Below it he posted two pictures side by side. On one side was a picture of a bunch of sticky notes on a wall. They read Depressed Kevin, Can't Do It Kevin, Guilty Kevin, Give Up Kevin, and Shame Kevin. The picture next to it was of the same sticky notes. *Kevin* had been crossed out and replaced by a committee member name: Depressed Dweezil, Bad Brad, Guilty Gabe, and so on. Except there was one sticky note that was crossed out entirely: shame. He explained, "Shame doesn't belong on the committee anymore. Shame doesn't get a name. Shame gets crossed out." Using something as simple as sticky notes, he pointed out that once he had recognized shame and taken away its voice, it didn't have a place to sit at the table anymore.

When you can stop listening to your committee, you are better able to direct that attention elsewhere. You can listen to your body and trust yourself. Once those blabbermouths lose their voices, you may notice less noise and clutter in your mind, which will open room for more space and freedom to move beyond your old identities and into someone new: yourself.

RIGHT NOW: START NAMING THE COMMITTEE MEMBERS

Pull out some sticky notes or a piece of paper. Take a few deep breaths. Start listening—inwardly. What committee members do you have in your head? Write them down. Give them names. Do they have a certain tone of voice? Then ask yourself, "Is this committee member helping or harming me?"

Start paying attention to when they pop up and give their opinions, judgments, commentaries, or commands. As you hear them, simply note them: "Oh, that's XX."

PART 3
A BIGGER BETTER OFFER:
DAYS 17–21

By now, you are well practiced at mapping out unhelpful habit loops and have been using awareness to become disenchanted with old habits. You've been leveraging the negative prediction error side of the reward value recalibration equation with the craving tool. You also have a sense for what it feels like to start stepping out of these old habit loops using RAIN, and you've learned how to build and stabilize your awareness using straight-up noting practice.

The tasks in the first two sections of the book—especially the bits about exploring how ungratifying these old habits loops are—can often feel like a lot of work. We have to climb the mountains of our minds in order to get to the top so that we can look around and enjoy the view. Postcards and pictures aren't the same as the real thing. And hopefully the climb hasn't all felt like a forced march. Some bits can be hard, especially when we're tired, our mind is resisting change, and we just want to eat the damn cookie.

Now for the fun part: forging new helpful habits. In this part you will utilize the positive prediction error side of things. You will use what you've already learned about your mind to provide a springboard for prolonged change. You've got gravity on your side. Going downhill is easier than going up. You've got momentum on your side.

Let's get started working with your brain's tendencies, employing its strengths instead of fighting against it to change your relationship to food, and possibly even to yourself.

CURIOSITY: OUR ZERO-CALORIE SUPERFOOD

I've been emphasizing awareness as a critical ingredient for changing your relationship to eating. You need awareness to notice if you're genuinely hungry or not. You need awareness to map out eating habit loops. You need awareness to change the reward value of different eating behaviors—both positive and negative. Noticing what it feels like to overeat helps break those deeply ingrained Corn Nut or clean-plate habits. Hands down, awareness is the critical currency for changing any behavior, in any direction.

In the chapters that follow, we're going to focus on a new mindset you can adopt in place of automaticity or habit—curiosity. We've touched on this a tiny bit with the RAIN practice. Now we'll explore it at length to discover its power. What you'll see in these chapters is that an attitude of curiosity is the other side of the mindfulness coin. Heads is awareness. Tails is curiosity. It's not a game of one or the other. You need both sides to win.

I get a lot of questions about what curiosity is and how to capitalize on it. For starters, there are two types of curiosity. If you are interested in learning more, you might be employing one or both types right now. Curious? Let's go.

The scientists Jordan Litman and Paul Silvia put names to the two main ways that we experience curiosity: D-type and I-type. D stands for deprivation and I stands for interest. Deprivation curiosity is well named. When we're deprived of information, we are driven to seek it out. Deprivation curiosity is that restless, itchy sensation that says, "Look that up" or "Find that out." At a neuroscientific level, the feeling is likely dopamine firing, driving us to do something. Once we get that information, we are no longer deprived—our thirst has been quenched.

Studies have even shown that in some cases, animals prefer getting a piece of information over a sip of water when they are thirsty. Curious to know how researchers figured this out? Basically, the researchers taught primates a gambling task and found that they reliably sacrificed water—which is a primary reward—for getting advanced information about a gambling outcome. And as your brain might have already predicted, this choice-making of getting a sneak peek of how the gamble is going to go involves the OFC. Just as an empty stomach signals us to get food, the thirst for knowledge drives us to seek out the equivalent of hydration for our brain in the form of information. Both calories and information help us survive. The internet is a bonanza for looking up trivia when you see a picture of someone famous and can't remember who they are—or an endless series of rabbit holes if you get sucked into reading their entire life history.

Interest curiosity, on the other hand, isn't about acquiring and consuming a specific piece of information. Whereas deprivation curiosity comes from a need to know, interest curiosity is more about the act of gathering that brain food. When we're starving, we might quickly shovel down some food to satisfy our stomach. In this situation, we often aren't paying attention to the how of eating. We miss the details of how the food tastes and so on. We don't notice what it feels like to eat. That's akin to deprivation curiosity—we're just trying to get that information into our brain. The process of chewing is analogous to what interest curiosity is all about. Eating can be joyful when we pay attention or can simply fill a void when we don't.

INTEREST VS. DEPRIVATION

Interest is that type of curiosity that we tap into when we are *in the process* of learning. We aren't just trying to get a certain piece of information. Instead, we are enjoying the process as we discover new things. When we need to know if the plant that our cat or dog just ate is poisonous, D curiosity sets us scrambling to look it up. When we find out that it is harmless for pets but notice that it is actually important for its symbolic nature in certain cultures, that's our I curiosity taking over. Deprivation curiosity feels closed down and narrows our focus—find that information fast. We ignore everything that seems superfluous. We're on a mission—driven—to get that piece of information. Interest curiosity opens us up to the experience. We don't feel rushed because we're focused on the process of learning. The joy of discovery feels good by itself. It is intrinsically rewarding because we don't have to get anything to feel its rewards.

You can remember the two types of curiosity this way: deprivation is about the destination. When you get that piece of information that you've been lacking, you're done—mission accomplished. Interest is about the journey. Even if you have a specific destination in mind, you are enjoying the process of learning. It doesn't matter if you get there or not.

Interest curiosity has been researched much less—from a brain standpoint—than deprivation curiosity. I don't think this is because of a lack of interest in interest curiosity, but instead because it is harder to pin down and study. It is relatively easy to put college students in a brain scanner and ask them trivia questions to tweak their deprivation curiosity. It is perhaps a little harder to teach a monkey to gamble. It is much more of a challenge to get humans to focus on the joy of discovery, or as the Zen folks would point out, the joy of not knowing while scanning their brains.

But we don't have to rely on fancy brain monitors to do our own experiments with interest curiosity. It is not hard to discover this for yourself. Being interested—truly curious—about something feels good. And because it is naturally rewarding, it feeds on itself. There is no hole to be filled because we're not deprived in the first place. It is possible to discover and even train ourselves that not having the answer is more than okay. In fact, letting go of needing or having to know can be freeing in itself when we see how heavy the burden of *needing to know* is, compared with the lightness of simply being, well, curious (in the I-type sense).

Interest curiosity sets us up for learning. When we're curious, we naturally move in and look more closely. We want to learn more. We are open to seeing what might seem to our predicting brains as the same thing in a fresh light. Oh wow, I didn't notice how the petal of that flower actually sparkles in the morning sun. How amazing. In *The Botany of Desire,* Michael Pollan put it this way: "Memory is the enemy of wonder, which abides nowhere else but in the present. This is why, unless you are a child, wonder depends on forgetting—on a process, that is, of subtraction." As we focus on the process, we subtract out our assumptions, which helps us see more clearly what is happening in the moment.

The attitude with which we approach life is critical for our survival. If we are in the habit of judging and assuming things are going to be a certain way, our brains close down, making it harder for us to learn. If we are constantly curious, we are open to new experiences. We move out of our comfort zone, where everything is familiar and safe, and into our growth zone, where we are open to learning. Interest curiosity helps us stay open, wondering instead of assuming. As Socrates reportedly said, "Wonder is the beginning of wisdom."

Hopefully you've already explored some of the powers of curiosity. Bringing interest curiosity to the explorations and practices that I've put forward so far in the book encourages an open-mindedness that helps you learn and grow instead of getting stuck in habit loops of self-judgment and shame. Building that mental muscle of curiosity as you move into this final section of the book will not only make it easier to learn but also make the journey more enjoyable.

The final section of this book will walk you through how to develop the freedom to choose helpful habits. These choices will come from listening to your body, as you become further disenchanted with the old "shoulding" habit loops that your mind promised would help but that never delivered for you. You'll learn how to show your brain the superior reward value of eating healthfully and caring for yourself in other ways so you can break old habits and replace them with better ones, which will hopefully stick with you for a long time as they build on themselves. As a bonus, you'll learn the power of kindness—how it can help heal mental wounds and dismantle those shoulding habits that you may have inadvertently set up along the way.

Curiosity and kindness are best friends. They support each other. They're also your friends: to your brain, they are a much more rewarding dynamic duo than guilt and shame. The more you learn to lean into them, the more they'll help and support you as well.

CHAPTER 20

Day 17: An Unforced Freedom of Choice

We've just spent the past two weeks teaching you how to break free of unhelpful food habit loops. If you smoked or were addicted to a drug, in this part of the book you'd be saying goodbye to your substance of choice, but you can't do that with food (well, maybe gummy worms). You don't have to smoke, but ya gotta eat to survive.

Total deprivation is not the answer. If you've ever tried to force yourself not to eat your favorite sweet, you know how that forbidden fruit becomes sweeter and sweeter in your mind as you can't stop fantasizing about it.

Now that you've identified and hopefully started to let go of the old habit loops, your brain can ask itself, "What do I really want?" What do you need that truly nourishes you instead of simply scratching the itch of a craving? Your brain has already started exploring what might be a better fit than your old habits. As you develop and refine your awareness, your brain is starting to figure out what qualities it's looking for that will ensure your chances of survival in the long run. What will leave you feeling fulfilled instead of crummy? Once you've identified new healthy habits around food—the types of food that are both tasty and nourishing, and the amount that doesn't send you off the cliff of overindulgence—you will be so satisfied that you won't think about those old unhealthy choices anymore.

In my clinic and digital therapeutic programs, I very unscientifically call this process finding the bigger better offer. I came up with the phrase after reflecting on that awkward rite of passage: high school dating. I'd line up a date for Friday night, and my excitement would build during the week, only to get a call at the last minute with what sounded like the world's lamest excuse when my date bailed on me. The proverbial "I'm washing my hair" was likely that person having some new and better option open up, like a date with someone else. She had gotten a bigger better offer. We'll call it the BBO for short.

Your OFC is always weighing the options, and it will always go with the BBO. As we've explored with willpower failure, the trick is to leverage its strength instead of fighting against it. This will increase the chances of success, ensuring that the new helpful habits will stick around.

As any good leader knows, a choice freely chosen will be embraced more deeply and more consistently than one that is dictated from on high, from the top of "Mount Should." This is why savvy parents don't make a fuss when their children refuse to wear a hat on a blustery morning. Wise parents know that children are much more likely to grab a hat voluntarily on Tuesday if on Monday they have learned from their own experience—*yeesh, my ears were really cold yesterday*—than if the parent insisted on putting a cap on the child after ten minutes of struggle. Warm ears are certainly a BBO than cold.

MAKE A MINDFUL CHOICE FREELY

My team and I discovered for ourselves how effective leveraging the OFC to find its own BBO is when our participants were able to make choices on their own.

As we were getting the Eat Right Now program up and running, a good friend of mine named Pete had been experimenting with mixing up how he taught physics to his college students at Cal Poly. He was exploring a "flipped classroom" model of teaching. The concept is that the lecture and the homework bits are flipped—lectures at home and homework in class. Pete recorded all of his physics lectures and had his students watch them whenever they wanted to. It freed up Pete's lecture time, so his students could come to class and do their problem sets during class time while he was there to help them by answering questions.

I wondered if we could use the same flipped classroom model at the Center for Mindfulness. The idea was that people could use the Eat Right Now app at home and attend a live weekly class where—in the same vein as MBSR and other group-based formats—they could get the benefits of a group. Instead of my standing up in front of the group going on and on about how reward-based learning works, they could learn the general concepts at home and then bring their questions to the group. Each week was dynamic. They brought topics to class from their struggles implementing the principles of the program in their daily lives. For example, if someone was stuck in a willpower habit loop, they could bring it up in class, where other members of the group and I would help them hash out where they were getting stuck and make suggestions for how to let go of willpower and start working with their survival and planning brains. Not only did the person who brought the problem up benefit from my and my co-facilitators' exploration with them, but the whole class got to learn by proxy.

After a year or two of running the group, I started to see a pattern emerge. When people joined the program, the first change that I noticed was that they were better at mapping out their habit loops. They could identify more of them and see them more clearly than before they joined the group. This wasn't a surprise. We were training them to do exactly that. It would have been more of a surprise (and frankly, a bummer) if they couldn't map a loop after a couple of weeks of using the app and being in the group. The second change that I noticed was that people were changing their eating habits. Not only that, but over the course of a couple of months of using the app and being in the group, people were coming back each week with lighter moods and more positive attitudes. Since I was in the thick of things leading the groups, it was hard for me to put my finger on the entire pattern. All I knew was that some shift was happening.

I brought in the experts to figure out what change process was driving these shifts. Ariel Beccia was a graduate student in my lab who happened to have a background in doing qualitative research. Most of the studies—and in fact most research that we think of as such—is done in ways that is measured and described by numbers. We calculate shifts over time in this or that and report percent changes. We look at brain activity differences between groups. That's all *quantitative* research.

This is where *qualitative* research comes in. It describes what is happening in people's lived experience that goes along with that quantitative shift. Qualitative research focuses on how people are experiencing the shifts in life that lead to or go along with the shifts in the numbers.

Ariel designed a qualitative study to figure out what was happening in the lives of our flipped classroom group. She sat down and listened to what the group had to say.

Ariel discovered that what was making all the difference in replacing an unhelpful eating habit with a helpful eating habit was people's ability to engage in making mindful choices. By going through steps 1 and 2, participants felt like they had an increased capacity to make positive choices about food and eating, and they were "adopting adaptive methods of coping with adverse experiences or emotions." One person summed the third step up this way: "You can have awareness at any time. But making the choice, that's what makes a lasting difference."

From this study, it was clear the key to success in step 3 is a choice that comes from listening to the body, not some "should" command that comes from the mind. Bringing together the language of our group, we defined step 3: an unforced freedom of choice, emerging from embodied awareness.

It was really gratifying to be able to put our fingers on what we'd been observing for years—another example of how reducing uncertainty in our brains makes us feel better. It was also nice to have this definition come from our group. We weren't white-coated researchers dictating how people should behave. We listened, and the group proved wise and eloquent.

Our group participants were describing over and over that this unforced freedom of choice fit perfectly with how our brains work: given a choice, we're going to pick the more rewarding option. Critically, we first have *to feel like we have a choice.*

Step 3 starts with seeing that we have a choice to step out of our old habit loops. Without awareness of what these loops are—step 1—we can't do this. Without awareness of how unrewarding the old habit loops are—step 2—we don't have the motivation to step out of the loop. We don't feel like we can do it. And only when we try out alternatives—stopping at the top of the pleasure plateau instead of going off the cliff of overindulgence—can we see that there are alternatives. Most important, we have to see that the alternatives feel better. We have to find the BBOs for ourself.

That is how our brain works, after all. The OFC is going to look at A and B and choose the one that is more rewarding. Our mission in step 3 is to teach the OFC there are foods out there—and amounts of food—that will be more pleasing than the ones it's become disenchanted with so your brain can freely choose the bigger better offer. For example, we discover that a piece of fruit gives some sweet satisfaction that doesn't make us crave more. Not overeating—stopping before going off the cliff—also counts. Not doing something—not overeating—is in itself a type of doing that also qualifies as a BBO because it feels better than overdoing it.

The BBO principle even applies to how we make decisions. For example:

Which feels better? Feeling as if you have no choice in a matter or being able to choose?

Which feels better? Forcing yourself to do something or feeling like that choice comes naturally?

Once our thinking brains start listening to our feeling bodies, it becomes a conversation that leads to agreement; together, they naturally pick the BBO. An unforced freedom of choice feels much better than being stuck in our old eating habits. It feels better than trying to force ourselves to stick to a diet or food plan.

In the chapters that follow, I'm going to walk you through how to use your brain to become enchanted with your bigger better offers.

RIGHT NOW: THE VIRTUE OF UNFORCED CHOICE

Habits are a powerful force, but as we've discussed, it is possible to break them. In fact, I'd guess you've broken a habit or two of your own already, simply by finding that B was better than A. Reflect on any habits that you've changed recently. Did you find that you were able to stick with the new behavior more easily when you felt you chose it freely? Are there other habits you have had more of a struggle with? And for those, have you chosen the new reward freely or were you directed to it by an outside source?

CHAPTER 21

Day 18: Leveraging the Food/Mood Relationship

I don't have many memories of my early childhood. It's a bit of a blur of skinned knees and playing in the woods. Yet there is one day when I was in first or second grade that stands out for me. I had gone to a sleepover at my friend Clayton's house. Sleepovers at Clayton's were special because his mom let us drink soda and eat doughnuts for breakfast, whereas the closest I generally got to sweets at home was carob (this weird chocolaty-esque thing that my health-conscious mom picked up at our food co-op in Indiana). The sugar bombs of doughnuts and soda blew my mind. I thought I had hit the jackpot. But then not long afterward, I experienced a terrible icky feeling in my stomach. When I got home and told my mother that my tummy was really upset, she asked, "What did you have for breakfast?" I thought back to the glazed jelly doughnut (or was it three?) that I'd polished off an hour earlier and something clicked in my brain. That may have been my first ever retrospective.

A few years later, when I was in middle school, I started seriously getting into racing BMX bikes—there's not a whole lot to do in Indiana, beyond the joke of watching the corn grow. Tearing up the dirt track on two wheels and landing big jumps was as thrilling as it got. The races were held on weekends in the summer and consisted of three heats. For each age category, the track officials added up where you placed in each of three races to determine the overall winner for the day. I kept careful track of my competition. I wanted to *win*.

To fuel up before each heat, I used money that I earned as a paper boy to buy my own food for the race because my mom wouldn't pony up for what I thought was proper race nutrition: soda and a candy bar. No more carob for this guy! The problem was that the heats cycled through all the age groups sequentially, so my races were spaced out over several hours. I generally did best in my first race, often finishing first or second. As the day wore on, my energy flagged, and so did my mood. By the third heat, I struggled to keep up with the others. As the sugar and caffeine high wore off, I became more irritable and sour.

One race day, my mom gently suggested that I try eating a peanut butter and honey sandwich instead of candy to give myself an energy boost. I guess I wanted to win more than I wanted to eat candy, so I gave the natural protein and energy alternative a shot. It worked. I was almost as fresh during my final heat as I had been for my first race of the day. I'd had no idea how much food could affect my energy level—and on top of that, my mood. Sure, it felt good to win. But switching up my food also helped me lose my grumpy-pants moods and remember why I was racing in the first place: it was fun to ride my bike (and catch some air), no matter if I won or not.

As a psychiatrist, I am not alone in this journey. Nutritional psychiatry is a new subfield of psychiatry that has sprung up in the last few years. Nutritional psychiatry is focused on what it sounds like: researching how the food we eat impacts how we feel emotionally. I would also add that it is a two-way street: how we feel affects what we eat. For example, correlations have been made between diets high in refined sugars and worsening symptoms of mood disorders such as depression. One cross-sectional study found that people who ate the highest glycemic index diets had greater odds of depression. Other studies have found that artificial food color and preservatives such as sodium benzoate increase hyperactivity in children. There is also a burgeoning area of research examining how the types of food we eat increase inflammatory markers in the body and brain, potentially playing a role in mood disorders. As scientists race to figure out the specific details of how all of this works, it may come back to a saying I learned as a kid: you are what you eat. Food = mood. Eat crap, feel like crap. Ironically, if we don't know how feedback cycles work in our minds, feeling like crap may trigger us to eat more crap, perpetuating the cycle.

Knowing how what we eat affects our energy, our mood, and our body's health allows us to find and choose bigger better offers. I've permanently moved on from soda—simply imagining how I would feel after drinking it as opposed to tea or water is all my brain needs to make that choice.

BLUEBERRIES—A HAPPY ENDING TO MY GUMMY WORM AFFAIR

When I was in my gummy worm phase, I did a little research experiment. In science the term *n of one study* highlights how you can learn a lot from single individuals. This single individual was about to learn a lot from comparing gummy worms to blueberries. This was during the part of my life when I couldn't even have those chewy worms in the house because even the most fleeting thought of them meant I had to have them.

Paying attention helped me become disenchanted with gummy worms, but that wasn't the whole of the story.

When gummy worms fell out of favor in my brain, that familiarity of eating them at night was still there. I would go up to the cabinet and linger. The craving hadn't gone away. My brain was looking for something else that could satisfy it—something sweet. My brain was looking for a bigger better offer.

If my brain wanted something sugary after dinner, I needed to do an experiment to see what sweet thing could win the contest that included how content I felt afterward—as in it didn't drive cravings for more mindless consumption—how it affected my energy level and mood, and so on. Plus, it needed to taste good. So I started comparing gummy worms to blueberries.

To begin with, I practiced mindful eating with each of them. The taste of the two foods was worlds apart. Gummy worms had that sickly sweet hint of petroleum. Blueberries had none of that. I don't really have great words for how they taste. It was as though blueberries had evolved to meet the perfect balance of mouthfeel, taste, and satisfaction for my brain and body, especially compared with gummy worms. Color: gummy worms psychedelic; blueberries a naturally inviting deep blue. Mouthfeel: gummy worms slimy; blueberries a slight pop and then soft but firm at the same time. Craving for more: gummy worms off the charts; blueberries easy to stop when I'd had enough. You get the idea.[1]

My brain—and all of our brains, for that matter—can tell when

---

[1] Yes, I'm deliberately being a bit hyperbolic here. As I pointed out earlier in the book, this doesn't mean that licorice or ice cream is going to suddenly taste bad when we pay attention. But we can explore the results of eating a cup of blueberries vs. a cup of gummy worms or licorice or whatever our sweet of choice is.

it's got a good thing as long as I provide it the opportunity to notice it. We don't have to read a study about the benefits of blueberries; our brains already know the real deal when we eat it.

I had found my BBO.

BUILDING ENCHANTMENT

My blueberry experiment highlights several important things. (1) Paying attention helps us tap into what is likely eons of evolution that helped us humans figure out what food is healthy. We have had to relearn this in the modern day, since we've become accustomed to eating manufactured foods. (2) Eating natural sources of sugar is very different from eating engineered objects when it comes to craving. With blueberries, for example, sugar is paired with fiber, so it is absorbed relatively slowly and steadily in our gut. Processed food is designed to be easily digested, freeing up sugar for rapid absorption. This leads to a compensatory insulin spike in our bloodstream. This is where the term *glycemic index* comes from. Foods get assigned a number—their glycemic index—based on how much they increase blood sugar. Blood sugar spikes and crashes contribute to cravings. Eating refined carbohydrates (basically sugar) only makes us want more. Remember, our bodies evolved this way so that we could weather famines. When we eat natural sources of calories, we can see in our own direct experience how these differ in how they make us feel—feeling content instead of craving more. We can much more easily coast to a stop at the top of our pleasure plateau instead of going off the cliff of overindulgence. (3) We can trust our brains to fill those voids that are left when we become disenchanted with a food.

Building trust starts with knowing how our brains work. We then build that trust by using our awareness to let our brains do the work for us. Trying to force ourselves to eat broccoli is a habit that is not rewarding and is exhausting. Awareness and curiosity are gifts that we give ourselves—they do the work for us.

POTENTIAL BIGGER BETTER OFFER FOODS

Your nutritional needs will be slightly different from everyone else's based on your genetic makeup, your exercise habits, your size, your sleep habits, and dozens of other factors. However, there are foods that tend to offer a higher reward value to everyone—and most of them fall into the category of simple, unprocessed foods, those that are as close to how they came out of the ground or off the plant as possible. (Unprocessed plant-based foods have the bonus of being gentler on the planet.) I'm not going to give you a list, because it is so easy to become obsessed with food rules and then put yourself in food jail if you don't follow them. Instead, pay attention. Listen to your body. Pay attention to what you get from eating different types of food. Your body is much wiser than some ever-changing list of what you should and shouldn't eat.

Yes, awareness not only helps you become disenchanted with unhealthy types and amounts of food, but it also helps you become more enchanted with those that serve your health and well-being. You don't have to tell yourself what food to eat or avoid. Your body will do this for you, as long as you build your awareness, paying attention to the results. The bonus is that this becomes a virtuous cycle between your body and mind. When you notice how a foul mood might lead you to eat junk food, which makes you even moodier, you become disenchanted with this cycle. When you notice that eating processed food or food with artificial additives can affect your mood, even tipping you into craving more unhealthy food, you can become disenchanted with that loop and step out of it. And then—as I have over the years—you can explore all the foods that help you boost your mood and maintain your energy levels.

Your body already knows what types and amounts of food are the BBOs—you just have to listen to it. Each time you do—and pay attention to the results—you build enchantment with those behaviors, simply because you feel better. Whether we are exploring eliminating food additives (e.g., artificial food coloring) and eating a natural-food diet, substituting seltzer for soda or blueberries for gummy worms, our bodies and brains know what is best for us. Doing a retrospective afterward helps lock these reward values in and makes them more accessible in the future.

It may not feel easy right now, but it is simple. I promise you that I have not oversimplified the concepts or the process. I haven't left anything out. The research from my lab's studies has backed it up. I'm also standing on the shoulders of many scientists who have researched the fundamental elements of reinforcement learning both in the brain and on our behavior.

RIGHT NOW: BUILD YOUR ENCHANTMENT DATABANK

By now, you should have a disenchantment databank full of useful information about foods that aren't all they were cracked up to be. The deposits you made in that databank were the result of negative reinforcement learning that came from eating more mindfully. But let's not forget about positive reinforcement. It's time to start making deposits in your enchantment databank—a group of foods that is satisfying in the short and long term. Choose a couple of foods you have started to enjoy more as a result of the practices you've learned so far.

MINDFUL EATING EXERCISE: Following the mindful eating guidelines I put forward earlier, pay careful attention as you eat these foods. Notice how each bite tastes. Notice how you feel after eating them.

RETROSPECTIVE ON THIS FOOD: After about twenty minutes and/or an hour after eating, take a few moments to notice how you feel. Do a retrospective on how it felt to eat in the moment. Repeat this as often as necessary to lock in how good it felt (and feels) to eat these foods.

You can do the same exercise with the amount of food you eat. Using the pleasure plateau, notice what it feels like to stop before going off the cliff of overindulgence. Do a retrospective later on to remember this, and see how much you can recall it when you are feeling the urge to overindulge in the future.

CHAPTER 22

Day 19: Kindness

A few years ago, a thirty-something woman was referred to my clinic for Binge Eating Disorder (BED). We'll call her Tasha.[1] When I looked at her chart, I saw she met all the criteria for BED: eating much more rapidly than normal; eating until feeling uncomfortably full; eating large amounts of food when not feeling physically hungry; feeling disgusted, depressed, or guilty after overeating. I knew what the traditional course of treatment would be—a mixture of medication to try to treat depression symptoms, cognitive behavior therapy to focus on negative thinking patterns, and perhaps some nutritional counseling (if necessary).

I'd been practicing medicine long enough to know that a bunch of criteria on my diagnostic checklist wouldn't tell me everything I needed to know about Tasha. As is true with every human being on the planet, her full story was much more complicated and would guide me to what would help her far more than her medical chart did.

As I talked to Tasha, I discovered she had a history of trauma. She had learned before the age of ten that eating allowed her to numb

---

[1] In contrast to everyone else in the book, she is not referred to by her real name. But she, like everyone else in the book, is a real person.

herself from negative emotions. By the time she came to see me, she had gotten to the point where she would binge on entire large pizzas roughly twenty out of thirty days a month. Sometimes she'd even binge on top of a binge. Her bingeing habits had taken a toll on her body and mind: she was at a very unhealthy weight, and she was depressed. She felt guilty when she binged, ashamed of herself that she couldn't stop, and somewhat hopeless about ever being able to step out of the cycle.

My heart went out to her—so many years of suffering.

But even though she had been bingeing for such a long time, I felt a lot of hope that we could work together to help turn things around. We mapped out her habit loop together: Trigger—negative emotion. Behavior—binge on pizza. Reward—numbing out. As we carried out the mapping process, it also became pretty clear how her bingeing made her feel ashamed, which was what led to her "binge on top of binge" behavior. The committee members in her head were in overdrive, judging her for bingeing. Then, feeling guilty for what she'd done, she became ashamed of who she was. She wasn't just judging her behavior. She was also judging *herself.*

Why would she binge again if bingeing itself sent her into guilt and shame spirals? Unfortunately, her brain had learned only one method for dealing with negative emotions, and that was to continue the unhelpful habit loop of bingeing.

When a binge leads to self-judgment, which leads to guilt and shame, which leads to another binge, it can feel like we're getting sucked into a never-ending vortex. The gravitational pull can be really, really strong. It's like a whirlpool: once we get sucked in, it speeds up and pulls us in even more. It can feel impossible to pull ourselves out of that "habit on top of habit" cycle, as they feed each other. What was going on in Tasha's brain wasn't her fault.

OUR SELF-JUDGMENT HABIT

Another unfortunate force of nature can add to the gravity of these situations: familiarity. Remember, our brains don't like change. It makes them so uncomfortable that they go out of their way to avoid that discomfort by seeking out the familiar. Let's look at an example of how this tug of familiarity can pull us in the wrong direction even when our planning brain can see it clearly would be better to change the behavior.

A team of researchers led by Yael Millgram at the Hebrew University performed a simple experiment. They showed depressed and non-depressed individuals a set of photographs. Some photos showed happy images, such as a bunch of cute kittens all crowded together and seemingly smiling at the camera. Other photos were sad pictures, such as someone crying. Still others showed neutral images, such as a clock or a stool. The scientists asked subjects to rate their mood after looking at a set of pictures. Across both groups, looking at happy pictures evoked happiness, while sad images evoked sadness. Not a surprise. But here's where it gets interesting: while depressed individuals did not differ in how many times they chose to look at happy pictures, they chose to view *significantly more* sadness-inducing images than those who were not depressed.

Millgram and her team repeated their experiment with the same setup, but instead of showing happy and sadness-inducing pictures, they had a new set of participants listen to happy and sad music clips. They found the same thing: depressed individuals were more likely to choose sad music.

The research team wondered what would happen if depressed individuals were given a cognitive strategy to make themselves feel either better or worse. What would they choose? A final round of participants was trained in how to increase or decrease emotional reactions to emotional stimuli using what is called cognitive reappraisal. By ascribing a different meaning or interpretation to the image, they could increase or decrease their emotional reaction. They were then shown the same types of happy, sad, and neutral images as the first experiment and asked to choose a strategy: make me happier or sadder. You can guess how this story ends. Indeed, depressed individuals chose not to make themselves feel better, but *worse.*

This might sound strange to the majority of nondepressed individuals in the world. But to those who have depression, it might sound or even feel familiar. Depressed people may simply be more familiar with feeling this way—it is their comfort zone.

We prefer that proverbial devil that we know simply because it is familiar. The fear of the unknown—that overwhelming feeling that comes when there is too much uncertainty—trumps our discomfort. Understanding how our minds resist change can help us open up to our experience and work with that resistance so that change can happen.

This is precisely what's going on when we judge ourselves for our eating. In a perfect world, we could just channel our inner Bob Newhart and say, "Stop it!" and poof, no more self-recrimination. But we are so accustomed to beating ourselves up for our unhelpful habits, we make a habit of that, too. We feel like it is our fault, when it isn't. It is an electrical fault in our brain due to a bit of miswiring—a fault that can be corrected.

On top of this, our brains rationalize our actions. We tell ourselves that we must be getting something out of judging ourselves. Otherwise we wouldn't be doing it, right? *Judging myself will make me stop the behavior!* Sadly, all it does is reinforce the habit of self-judgment. For many people, engaging in self-judgment feels better than not doing anything at all—especially if they are carrying a lot of baggage.

Despite the fact that the something happened in the unchangeable past, they feel the need to do something about it, and what they can do right now is beat themselves up. Ah, control. The more they do it, the more familiar it becomes, which then makes it even harder to step out of the loop. Control and comfort are powerful friends, especially when they come together.

Someone in our program reflected, "I've often wondered why I seem to self-sabotage, to eat even when I distinctly remember hating myself for doing so. In the past I've thought maybe the answer is that I need to hate myself more vividly so it serves as a restraint in my memory next time."

Which brings me back to Tasha, who was stuck in her own binge-shame-binge cycle. As part of our work together, she learned to leverage her OFC, starting with exploring what she got from self-judgment. That part was pretty straightforward. She could see how her OFC didn't really get anything from self-judgment except more bingeing. Not rewarding. Through that negative prediction error, her brain was helping her break her habit loop and binge less often.

Yet that was only half the story. What about alleviating the self-judgment itself? She needed to find something better for her mind in those moments.

KINDNESS AS A BIGGER BETTER OFFER

Tasha's self-judgment committee member was working overtime. Yet Tasha herself was starting to learn how to step out of self-judgment habit loops by seeing how unrewarding they were. It was time to bring in the secret sauce: kindness. We began having her explore kindness— toward herself.

Often people use the terms *kindness* and *compassion* somewhat interchangeably, especially when applied toward oneself. Compassion comes from the root *compati*: *com* means "with," and *pati* means "to suffer." When we are in the face of suffering—others or our own—there is often a natural response: we're moved to help in some way. And what is the attitude of this compassionate response? Kindness. So compassion and kindness are related but not the same. We can be kind in the absence of suffering. When we are suffering, kindness is a natural compassionate movement to alleviate that suffering. Why might kindness arise in situations like this?

My lab did a research study to see where kindness stood when it came to reward value. We asked hundreds of people to rank a bunch of different mental states and behaviors, the most preferable at the top and the least preferable at the bottom. The mental states ranged from anxious, fearful, angry, frustrated, and worried to grateful, content, connected, and kind. Kindness ranked number two overall—second only to feeling joyful. You can repeat that experiment right now, for yourself. What feels better? When you judge yourself or you are kind to yourself? Another no-brainer.

If you tend to judge yourself or even judge yourself for judging yourself, this might be a good time to take a step back, map it out, and ask, "What am I getting from this?" You don't need to kick a self-judgment habit to the curb—remember, willpower is more myth than muscle—you simply need to call up your awareness and kindness. Awareness helps your OFC see that judgment is not rewarding, so it naturally drops out of favor. Kindness steps in, asking innocently, "How'd it feel the last time you walked with me?" Kindness is the bigger better offer. And in the face of suffering—such as when we are judging or beating ourselves up—we can learn to develop and lean on kindness as a new habit.

Here's an example. The day before I wrote the first draft of this chapter, I was working with a man named Alex during our live weekly group video meeting. He told me how he was struggling with self-judgment. I asked him to explore what it felt like to judge himself. He was putting himself out there in front of about two hundred other people in the meeting, so he kept it short and to the point: it didn't feel good.

I then asked him to think of a time when he had experienced kindness. I anticipated that he would relate an anecdote about someone letting him get in front of them in line at the grocery store, or a time a child gave him a spontaneous hug, but instead he surprised me by saying, "I cooked my roommate an egg the other morning for breakfast." Not what my brain was expecting. Interesting.

I asked him how it felt to extend that act of kindness to his roommate, and he assured me it felt good. Very good. He was demonstrating how kindness to others has a positive effect on our mood. I asked him to do that comparison for himself: kindness vs. judgment. Alex did a quick retrospective so he could feel what self-judgment feels like (not good) and what kindness feels like (good!). Then I had him compare the two so he could clearly see which one had a higher reward value.

Often it is easier to practice kindness toward others than to turn it toward ourselves. So at the end of our roughly five-minute inquiry, I gave Alex his mission: when you notice self-judgment, remind yourself what it felt like to cook an egg for your roommate. Take a moment to mentally cook yourself an egg. He accepted.

Kindness feels good. Whether someone does something kind to or for us—especially when it is unconditional, so they aren't paying us back or looking for something in return—it feels open and warm, like we're getting cozy in our favorite blanket. Tracy, who now teaches mindfulness to college students, described it this way: "Kindness is like wearing one of my softest sweaters, but I don't just feel the soft sweater on my skin—I feel it all the way through my body. It's a comfort." Here's a bonus: with self-kindness, we are both giving kindness (to ourselves) and receiving kindness (from ourselves). That's quite a sweater.

Tracy's and Alex's felt experience of the rewards of kindness is backed up by neuroscience. My lab has done neuroimaging studies that could be summed up with the headline THIS IS WHAT YOUR BRAIN LOOKS LIKE ON KINDNESS. I've written extensively about our research elsewhere, but I'll summarize it here. We've done several studies on how kindness affects the brain, including when people practice a meditation called loving-kindness (you'll learn how to do this later in the chapter). Over and over, we found that the posterior cingulate cortex—that region that gets fired up when we want more chocolate, judge ourselves, or worry about the future—gets pretty darn quiet when we're practicing kindness. The main point can be summed up in a tweet: kindness cools the brain regions that heat up with craving.

We all can pay attention to what that sweater of kindness feels like, whether someone is being kind to us, we're being kind to someone else, or we're being kind to ourselves. What kindness sweaters can we mentally knit for ourselves and others?

HOW KINDNESS LEADS TO SUCCESS

Research led by the British psychologist Paul Gilbert has shown that kindness—especially toward ourselves—can be scary. For those of us who have loud self-judgment and self-criticism committee members, Gilbert's research suggests that we can develop a fear of compassion or kindness, and that this fear is linked to self-criticism, stress, anxiety, and depression. When we're in the habit of self-unkindness, being kind to ourselves can be scary simply because it is different from what we are used to doing. There can be fear that we simply can't be kind to ourselves and/or that we don't deserve it. We can also be afraid that we might lose our edge or lose control. Self-indulgence gets lumped together with self-control when our mind convinces us that we're being kind to ourselves by eating that extra helping of ice cream. Ironically, the kindest thing we can be doing in these moments is checking in with ourselves.

Our qualitative study of Eat Right Now participants showed how understanding what was going on in our minds when we judge ourselves or got caught up in a self-indulgence or stress eating habit loop empowered people to let go of and break that stubborn habit loop. Here's how we described our findings in the paper:

> For many, these behaviors were coping mechanisms, and they identified stressful or traumatic life events as triggers. As one woman stated, "I don't think we questioned our binges. Now I can go back and say, well, I had just gotten devastating news. No wonder I needed a way to cope!" Understanding the role disordered eating played in their lives decreased feelings of shame or guilt (e.g., "There's less judgment. I'm just human, and this is what I'm feeling"), and this was often contrasted with previous attempts to "control" their eating, such as through dieting. For example, one woman explained, "That's the main thing about this program versus others where it was either you lost weight or you didn't, meaning you're a good person or a bad person."

Letting go of guilt and shame empowered people, opening the space for self-kindness and even a desire to address the root causes of their emotional distress, rather than avoiding them through eating. One person reported: "This is very empowering for me because now that I know what's going on, I can make changes."

When we feel empowered, we have a greater capacity to make choices for ourselves, which makes us feel good about ourselves. Instead of judging ourselves for being weak or failures, we treat ourselves with compassion and understanding, knowing we are just trying to protect ourselves.

Someone in the program put it simply: "With kindness, I've found that a lot of my old committee members' voices have completely disappeared. Instead of being plagued with constant what-ifs that drive me to despair, there is the constant voice of kindness. It has completely changed my life!"

We can become disenchanted with old, unhelpful committee members, and as their reward value drops, they drop out of our heads and our lives. In the same way, when we notice how good kindness feels, its reward value becomes even more clear, so it becomes clearer and easier to listen to—especially when the old voices have left the room. It certainly is a BBO, especially when compared with the what-ifs and other naysayers.

PRACTICING KINDNESS

There are many ways to practice kindness toward ourselves. These come in all flavors and forms, from different religious and cultural traditions. If you are looking to learn to create yourself some kindness, I'd suggest starting very simply. As I explored with Alex, map out self-judgmental or other unkindness habit loops. When you talk to yourself, what tone of voice do you use? Do you force yourself to keep sitting at your desk instead of listening to your body asking for a stretch break? These mental and physical acts of unkindness can be really subtle. When exploring their myriad manifestations, I noticed that I was even bringing a lack of self-care to brushing my teeth—I was brushing them quickly and harshly. When you notice that you're falling into any of these automatic behaviors—mental and physical—ask, "What am I getting from this?" Pay careful attention to the results.

Then take a moment to practice some genuine kindness toward yourself. It could be as simple as a phrase that would remind you not to be so hard on yourself: "It is completely understandable for you to feel this way right now"; "You're doing the best you can"; "You're good enough as you are (because you are!)"; or whatever resonates with you. Accepting or allowing our experience is an act of kindness. Accepting that something is happening is very different from rejecting reality. (As an aside, if someone is doing something to us that is harmful, it isn't condoning their behavior—accepting rather than denying that something is happening empowers us to call it out and take appropriate action.) You can also practice small random acts of kindness toward others to build up your kindness enchantment databank. You'll notice that holding the door for someone without looking for anything in return feels pretty good. Pay attention to those results and your brain will groove it so that it becomes more automatic.

To make a lasting change, however, remember that you'll need to allow your OFC to make a freely chosen choice between two options. To show the OFC the full potential and reward value of kindness, you'll need to pair it with the power of awareness. You'll groove those habits better when they're together. Notice what kindness—in any form—feels like in your body. Remember what that feels like. Repeat until that feeling is easy to access.

Here's how we teach kindness in the Eat Right Now program. (It can be hard to do a meditation by reading it. You can find an audio recording of me leading this on my website: https://drjud.com/mind fulness-exercises/.)

KINDNESS EXERCISE

To begin, sit in a comfortable position in a quiet place and let your mind just rest on the feeling of your body breathing.

Now, and as a contrast to kindness, remember a situation in which you were unkind to yourself recently. Notice what it feels like in your body. Note the sensations that arise for a few moments.

Now imagine a dear friend coming through the door—perhaps someone whom you haven't seen in a long time. What does this feel like?

Notice any differences between this feeling and the feelings that arose when you were unkind to yourself. Is there warmth coming from your heart or chest? Or maybe you just feel a little less clenched, restless, or agitated.

Now bring to mind this dear friend or someone who has been a real role model in your life. Perhaps they were unconditionally loving, generous, or wise. This can even be a family pet—pets are really good at displaying unconditional love.

Now think about their beneficial qualities. Notice if there is a feeling that arises in your body similar to imagining a dear friend coming through the door. Maybe warmth, expanding, etc. Often this is in the chest/heart.

If you don't notice anything right now, that's okay, too. Just keep checking in with your body as we do this exercise.

Now pick a few phrases of well-wishing that you're going to offer to this being whom you just brought to mind. We'll give you some suggestions here, but feel free to pick whatever phrases work best for you.

Holding this being in mind, now offer them the first kindness phrase: for example, "May you be happy." Breathe it in—*May you be happy*—and breathe it throughout your body. *May you be happy.*

Now offer them the second kindness phrase: "May you be healthy." Breathe it in—*May you be healthy*—and breathe it throughout your body. *May you be healthy.*

Now offer them the third kindness phrase: "May you be free from inner and outer harm." Breathe it in—*May you be free from inner and outer harm*—and breathe it throughout your body. *May you be free from inner and outer harm.*

Now offer them the final kindness phrase: "May you care for yourself joyfully." Breathe it in—*May you care for yourself joyfully*—and breathe it throughout your body. *May you care for yourself joyfully.*

Repeat these phrases silently at your own pace for the next minute or so. Use the phrases and the feeling of unconditional love in your body as anchors to keep you in the present moment. If the feeling feels weak or forced right now, just relax and focus on the phrases. As you reawaken this natural capacity, it will strengthen with time; don't try to force it.

Also, when your mind wanders, just note where it has gone off to and return to the phrases and the feeling of unconditional love there in your chest.

Now bring yourself to mind. Bring to mind some of your own good qualities. Notice if there is some resistance to doing this. Yes, we're good at judging ourselves as not worthy. Just notice what you get from this and see if you can place it off to the side. Ask yourself, "Do I want to be happy?" Let that question sink in.

Offer yourself the first kindness phrase: "May I be happy." Breathe it in—*May I be happy*—and breathe it throughout your body. *May I be happy.*

Now offer yourself the second kindness phrase: "May I be healthy." Breathe it in—*May I be healthy*—and breathe it throughout your body. *May I be healthy.*

Now offer yourself the third kindness phrase: "May I be free from inner and outer harm." Breathe it in—*May I be free from inner and outer harm*—and breathe it throughout your body. *May I be free from inner and outer harm.* Yes, this one is about not harming ourselves or being harmed by others, verbally, emotionally, or physically.

Now offer yourself the final kindness phrase: "May I care for myself joyfully." Breathe it in—*May I care for myself joyfully*—and breathe it throughout your body. *May I care for myself joyfully.*

Repeat these phrases silently at your own pace. Use the phrases—these or whatever phrases you chose that work for you—and the feeling of unconditional love in your body as anchors to keep you with the present moment. When your mind wanders, just note where it has gone off to and return to the phrases and the feeling of kindness in your chest. If you notice resistance or tightness or other body sensations, just note these and return to repeating the phrases.

If this kindness practice doesn't resonate with you, here's an alternate one that Jacqui shared with me:

Take a moment to settle into any position that feels nourishing for you right now. This might be sitting in a chair or lying on your bed. Close your eyes or soften your gaze. Take a few deeper breaths just to settle in. Each time you breathe out, allow any unnecessary tension in your face and body to soften. Feel the weight of your body resting a little deeper into whatever is supporting you.

Gently check in with how you're feeling right now. Kindly and tenderly explore your whole experience. Notice any thoughts moving through the mind right now. Become aware of any emotions you might be feeling. Explore how your body feels in this moment.

If you're experiencing any difficulties, remember you're not alone. Human beings experience a whole spectrum of feelings and emotions and experiences. This is what it's like to be a human being, something we all experience. Often we try to change our experience. We might resist it or try to fix it. When we start to explore our experience with compassion, we can learn how to hold any experience, even the difficult ones, in a warm, kind, tender embrace. And this helps us to care for ourselves while we're experiencing the difficulties.

So explore right now how it feels to honor your experience, whatever it may be. If your experience is hard, then honor that and validate that, saying to yourself, "This feels hard, this is difficult, it's understandable for me to feel this way."

And offer yourself the kindness and care that you'd offer a friend experiencing this. You may like to use touch. Place a hand on your heart or on your belly or arm, or maybe hold one hand in the other, noticing the warmth and the care within that touch.

It may feel helpful to offer yourself some words or phrases of support. *May I care for myself, kindly and gently. I'm doing the best I can right now.* Choose any words or phrases that feel most supportive for you.

And you can explore offering yourself feelings of care and compassion. Notice how it feels to honor and care for yourself throughout this experience. Know we all have these innate qualities of care and compassion, and we can tap into them anytime. Stay with this practice as long as you like.

When you feel ready to transition out of the practice, remember you can take this care and compassion with you as you move into the rest of your day, and you can call upon it anytime. It's always here within you. Thank you for taking good care of yourself with this practice today. May you continue to care for yourself with kindness and compassion.

You can do a kindness practice while sitting in a chair or on a meditation cushion or when you lie down to go to sleep. You can even do this as you're walking down the street—offering these phrases to yourself and anyone who walks by. One really important note is that these phrases don't resonate with everyone. That's okay. These particular phrases are just suggestions. Find whatever phrases work for you.

You might find that practicing kindness is hard to start. I know I did. I heard about loving-kindness when I was first learning about mindfulness, and I thought it was straight out of the 1970s—a bunch of crap that stank of hippie love. It wasn't until I tried it instead of judging it—yes, note the irony here—that I realized for myself how extraordinarily helpful it was. I would practice kindness while riding my bicycle to work at the hospital when I was in residency. I would offer a short phrase of kindness to anyone who honked at me, and then one to me as well: *May you be happy, may I be happy.* It helped set the tone for my day: I could be more present and bring kindness to my interactions with my patients and colleagues, quite a contrast to when I went in grumpy because someone had honked at me.

You might judge the practice, judge yourself, or worry that you can't do it or can't do it correctly or are too broken to be able to do it at all. If this is the case for you, I'll paraphrase some sage advice from Leonard Cohen's song "Anthem": Forget about being perfect. Your imperfections are how the world's light gets in to you. I'll add that it is also how you can uniquely and authentically shine your light on the world.

KINDNESS AT WORK

I suggested that Tasha, my pizza-eating patient, try practicing some self-kindness, especially in moments when she noted she was spiraling through shame. After she worked with this for a few months, the practice became the backbone of a different outlook on her life. She stopped bingeing almost entirely, describing how she could eat a single piece of pizza and actually enjoy it. Pizza wasn't the enemy here, and she could clearly see that now. Instead of being her own enemy, she began befriending herself. She even began dating instead of writing off the possibility of a relationship because she thought herself worthy.

If you are craving more extensive kindness or self-compassion training, there are many ways to "learn" or practice building your ability to tap into this feeling. For example, Kristin Neff created an entire self-compassion course. More traditional approaches come in the form of prayer and other practices in all major religions, so if you are steeped in one of these traditions, I'd suggest checking in with your clergy or community leaders. It doesn't matter exactly what form your practice takes. The important thing is that you pay attention to how much higher the reward value is when you offer yourself self-love instead of self-judgment. That's how you'll break free.

RIGHT NOW: PRACTICE SELF-KINDNESS

During the day, check in with your actions, both mental and physical. When you recognize habits of unkindness, ask yourself: "What am I getting from this?" If you go through your day—as Jacqui puts it— habitually viewing the world through your "judge and jury" glasses, how does it change your look and outlook when you swap them out for your "care and kindness" glasses? Can you practice at least one random act of kindness toward someone else? How about one toward yourself? And once you get in the habit, don't limit yourself to one-and-done for the day, especially as you reflect on how much better it feels and how much brighter your day is when that habit feeds itself.

Before you go to sleep, set aside a few minutes to listen to the loving-kindness meditation on my website (https://drjud.com/mindfulness-exercises/) or simply read through the practice on page 233 until you get the hang of it. During the day, see how often a voice of kindness starts to show up in your head. Name it. Note it. And notice how helpful it is for your well-being. Perhaps give it promotion on the committee and a microphone so you can more easily hear it as you go through your day.

CHAPTER 23

A Note About Trauma

There's an interesting tension between science and people. The Rescorla-Wagner model has predicted and explained behavior from mice to humans for half a century. The theoretical model for reinforcement learning can be traced back to ancient Buddhist psychology—hundreds of years before paper was even invented. We can show, in randomized controlled clinical trials, that applying these methods has a meaningful and real-world impact on behaviors, ranging from smoking to anxiety to overeating.

Yet when you look at the Rescorla-Wagner model—the one that says that positive and negative prediction errors are what change behavior, and that awareness is needed to do this—there is a conspicuous absence of a place for someone's history. I say conspicuous because I notice this when I sit down with my clinic patients. When I ask them who they are and what brought them to my clinic, knowing their story is critical for being able to help them.

This is especially true for individuals who have a history of trauma. Trauma is talked about in many different ways, and because it is very personal, even the way it is talked about can trigger a reaction. If you notice this happening as you read on, at any time, you can take a step back and ground yourself with one of the practices you've been learning in this book such as noting and loving-kindness. Or you can skip to the Right Now section at the end of this chapter to learn a practice called five-finger breathing. Use a grounding practice that you've learned from a therapist or reach out to someone in your support network. Please don't continue until you feel ready.

One pragmatic way that has helped me bring together science and my patients is to identify how eating patterns may have been set up as protective mechanisms. Reinforcement learning is set up to shield us from danger. If something bad happens, we learn how to avoid it in the future. When it comes to trauma, our brain is a one-trick pony. No matter where we are on the trauma spectrum—capital T trauma to microtrauma—our brain applies the same avoidance mechanisms: learn what helps avoid it in the future, and repeat the behavior if it works.

For example, as I mentioned in a footnote earlier, one of my patients had deliberately gained weight to protect herself from unwanted sexual advances. Others—for example, Tasha—learned to eat as a way to numb themselves from distressing memories and emotions. Sitting with my patients as they talk about their trauma history breaks my heart. So many people feel guilty, thinking they could have done something to avoid what happened, and then spin out into a spiral of shame as, triggered by guilt, they feel ashamed of themselves. They often feel like something is wrong with them. I gently remind them that it wasn't and isn't their fault. There is nothing wrong with them. I do this as consistently as possible to support them to step out of these habit loops—many people have had that "it is my fault" story going so long that they never even stopped to consider that it might not be true. This story of shame can be especially entrenched when it comes to childhood trauma. Children have so much less control over their circumstances than adults so that the *my fault* story often is the only coping strategy their minds can come up with. And the longer they carry it with them, the more deeply it gets entrenched.

If you've experienced trauma, my heart goes out to you. It isn't your fault. You have the power to change that old "my fault story" and work through the shame that comes with it.

So, with the whole human in mind, is the Rescorla-Wagner model wrong? Is it missing something? Does it need a variable for childhood or history? Yes and no. Let's start with the no. Earlier I maintained that a consideration of one's childhood was not necessary for the model to work. Let's look at a more nuanced version of that statement now. Our past has set up our habits for the present, how we behave right now. How we behave right now sets up our habits for the future. If we pay careful attention to the results of our behaviors, we'll see one of three things happen: (1) if it is more rewarding than expected, we'll get a positive prediction error and be more likely to repeat it in the future; (2) if it is less rewarding than expected, we'll get a negative prediction error and be less likely to repeat it in the future; (3) if it is as expected, we won't get any discrepancies from what is expected, and we'll keep repeating it in about the same way as we've done in the past—the habit is still there and hasn't increased or decreased. But all of this is contingent on zooming in and really paying attention to the behavior itself. If we focus solely on the behavior and what its results are, the model works. It isn't missing anything.

Now for the yes. It is missing something. As humans, what makes us human is our history, our story. We reminisce about our past, and we worry about our future. We do this a lot—a now-classic study suggests that our minds are wandering to the past and the future about 50 percent of our waking life. When we experience trauma, our brains learn how to avoid the past and/or prevent it from being repeated in the future. Eating to feel better or numb ourselves from negative emotions helps us avoid memories from the past that trigger feelings in the present. Our brains learn to associate eating with protection from future occurrences of things that have happened to us in the past. As a reminder, this can be an unconscious process; it is not our fault. Our brain is trying its best to protect us.

So how do we bring the yes—yes, the formula is correct—and no—no, the formula needs to account for our story—together?

The only place that the past and the future meet is in the present. The here and now is the only time that we can work with the past to change the future. By work with, I mean that we can see the past for what it is and learn to not inadvertently and habitually drag it into the present—which sets us up to carry it forward into the future. (Again, this is not our fault. Our brains are just trying to help.) For example, when my patients struggle with anxiety, panic, overeating, or all of the above, often their brains have gotten in the habit of signaling danger when there isn't any. The danger from the past is no longer present, but the alarm is still going off, putting them on high alert or triggering them to eat. One analogy to this is a smoke detector in the kitchen. If it is set incorrectly—for example, it goes off not just when it detects smoke, but when it detects steam—we're going to get a lot of false alarms. It's going to tell us to run out of the kitchen not only when there is a real fire but also when we're boiling a pot of water. In the kitchen, we can learn to ignore the sound. It can be annoying, but we can live with it. This is harder to do if the alarm is going off in our head.

When those alarm bells signal us to run or eat, or run and eat, they are really hard to ignore. Here we can bring the past into the light of the present. For my patients or for people using our programs, I start by having them learn some foundational grounding practices—such as noting, RAIN, loving-kindness, a focus on simply hearing the sounds around them and seeing what is in front of them, or five-finger breathing (see the next section). The idea is that if we're panicking or in the middle of a binge, our brain is on autopilot bulldozer mode. It has a lot of momentum. You can't just jump in front of it and make it stop. But you can learn to turn off the engine. In other words, if your prefrontal cortex is offline, the first thing to do is to get it back online. Grounding practices help anchor us in the present moment, thereby helping slow down and eventually stop whatever behavior we're bulldozing forward with. They help us care for ourselves while acknowledging strong emotions with curiosity and kindness.

Once we are grounded and our prefrontal cortex is back online, we can use it. I have people ask this simple question: "Am I in danger right now?" As they're asking the question, I have them look around at their environment—grounding them even more in the present—to see if they really are in danger. Is it real? Or is it a habit?

By grounding ourselves, anchoring our senses and awareness in the present moment, we can do two critical things. First, we can separate the past from the present. If our response to the danger signal is to eat, we can learn to separate out the eating as a habitual behavior and focus on the present-moment results of it. This helps us really zoom in and use the power of negative prediction to change the behavior. And this sets us up for number two. Just as we readjust a smoke detector to cut down on false alarms, we can learn to recognize and recalibrate these danger signals.

There is quite a bit of research on a number of different techniques and therapies that can help with this recalibration, ranging from mindfulness training to Eye Movement Desensitization and Reprocessing (EMDR) therapy. And these seem to have at least one thing in common: they help us experience our emotions as emotions in the present moment and to see these as separate from our thoughts and memories. Memories can be decoupled from the emotional reactions that they habitually trigger. We can learn to see a memory as a memory from the past, but not habitually react with a mental or physical behavior. And with this, we decouple the two and step out of the habit loop.

As we learn to recalibrate our danger signals and the alarms become less noisy, we can also start to recognize and see clearly how our old mental patterns might be harming us today. What might have served as a protective mechanism in the past went from temporary to semipermanent as a habit. Ironically, it may be hurting us now and continue to do so into the future. It's like a favorite shoe that no longer fits because we've outgrown it. We continue to wear it because it is familiar. We also ignore the pain that it is causing right now, because the pain is familiar.

The more we learn that we can actually be with strong emotions without reactively eating or falling into any number of now no-longer-helpful protective habit loops, the more we can heal from our past. We can honor our childhood or earlier self, knowing we did our best in terrible circumstances, and with this honoring, move forward to change the habits that were carried forward. When our brains see that the old shoes don't fit—and in fact hurt our feet—they naturally start looking for a new pair.

Here's an example. On one of our live weekly Zoom groups, someone asked if we could discuss how to work with childhood trauma. The way these discussions work is that we have a one-on-one conversation with the person who asks about the topic about their own experience—in front of two hundred or more people. So after I asked him for permission to "go there" and warned the group that we were going there, we dove in.

I asked him to describe what habit loop he had developed. He described the habit loop: ever since his childhood trauma, he protected himself by worrying. It was his way of keeping him safe. We talked about how it might have been the only way he could feel in control at that time. And through our Unwinding Anxiety program, he had also learned that worrying wasn't helping him now—the shoe was hurting his foot. I asked if he had outgrown that strategy and had learned new ways to care for himself. He had.

I then asked if he could honor his childhood self and acknowledge all that it had done to protect him so that he could now let the past go and move forward in the present. He replied that he could, adding that honoring his child was a really important part of this. He could try on a new pair of coping shoes, ones that would fit him now and possibly help him going forward.

This story isn't to say that this process is easy or the way to go for everyone. Yet it highlights that when we combine this type of honoring of ourselves with learning to step out of present-day habit loops— as well as other old habits that no longer serve us—we can learn that it is indeed possible to leave the past in the past and move on to a brighter future.

RIGHT NOW: TRY FIVE-FINGER BREATHING

The thinking and planning part of your brain is called the dorsolateral prefrontal cortex, or dlPFC for short. It is toward the front and to the side of your brain. The dlPFC is important for working memory, meaning it is concerned with immediate conscious perceptual and linguistic processing. Basically, it holds information for you to use right now, like remembering a grocery list or a phone number.

Have you noticed that it is harder to remember these types of things when you're stressed or anxious? Your brain is similar to your computer. It can hold only so much information in working memory. If you're really worried about something, that worry thinking takes up a lot of space, so it is harder to remember your grocery list or what someone just said a few minutes ago on a conference call. So how can you free up that space, to get your brain working more effectively?

I've mentioned before that mindfulness practices can help get your thinking brain back online. But sometimes this can be really challenging. You bring your awareness to your breath or your feet for a few moments, but because your working memory has been filled with worry thoughts, this step can feel forced or inadequate to help your mind and body calm down. So here's a little trick you can play to reboot that RAM in your brain. I love this because you can use the excuse of teaching it to your kids and practicing it with them, but really it works for all ages. It's called five-finger breathing.

Start by placing the index finger of one hand on the outside of the pinkie finger on your other hand. As you breathe in, trace up to the tip of your pinkie, and then as you breathe out, trace down the inside of your pinkie. Then on the next inhalation, trace up the outside of your ring finger, and on the exhalation, trace down the inside of your ring finger. Inhalation up the outside of your middle finger. Exhalation down the inside of your middle finger. Continue until you've traced your entire hand, and then reverse the process as you trace from your thumb back to your pinkie. What's it like to even trace a few fingers? Better than getting caught up in worry, no?

Five-finger breathing is great because it brings several of your senses together at the same time. You watch and feel your fingers at the same time that you are paying attention to your breath. Not only is this multisensory—seeing and feeling—but it requires an awareness of multiple locations as well: hands and breath. This takes a lot of your brain's RAM to do, perhaps enough to crowd out those worry thoughts. If you pay attention only to your breath, those worry thoughts can still be pretty loud and take up that memory space. If you use up all that RAM with multisensory and multilocation awareness, you might forget what you were worrying about for a moment. And as you also calm down, those thoughts won't have the same power because they won't have the same emotional tone. Without that arousal they have less energy and are easier to let go or to see simply as thoughts instead of something that you have to act on right now.

CHAPTER 24

Day 20: Building Trust in Yourself Through Experience

Are you wondering how this book is going to end? Maybe you've already flipped ahead to see how many pages are left or skimmed the next chapter to see what secret nuggets of wisdom I've saved for last.

Over the years, one of the most common questions I've gotten from plan participants is some variation of this: Will this work? Will it lead to lasting change? This is what I love about the brain. When it comes to changing habits—whether letting go of old ones or developing new ones—it follows one path and one path only: changing reward value. We can be fooled for a while, but once we clearly see how the results of a behavior are not serving us, we can't unsee what we've just seen.

I asked Tracy to reflect back on her experience to see how her relationship with food has changed since she started bringing awareness into the fold. She wrote me an email that began by describing how it has taken some time, "but the results of mindful eating feel irreversible at this point." She used to struggle with thoughts around how whatever issue she was dealing with wasn't going to be solved with eating, especially when the urgency to get quick comfort would battle with that very rational—and correct—idea. She put it this way:

Now, my body knows this beyond thought. When I'm
feeling anxious, angry, sad, bored, or some other discomfort
(whether mediocre or existential), I know *in my bones* that eating
more than my body needs won't solve anything. Sometimes I still
pout about it—there's no perfect practice: I'll reach for something to
quickly scarf down, but I usually pause now, "ugh . . . I *know* this
won't work . . . must raise white flag to the uncomfortable emotions.
AGH!" The deep or shallow pain of any day won't be healed by that
overly sugary or fatty snack, nor by a cocktail, a cigarette,
a new purchase (or any of the other things I've reached out to). And
even better, I don't have to deal with as many carb crashes, sugar
headaches, cocktail hangovers, or debt guilt. At this point, after all
these years of noticing my eating habits—and most important, letting
myself dive into those unhelpful eating habits and watching what
happened next in some kind way—I know that eating helps only up to
the point of satisfying true physical hunger, and then after that, no
emotional hunger is really soothed by it. What helps is crying out
sadness, hiking out anger, pausing with anxiety . . . and it always
passes. I no longer have to try to convince myself of this. I really, truly
know it.

As Tracy's story shows, once we collect enough data, we can't
go back. Once we see in our own experience that the fairy is not real,
the tale changes. We can see it for what it is—a story—and nothing more.

You can trust your brain to help you learn. Your OFC will never
fail you, as long as you have a curious awareness.

But it can take some time to start to trust your brain. Especially if
you've run down so many different paths over the years, only to find
dead end after dead end.

BUILDING TRUST IN YOURSELF

You've gotten a whole lot of concepts in this book. Hopefully you now have a much better sense of how your mind works. Yet you can't just read a book and magically have that change your eating habits. As I've stated before, if your thinking brain was stronger than your feeling body, you'd be in a very different place. The only concept you'd need to know is "Stop it."

Your feeling body is what drives behavior. The good news is that it is wise enough to drive healthy behavior, as long as you pay attention and listen to it.

So whether you binged on this book, quickly reading through it as a type of brain candy—feeling that urge to get the right information— or carefully consumed it with highlighter in hand, taking notes along the way, the key next step is to dive into your own experience to make the concepts stick. Only experience turns concepts into wisdom.

There are two types of trust. The first is that leap of faith when you try something new. We often take these leaps when we've seen someone else go ahead of us. If you're about to jump in a lake or a swimming hole but don't know how cold it is, you might wait for your friends to go first. When they go for it and come back to the surface with smiles on their faces, you trust them enough to take the plunge yourself. My patients have to take that leap of faith when I encourage them to go ahead and smoke or eat food they have forbidden themselves. Yes, that's what the doc recommended. When they give it a shot—paying careful attention to the results—they get that first glimpse of the second and more important type of faith: what I call evidence-based trust. In evidence-based medicine, we use experience (studies) to dictate treatment. But here I want to move beyond "trust me, I'm a doctor." I want my patients to start trusting themselves.

If you've followed the one-chapter-per-day plan of the book, you've been practicing the Right Now exercises. Along the way, you were collecting important data for yourself. The practices you've been learning from this book help you develop your own evidence base. That disenchantment databank that I've been talking about—how much have you filled it already? How much evidence have you already gathered to help your brain become disenchanted with stuffing yourself with unhealthy food, eating when you weren't hungry, or going off the cliff of overindulgence? And how much evidence have you already gathered to build your enchantment databanks, whether it's eating a certain type of food that keeps you in a good mood and gives you energy for the day or stopping when you've hit the pleasure plateau with a dessert?

Notice how I'm *not* asking you to put faith or trust in the concepts of this book because I'm a neuroscientist or a doctor or even because I'm a neuroscientist doctor. I'm not asking you to put faith in this program because I've done the research to show that it works for other people. I'm not even asking you to put any trust in this program beyond trying it. You now have the tools. Now all you can do is take that leap—and observe for yourself that you can swim. You can do this.

A participant in our Eat Right Now program offered the following reflection:

> We need to have faith that we can keep up these practices, and this faith can be strengthened by the personal evidence we've collected . . . I have seen this program working and the benefit of these practices when I practice them well. I have also seen how easy it is to return to my old habits when I let these practices slide. Diligence is necessary to really ingrain these as new habits. Part of that will take faith that I can make these practices my new habits so that I don't just give up and go back to my old ways.

See how much evidence you can build for yourself every day. Wisdom comes from experience. You already have a lot of wisdom—your own life experience. You can build on this each day by leaning on curiosity and kindness as you gather more and more data from your own life as it unfolds.

RIGHT NOW: TAKE STOCK

Take a few minutes to take stock of how far you've come. How much evidence have you built—from your own experience—that you can do this? How many times have you eaten something mindfully? Explored the pleasure plateau? Taken the hunger test? Used the craving tool (parts 1 and 2)? How many retrospectives have you done, and how much have they helped your memories become clearer and more vivid? If you haven't gathered a whole lot of data, now is a good time to go back and move more slowly through the action chapters of the book. Spend a few days collecting data from each chapter's exercise before moving on to the next. See how much data you can collect over the next few weeks. And don't stop there—keep collecting!

CHAPTER 25

Day 21: The Ultimate Bigger Better Offer (The Biggest Bestest Offer)

MEETING OUR NEEDS INSTEAD OF FEEDING OUR WANTS

Someone who had recently started our program asked the following question: "What should I do when I am really tired but need to work? Chocolate always gives me the energy boost I need to be productive, but I want to get rid of that habit. I just don't know how to handle the tiredness and the feeling of being stuck."

This question highlights how we often try to hack our way through life. When we're tired, we eat chocolate or drink more caffeine. When we're short on time, we multitask to get more done. Of course we want to be less tired. We want to be more productive. Heck, who wouldn't rather be happy than be stressed—preferably all the time?

We get stuck in these short-term "solutions" in which we get a little boost from chocolate or caffeine but don't pay attention to the results: we need more chocolate and caffeine, and at some point we crash. Why? We're focusing on and feeding our short-term wants instead of meeting our needs to help us survive and thrive. Think of Maslow's hierarchy of needs here.

Abraham Maslow was an American psychologist who was really interested in what instinctive needs we have and which ones had to be fulfilled for physical and psychological health. He wrote extensively about what became known as Maslow's hierarchy of needs. This is a multilayer model like a pyramid-shaped multilayer cake that starts at the bottom with basic physiological needs, such as food, water, warmth, and rest. The next layer is our safety needs. The next two layers above these are needs for belongingness and love, such as friendship and intimate relationships. Above those layers are our needs for esteem, such as feelings of accomplishment. These two layers, belonging and esteem needs, together make up our psychological needs. We generally start with meeting our basic needs first, then add in our psychological needs as we build upward. But at times we short-circuit this process, eventually learning to ignore our bodies and minds.

Our wants are generally driven by our needs. We need calories, so we want food. We need to feel a sense of belonging, so we want friends and close relationships. Yet as you've seen throughout the book, we can get caught in cycles of wanting that aren't based in our actual needs. Wanting chocolate can come from a need—hunger—or because we've learned to eat chocolate when we're bored or lonely. Over time, we listen more and more to our wants, because our wanting has such a loud voice. When we feed our wants, they quiet down for a while, but only for a while. With each feeding, we reinforce these wanting cycles. Eventually we spend all our time feeding our wants, to the point where we ignore or don't even have a good sense of what our needs are anymore.

It's amazing how taking care of ourselves by attending to our needs seems like a foreign concept at first. We no longer default to focusing on taking care of our needs. Yet pretty quickly, we learn that taking care of our needs works better than trying to find that special brain hack. If you are in the habit of looking for that magic bullet, here's a radical concept: ask yourself, "What do I need right now?" Of course, eating the wrong food is a great example of indulging our wants—energy hack or otherwise—instead of meeting our needs. Our inner children scream so loudly that we can't hear ourselves think. We impulsively give them what they want, inadvertently feeding our short-term cycles of indulgence through negative reinforcement.

Have you explored what it feels like—both short and long term—when you meet your needs, as opposed to scratching that itchy urge of wanting? After investigating which provides a bigger better—and more lasting—offer, Jacqui put it this way:

> A huge change [for me] was learning to care for my other needs like sleep, recreation, and being kind to myself. I still experience the kinds of difficulties every human faces—stress, deadlines, bereavement, sadness, overwhelm, etc. But by not eating my feelings, I am able to learn how to understand my needs and care for them in ways that don't have negative consequences. Instead of wasting time and energy on eating habits/food jail, I have the time and energy to return to hobbies I enjoy like dressmaking, creating art, and being in nature. They are far more rewarding and pleasurable than eating my body weight in cake. I have also developed a much broader approach to meeting my real needs by asking "What do I really need right now?"

Remember the key to succeeding at changing unhelpful habits, that definition that came from our focus groups—an "unforced freedom of choice, emerging from embodied awareness"? Jacqui had discovered the biggest bestest offer: we feel good when we make choices that help us not only survive but thrive. Being constantly curious—asking ourselves, "What do I need?" instead of "What do I want?"—helps us naturally move in the direction of meeting our needs, because it feels good. It is rewarding in a contented sort of way. As a bonus, not only does our survival brain love us for getting enough sleep and feeding it nutritious food that is going to keep our energy at optimal levels, but it loves us for the feeling of—you guessed it—control it gives us.

When Ariel Beccia studied our Eat Right Now participants, that feeling of control was one of the key findings. This made complete sense. Our brains hate being at the mercy of outside forces (any of those outside forces could be a threat to our survival), so when we feel like we are at the helm, consciously making choices by aligning our planning brain with our survival brain, we have harmony.

Rob described his experience with establishing helpful habit loops through becoming more aware:

> I was in a very consistent rhythm of paying attention to the present-moment experience of my habit loops, as well as bringing to memory times when I was engaged in binge eating and eating junk food and sitting with the very real feelings of what doing that felt like in my body and in my mind. When I really allowed myself to see and feel the truth about those habit loops in a kind and nonjudgmental way, and really saw how I was harming myself, and even expanding out to how my binge-eating habits were indirectly harming others I loved, it was enough to not want to do it anymore.

He added:

> The learning was there and I didn't want to numb out anymore because feeling alive felt SO. MUCH. BETTER. This wasn't about anxiety, and it damn sure wasn't about ice cream. This wasn't about being afraid to die; I already knew all too well what being dead felt like. It was about being terrified to live, and my wise old friend awareness helped me see that I could, one moment at a time.

The more you practice the techniques in this book, instead of judging yourself or beating yourself up for things that happened in the past or that you anticipate might happen, the more you'll get in the habit of being present, allowing yourself to be human. It's as if we have replaced our entire unruly committee with two key members: Curiosity and Kindness. Curious awareness reminds us that life is a journey and to be constantly curious with each step that we take. Kindness tells us again and again, "You're human. Be gentle with yourself along the way." These best friends can become our best friends—the biggest bestest offer of all.

KEEP CURIOUS, KEEP GOING

Often when we speak about mindfulness, we do so in almost mystical terms. It's almost as if we are saying, "Mindfulness is magic! It will cure what ails you!" I'm sure you already know this at some level, but I'll say it anyway: it won't. Mindfulness is not some magic cure-all. Mindfulness won't make all of your moments feel golden (though it might help you not judge them all as terrible). But it will help you learn. And the best way to learn is to have an open mind. Learning from your own experience builds wisdom.

In Zen circles, you'll often hear people speak about "don't know" or "beginner's" mind. It is *the attitude* one can bring to the present moment. Either we can see the world through the lenses of our biases and judgments—these are learned through the same reinforcement learning mechanisms as other habits—or we can take those glasses off and see the world fresh.

Vipassanā, a Buddhist term derived from the ancient Pali language that literally means "special seeing," is often translated today as "seeing clearly." It's like a trail in the woods clearly marked with signposts pointing us in the right direction; we can clearly see what we need to do to move forward even if the path is long or full of obstacles. This removes uncertainty so that doubt doesn't spring up in our mind. If I know that the journey is a thousand miles, I can prepare myself for it—and even enjoy the journey. This is very different than being yanked around by our impulses that say, "Go this way!" only to change tack and say, "Never mind, go that way!" When we don't know how our minds work, we end up going down all sorts of different side streets and blind alleys, adding unnecessary miles to our trip.

It's not magic. When we cultivate clear seeing, we place our learned biases off to the side and become more curious about the world as it truly is instead of how we perceive it to be. I have heard the results of having had cataract surgery described as suddenly seeing the world in brilliant color after having previously seen it as if it had been dipped in sepia-toned tea. That is what can happen when we foster a curious awareness. The world looks and feels fresh.

A curious attitude helps us remove the glasses of expectation we've been wearing for years, preventing us from approaching experiences with the thought of "Oh, I know how this is going to go; I've seen it a million times before." Instead, curiosity brings the attitude of "Ohhh! I've seen this before; I wonder if it will go the same way?" That hint of wonder helps us open our minds and turn toward our experience, instead of turning our backs on it or not paying attention because we assume we know how things will turn out. When we prejudge or assume, we are more likely to meet those moments with our habitual reactions, which keeps us in an unhelpful feedback loop.

We can lean on curiosity when we have strong cravings. Because cravings are unpleasant, our brain can easily jump into survival mode: unpleasantness triggers us to do something to make it go away—the "Oh no!" that comes with a craving, urging us to do something. We'll either satisfy the craving—scratch the itch—to make it go away, only to keep the habit going, or fight it as long as we can. Curiosity helps flip that "Oh no!" into an "Oh?" In these moments we can explore what a craving feels like in our body. Here we can use noting practice to take good notes and leverage the observer effect such that we're not caught up in the craving, or use RAIN to ride it out.

I often ask my patients to investigate curiosity itself as a bigger better offer. I ask them a simple question: "What feels better, a craving or curiosity?" Of course, curiosity feels better than a craving, so remembering that it is a BBO, the next time they have a craving, they can call in the curiosity cavalry and (kindly) RAIN on the craving until it subsides. The more they open to their experience (that's what the A in RAIN is all about), the less they resist what is happening. Remember, what we resist persists. At the risk of sounding too goofy, I'll add a second part that I learned recently: what we resist persists; what we feel heals. Sappy as that may sound, it points to one of my favorite sayings: the obstacle is the way.

We often think of cravings as obstacles that we need to endure or fight—but when we look at our experiences with curiosity, we can instead see cravings as teachers. Curiosity helps disarm us: instead of bracing ourselves for a fight, we can bow to the craving, asking, "What can I learn from this?" In this way, the obstacle becomes the way forward. We lean in. We learn. We grow. And then we are grateful for the lesson.

Remember that radical notion that I put forward in chapter 15 on retrospectives—that there is no such thing as moving backward if we're learning from the experience. With curiosity as our superpower, *every* obstacle becomes the way. Life becomes a constant journey of learning; every step is a step forward. And learning certainly is a BBO when compared with being stuck in the mud of old habits.

CULTIVATING CURIOSITY WITH OUR EARS AND EYES

How can we help our prediction-focused brains not go on auto-pilot?

One of my favorite ways to help people stay curious (and I'm referring to interest curiosity here) is to check in with their ears and eyes. When they are approaching a situation, I have them listen to how they are talking to themselves. If they are about to eat something, for example, what is their inner tone of voice? Is the Judgy McJudgerson committee member saying, "Uh-oh, I know how this is going to go." That's a sign other committee members are more interested in predicting the future than exploring the present. The shift we are trying to make here—the bigger better offer we are trying to find—is to be in the present. To discern the voice of I curiosity from the cacophony of other committee members. Instead of "Oh no!" is there or can there be a little sound of upward movement in the voice? "Oh?" That upward-inflecting *Oh?* opens a window, a willingness to explore that doesn't take willpower. Listening to ourselves helps us identify old habits of *Oh no!* so that we can see what we get when we are on autopilot, making assumptions that keep us in our fixed mindsets.

That's the ears. What about the eyes? Try this out yourself: Think of an eating scenario that went poorly in the past. Try out that "Oh no!" voice. Does your forehead wrinkle up a bit as your brow furrows? Do your eyes get a bit narrower—perhaps looking a bit accusing—as you judge how that went? Now see if you can simply flip the *Oh no!* to *Oh?* What do your eyes naturally do? Do they follow that tone of voice and open up a bit? Try it again. *Oh no!* vs. *Oh?*

Try to get the hang of checking in with your ears. Listen for the end of curiosity: *Ohh!* Let it be a signal to open your eyes and look around. You can literally open your eyes really wide to help jump-start the process. And with this more open perspective, see if you can see what is right in front of your eyes, whether it is a food you've eaten your whole life or an amount of food that you think can't possibly be filling enough. And don't stop with food. With eyes and ears wide open, we can drink in the world, appreciating sights, sounds, smells, and sensations wherever we are, whenever they happen. We can take a walk in nature, fully experiencing life. When listening to music, even the musical tone of laughter, we can fully open to it.

Pausing, collecting ourselves, being present in the moment, recollecting our experiences—all of these are bigger better offers than rushing, pushing, doing things automatically or mindlessly. Paradoxically, by taking that moment to be with ourselves and our experience, we give our bodies and minds time to remember what we have learned from past experiences. We can remember what we get from trying to force things. We can remember what we get from working with ourselves and our brains. We can see that life moves at its own pace, that change happens at its own pace, and that our impatience slows us down instead of speeding us up. Patience is an act of kindness, a way of caring for ourselves. The more we practice patience, the more we learn that not only does it feel better, but it is also the fastest way forward.

I asked Jacqui to reflect on the past five years. She wrote me a heartfelt note, pointing out how simply doing this retrospective was a "lovely reminder of how [her] life is now." She described how one of the biggest changes for her was stepping out of diet jail ("FOR-

EVER!!!!"). She now enjoys life, food, and self-care in ways that she never thought possible. She can eat, savor, and feel satisfied with "polite amounts" of previously forbidden foods, without having the craving monster haunt her or lurk in the background building energy until she has to eat them. She put it this way:

> I literally can "have my cake and eat it." Instead of being in diet jail or a food fugitive on the run—I just simply explore all the effects of eating in a kind and honest way. For example, eating that at that time = this. Or eating that amount of x = y. I don't take the effects, whether they are helpful or not, personally—they are simply data points that help me travel forward. I have learned to trust my body and my body has learned to trust me—after years of disconnect and fighting, we are now very, very good friends. That is not something I expected at all and is a wonderful side benefit. I also enjoy shopping, cooking, and EATING much more than I ever did! Eating was always so stressful whether dieting or bingeing—but now eating is another act of mindful self-care and pleasure.

Reading Jacqui's reflection brings tears to my eyes. Her curiosity and self-kindness are contagious. And we can all catch that bug! With each bite of food, we can learn and grow. Using the principles of how all of our brains work, collectively, we can find a path that works for each of us, individually. As we learn from our own experience, we build our own wisdom—a wisdom that comes from knowing, because we've been there, we've been down that road so many times before. We learn to listen to our bodies and grow from our direct experience. All of this feeds forward to build a wisdom-based trust in ourselves that is unshakable.

Simply take it one moment, one bite at a time.

RIGHT NOW: A RETROSPECTIVE FOR THE ROAD

It's time for one final retrospective. This one is the 30,000-foot view, as they like to say in corporate speak, where you take a look at how far you have come. If it seems helpful, pull out your notes and reflections from Day 1. You're not comparing one food to another, you're comparing one approach to another—old vs. new. For this practice, I'd like for you to sit quietly for a moment and really feel in your body the difference between eating as you did on the first day of this program and how you are eating now.

What are your relative energy levels like? What about your attitude toward yourself? Have you found less judgment? More moments of calm? Do you feel less beholden to your cravings? Which feels better, getting caught up in a craving or being curious and exploring what it feels like in your body? Have you been able to recognize habitual self-criticism and replace it with self-care? If your mind is stuck in "Wow, this is a lot of information," "I feel like I'm just getting started," "I don't yet feel like a completely new me," or some other thought pattern, that's the beauty of books. You can go back, reread, and repeat any or all of the practices until they become habit.

As you are doing this retrospective, you are, of course, finding your ultimate bigger better offer: eating mindfully has a higher reward value than perpetuating unhelpful habit loops. Congratulations. Your journey has begun. With curiosity and kindness as your constant companions, you are on your way to a lifetime of continuous learning, a deepening friendship with yourself, and a completely different relationship to eating. There's no going back.

Enjoy the ride.

ACKNOWLEDGMENTS

First and foremost, I offer a deep bow of gratitude to all of the voices that are at the heart of this book: Jacqui, Rob, Anne, Tracy, Jack, Mary Beth, and others who took the plunge of vulnerability and—cribbing from Brené Brown here—turned it into strength: the strength to give this story of struggle a voice. You also showed that the struggle doesn't have to be a struggle. It can be turned into a dance as we move through life. Thank you. Thank you. Thank you.

I am forever indebted to the many individuals who volunteered for my lab's research studies, and to my current and former lab members who, with a shared vision of making the world a better place, form(ed) a great team to carry out our work, including Alex(andra) Roy, Véronique Taylor, Bill Nardi, Remko van Lutterveld, Susan Druker, Lia Antico, and others. Also, a special shout-out to Ashley Mason (and her lab at UCSF), who led the first mechanistic study of the Eat Right Now app.

My patients are a constant source of inspiration and humility, and have taught me more about the practice of psychiatry and medicine than any textbook ever could. To all of you out there, thank you!

A big thanks to my editor, Caroline Sutton, who challenged me to write this book, and then gave extremely insightful feedback (in addition to helping the book flow). I am also grateful to Becky Cole and Liz Stein for their helpful editing and conversations.

I'd like to thank my wife, Mahri Leonard-Fleckman, who, in addition to being the best life partner I can imagine, has been a really helpful sounding board for everything from the overall framework to what examples and stories are helpful for conveying concepts. Much gratitude goes to Robin Boudette, with whom I've had the honor of coleading groups, coteaching and training facilitators, having deep discussions about all things related to helping people awaken and live happier healthier lives, and much more. Thank you for your friendship, wisdom, and generosity.

I have been fortunate enough to get to work with a wonderful team of people at MindSciences (now part of Sharecare, Inc.), who share a mission of helping to make the world a better place: Josh Roman, Maria Neizvestnaya, and many others who make up our amazing team.

I'm indebted to my agent, Melissa Flashman, who was really helpful in the early conceptualization of the book and has been instrumental in all things promotional.

A number of people not only volunteered to read various drafts of this book, but also offered very helpful feedback and suggestions, including Jacqui, Rob, Anne, Tracy, Diana Hill, Robin Boudette, Michelle Brandone, Dianne Horgan, Bill Nardi, Shannon McNally, and others whom I may have inadvertently forgotten to mention.

NOTES

INTRODUCTION

xvi. craving-related eating by 40 percent: Ashley E. Mason et al., "Testing a Mobile Mindful Eating Intervention Targeting Craving-Related Eating: Feasibility and Proof of Concept," *Journal of Behavioral Medicine* 41, no. 2 (2018): 160–73; doi: 10.1007/s10865-017-9884-5.

CHAPTER 1. HOW DID WE END UP IN THIS MESS?

8. "The Extraordinary Science of Addictive Junk Food": Michael Moss, "The Extraordinary Science of Addictive Junk Food," *The New York Times Magazine*, February 20, 2013, https://www.nytimes.com/2013/02/24/magazine/the -extraordinary-science-of-junk-food.html.

9. "Doritos Celebrates One Millionth Ingredient": "Doritos Celebrates One Millionth Ingredient," *The Onion*, May 14, 1996, https://www.theonion.com /doritos-celebrates-one-millionth-ingredient-1819563896.

CHAPTER 2. HOW FOOD HABITS FORM

11. cancha in Peru and chulpi in Ecuador: Silverio García-Lara and Sergio O. Serna-Saldivar, "Corn History and Culture," in ed. Sergio O. Serna-Saldivar, *Corn: Chemistry and Technology*, 3rd ed. (Duxford, UK: Woodhead Publishing, 2019), 1–18.

11. cancha in Peru and chulpi in Ecuador: Paul C. Mangelsdorf, "The Origin of Corn," *Scientific American*, August 1986, 80–87.

15. we don't miss the message: Christopher A. Zimmerman and Zachary A. Knight, "Layers of Signals That Regulate Appetite," *Current Opinion in Neurobiology* 64 (2020): 79–88; doi: 10.1016/j.conb.2020.03.007.

20. when strong emotions arise: Amy F. T. Arnsten, "Stress Signalling Pathways That Impair Prefrontal Cortex Structure and Function," *Nature Reviews Neuroscience* 10, no. 6 (2009): 410–22; doi 10.1038/nrn2648.

21. aiming to steer you to safety: Amy F. T. Arnsten, "Stress Weakens Prefrontal Networks: Molecular Insults to Higher Cognition," *Nature Neuroscience* 18, no. 10 (2015): 1376–85; doi: 10.1038/nn.4087.

21. aiming to steer you to safety: Amy F. T. Arnsten et al., "The Effects of Stress Exposure on Prefrontal Cortex: Translating Basic Research into Successful

Treatments for Post-Traumatic Stress Disorder," *Neurobiology of Stress* 1 (2015): 89–99; doi: 10.1016/j.ynstr.2014.10.002.

27. The OFC sits at a crossroad: M. L. Kringelbach and E. T. Rolls, "The Functional Neuroanatomy of the Human Orbitofrontal Cortex: Evidence from Neuroimaging and Neuropsychology," *Progress in Neurobiology* 72, no. 5 (2004): 341–72.

27. but with a twist: R. A. Rescorla and Allan R. Wagner, "A Theory of Pavlovian Conditioning: Variations in the Effectiveness of Reinforcement and Nonreinforcement," in ed. Abraham H. Black and William Frederick Prokasy, *Classical Conditioning II: Current Research and Theory* (New York: Appleton-Century-Crofts, 1972), 64–99.

31. to explore new territory or stick with a good thing: Vincent D. Costa and Bruno B. Averbeck, "Primate Orbitofrontal Cortex Codes Information Relevant for Managing Explore–Exploit Tradeoffs," *Journal of Neuroscience* 40, no. 12 (2020): 2553–61; doi: 10.1523/JNEUROSCI.2355-19.2020.

31. exploitation gets us stuck in habits: M. A. Addicott et al., "A Primer on Foraging and the Explore/Exploit Trade-Off for Psychiatry Research," *Neuropsychopharmacology* 42, no. 10 (2017): 1931–39; doi: 10.1038/npp.2017.108.

31. plays a major role in the explore/exploit trade-off: Vincent D. Costa et al., "Dopamine Modulates Novelty Seeking Behavior During Decision Making," *Behavioral Neuroscience* 128, no. 5 (2014): 556–66; doi: 10.103/a0037128.

32. while the opposite moves us toward staying put and exploiting: Jeff A. Beeler, Cristianne R. M. Frazier, and Xiaoxi Zhuang, "Putting Desire on a Budget: Dopamine and Energy Expenditure, Reconciling Reward and Resources," *Frontiers in Integrative Neuroscience* 6 (2012): 49; doi: 10.3389/fnint.2012.00049.

CHAPTER 3. WHY DIETS (AND MEASURING) DON'T WORK

35. the weight-loss industry: Vicky Allan, "The Fat Controllers," *The Herald* (Scotland), January 7, 2006, https://www.heraldscotland.com/default_content /12445279.fat-controllers-battle-new-year-bulge-begins-vicky-allan-weighs-lives -behind-diets/.

36. weight-loss program run by the New York City Board of Health: Vicky Allan, "The Fat Controllers."

38. Alan Marlatt and Judith Gordon: Susan Curry, G. Alan Marlatt, and Judith R. Gordon, "Abstinence Violation Effect: Validation of an Attributional Construct with Smoking Cessation," *Journal of Consulting and Clinical Psychology* 55, no. 2 (1987): 145–49; doi: 10.1037/0022-006X.55.2.145.

39. to build that critical muscle of self-control: Brian Resnick, "Why Willpower Is Overrated," *Vox*, January 2, 2020, https://www.vox.com/science-and-health/2018 /1/15/16863374/willpower-overrated-self-control-psychology.

39. more of a myth than a usable mental muscle: Daniel Engber, "Everything Is Crumbling," *Slate*, March 6, 2016, https://www.slate.com/articles/health_and _science/cover_story/2016/03/ego_depletion_an_influential_theory_in_psychology _may_have_just_been_debunked.html.

39. the more depleted and exhausted they felt: Marina Milyavskaya and Michael Inzlicht, "What's So Great About Self-Control? Examining the Importance of Effortful Self-Control and Temptation in Predicting Real-Life Depletion and Goal Attainment," *Social Psychological and Personality Science* 8, no. 6 (2017): 603–11; doi: 10.1177/1948550616679237.

39. Over the course of human history: Sandra Aamodt, "Why Dieting Doesn't Usually Work," TEDGlobal 2013, https://www.ted.com/talks/sandra_aamodt_why _dieting_doesn_t_usually_work/transcript?language=en.

45. ambivalence and certainty activate different brain networks: Andrew Luttrell et al., "Neural Dissociations in Attitude Strength: Distinct Regions of Cingulate Cortex Track Ambivalence and Certainty," *Journal of Experimental Psychology: General* 145, no. 4 (2016): 419–33; doi: 10.1037/xge0000141.

46. the adverse childhood experiences, or ACE, study: David A. Wiss and Timothy D. Brewerton, "Adverse Childhood Experiences and Adult Obesity: A Systematic Review of Plausible Mechanisms and Meta-Analysis of Cross-Sectional Studies," *Physiology & Behavior* 223 (2020): 112964; doi: 10.1016/j.physbeh.2020.112964.

47. the highest mortality rate of any psychiatric disorder in young females: C. Laird Birmingham et al., "The Mortality Rate from Anorexia Nervosa," *International Journal of Eating Disorders* 38, no. 2 (2005): 143–46; doi: 10.1002/eat.20164.

48. weighing in at roughly a billion trillionth of a gram: Celeste Biever, "World's Most Sensitive Scales Weigh a Zeptogram," *New Scientist*, March 30, 2005, https://www .newscientist.com/article/dn7208-worlds-most-sensitive-scales-weigh-a-zeptogram/.

48. a digital device to track their health in some way: Research2Guidance, *Mobile Health Market Report 2013–2017*, https://research2guidance.com/product /mobile-health-market-report-2013-2017/.

49. One of them is called completion bias: Francesca Gino and Bradley Staats, "Your Desire to Get Things Done Can Undermine Your Effectiveness," *Harvard Business Review*, March 22, 2016, https://hbr.org/2016/03/your-desire-to-get-things-done-can-undermine-your-effectiveness.

50. collapse once pressure is placed upon it for control purposes: Charles Goodhart, "Problems of Monetary Management: The U.K. Experience," *Papers in Monetary Economics* 1 (1975).

50. who had become obsessed with tracking his step count: James Tapper, "A Step Too Far? How Fitness Trackers Can Take Over Our Lives," *The Guardian*, November 10, 2019, https://www.theguardian.com/lifeandstyle/2019/nov/10/counting-steps-fitness-trackers-take-over-our-lives-quantified-self.

CHAPTER 4. DAY 1: WELCOME TO YOUR 21-DAY CHALLENGE

59. break an unhelpful or form a helpful habit: Judson Brewer, *Unwinding Anxiety: New Science Shows How to Break the Cycles of Worry and Fear to Heal Your Mind* (New York: Avery, 2021).

CHAPTER 8. DAY 5: IDENTIFYING YOUR URGES—HUNGER OR SOMETHING ELSE?

81. the Food Cravings Questionnaires (FCQs): Adrian Meule, "Twenty Years of the Food Cravings Questionnaires: A Comprehensive Review," *Current Addiction Reports* 7, no. 21 (2020): 30–43; doi: 10.1007/s40429-020-00294-z.

83. a core area involved in the brain's reward system: Andreas Heinz et al., "Identifying the Neural Circuitry of Alcohol Craving and Relapse Vulnerability," *Addiction Biology* 14, no. 1 (2009): 108–18; doi: 10.1111/j.1369-1600.2008 .00136.x.

83. difference between liking and wanting: Kent C. Berridge, "'Liking' and 'Wanting' Food Rewards: Brain Substrates and Roles in Eating Disorders," *Physiology & Behavior* 97, no. 5 (2009): 537–50; doi: 1016/j.physbeh.2009.02.044.

83. these neurotransmitters don't show up on marijuana drug tests: David A. Raichlen et al., "Wired to Run: Exercise-Induced Endocannabinoid Signaling in Humans and Cursorial Mammals with Implications for the 'Runner's High,'" *Journal of Experimental Biology* 215, no. 8 (2012): 1331–36; doi: 10.1242/ jeb.063677.

87. carbohydrates to prevent diabetes, heart disease, and stroke: George McGovern et al., *Dietary Goals for the United States*, 2nd ed., Report of the Select Committee on Nutrition and Human Needs, United States Senate, December 1977, https://naldc.nal.usda.gov/download/1759572/PDF.

87. have higher amounts of sugar: P. K. Nguyen, S. Lin, and P. Heidenreich, "A Systematic Comparison of Sugar Content in Low-Fat vs Regular Versions of Food," *Nutrition & Diabetes* 6, no. 1 (2016): e193; doi: 10.1038/nutd.2015.43.

88. this is called hedonic hunger: H. M. Espel-Huynh, A. F. Muratore, and M. R. Lowe, "A Narrative Review of the Construct of Hedonic Hunger and Its Measurement by the Power of Food Scale," *Obesity Science and Practice* 4, no. 3 (2018): 238–49; doi: 10.1002/osp4.161.

88. this is called hedonic hunger: Michael R. Lowe et al., "Hedonic Hunger Prospectively Predicts Onset and Maintenance of Loss of Control Eating Among College Women," *Health Psychology* 35, no. 3 (2016): 238–44; doi: 10.1037 /hea0000291.

88. this is called hedonic hunger: Michael R. Lowe and Meghan L. Butryn, "Hedonic Hunger: A New Dimension of Appetite?," *Physiology & Behavior* 91, no. 4 (2007): 432–39; doi: 10.1016/j.physbeh.2007.04.006.

PART 2. INTERRUPTING YOUR HABIT LOOPS WITH AWARENESS: DAYS 6–16

93. still the standard today: Agency for Healthcare Research and Quality, "Five Major Steps to Intervention (The '5 A's')," https://www.ahrq.gov/prevention /guidelines/tobacco/5steps.html.

94. five times more effective: Judson A. Brewer et al., "Mindfulness Training for Smoking Cessation: Results from a Randomized Controlled Trial," *Drug and Alcohol Dependence* 119, no. 1–2 (2011): 72–80; doi: 10.1016 /j.drugalcdep.2011.05.027.

CHAPTER 9. DAY 6: THE POWER OF PAYING ATTENTION

97. make empathetic connections with others: Judson A. Brewer, *The Craving Mind: From Cigarettes to Smartphones to Love—Why We Get Hooked & How We Can Break Bad Habits* (New Haven and London: Yale University Press, 2017).

97. make empathetic connections with others: Judson A. Brewer, "Feeling Is Believing: The Convergence of Buddhist Theory and Modern Scientific Evidence Supporting How Self Is Formed and Perpetuated Through Feeling Tone (*Vedanā*)," *Contemporary Buddhism* 19, no. 1 (2018): 1–14; doi: 10.1080/14639947.2018 .1443553.

CHAPTER 10. DAY 7: MINDFUL EATING

105. listen to the wisdom of our bodies: "10 Principles of Intuitive Eating," http:// intuitiveeating.org/10-principles-of-intuitive-eating/.

109. a useful tool for evaluating how mindful: Celia Framson et al., "Development and Validation of the Mindful Eating Questionnaire," *Journal of the American Dietetic Association* 109, no. 8 (2009): 1439–44; doi: 10.1016 /j.jada.2009.05.006.

CHAPTER 11. DAY 8: RECONNECT WITH YOUR BODY

118. hyperactive in people with anxiety disorders: Richard Gray, " 'Island of the Brain' Explains How Physical States Affect Anxiety," *Horizon: The EU Research & Innovation Magazine*, August 2, 2018, https://ec.europa.eu/research-and -innovation/en/horizon-magazine/island-brain-explains-how-physical-states -affect-anxiety.

CHAPTER 12. DAY 9: GET TO KNOW YOUR PLEASURE PLATEAUS

129. Liking is very different from wanting: Kent C. Berridge, "Wanting and Liking: Observations from the Neuroscience and Psychology Laboratory," *Inquiry* 52, no. 4 (2009): 378–98; doi: 10.1080/00201740903087359.

133. time to process what and how much you've eaten: Kathleen M. Zelman, "Slow Down, You Eat Too Fast," WebMD, https://www.webmd.com/diet/obesity/features/slow-down-you-eat-too-fast.

133. time to process what and how much you've eaten: Juliette Steen, "We Found Out If It Really Takes 20 Minutes to Feel Full," *HuffPost*, November 9, 2016, https://www.huffpost.com/entry/we-found-out-if-it-really-takes-20-minutes-to-feel-full_n_61087613e4b0999d2084fcaf.

CHAPTER 13. DAY 10: THE CRAVING TOOL (PART 1)

134. "Overeating and Mindfulness in Ancient India": Bhikkhu Anālayo, "Overeating and Mindfulness in Ancient India," *Mindfulness* 9, no. 5 (2018): 1648–54; doi: 10.1007/s12671-018-1009-x.

135. just how far the gratification in the world extends: Bhikkhu Bodhi, *In the Buddha's Words: An Anthology of Discourses from the Pāli Canon* (Wisdom Publications, 2005), 192–93.

143. they went through the Eat Right Now program: Véronique A. Taylor et al., "Awareness Drives Changes in Reward Value Which Predict Eating Behavior Change: Probing Reinforcement Learning Using Experience Sampling from Mobile Mindfulness Training for Maladaptive Eating," *Journal of Behavioral Addictions* 10, no. 3 (2021): 482–97; doi: 10.1556/2006.2021.00020.

CHAPTER 16. DAY 13: THE CRAVING TOOL (PART 2)

165. the word *mindfulness* is a modern-day translation: https://encyclopediaofbuddhism.org/wiki/Sm%E1%B9%9Bti.

CHAPTER 19. DAY 16: FIRE YOUR COMMITTEE

195. different lighting conditions affected worker output: "Hawthorne Effect (Observer Effect): Definition and History," Statistics How To, https://www.statisticshowto.com/experimental-design/hawthorne-effect/.

PART 3. A BIGGER BETTER OFFER: DAYS 17–21

202. D-type and I-type: Jordan A. Litman and Paul J. Silvia, "The Latent Structure of Trait Curiosity: Evidence for Interest and Deprivation Curiosity Dimensions," *Journal of Personality Assessment* 86, no. 3 (2006): 318–28; doi: 10.1207/s15327752jpa8603_07.

203. over a sip of water when they are thirsty: Tommy C. Blanchard, Benjamin Y. Hayden, and Ethan S. Bromberg-Martin, "Orbitofrontal Cortex Uses Distinct Codes for Different Choice Attributes in Decisions Motivated By Curiosity," *Neuron* 85, no. 3 (2015): 602–14; doi: 10.1016/j.neuron.2014.12.050.

CHAPTER 20. DAY 17: AN UNFORCED FREEDOM OF CHOICE

211. ability to engage in making mindful choices: Ariel L. Beccia et al., "Women's Experiences with a Mindful Eating Program for Binge and Emotional Eating: A Qualitative Investigation into the Process of Change," *Journal of Alternative and Complementary Medicine* 26, no. 10 (2020): 937–44; doi: 10.1089/acm.2019.318.

CHAPTER 21. DAY 18: LEVERAGING THE FOOD/MOOD RELATIONSHIP

215. Nutritional psychiatry: Eva Selhub, "Nutritional Psychiatry: Your Brain on Food," *Harvard Health Blog*, September 18, 2022.

216. highest glycemic index diets had greater odds of depression: Fahimeh Haghighatdoost et al., "Glycemic Index, Glycemic Load, and Common Psychological Disorders," *American Journal of Clinical Nutrition* 103, no. 1 (2015): 201–209; doi: 10.3945/ajcn.114.105445.

216. sodium benzoate increase hyperactivity in children: Donna McCann et al., "Food Additives and Hyperactive Behaviour in 3-Year-Old and 8/9-Year-Old Children in the Community: A Randomised, Double-Blinded, Placebo-Controlled Trial," *The Lancet* 370, no. 9598 (2007): 1560–67; doi: 10.1016/S0140-6736(07)61306-3.

216. potentially playing a role in mood disorders: Joshua D. Rosenblat et al., "Inflamed Moods: A Review of the Interactions Between Inflammation and Mood Disorders," *Progress in Neuro-Psychopharmacology & Biological Psychiatry* 53 (2014): 23–34; doi: 10.1016/j.pnpbp.2014.01.013.

CHAPTER 22. DAY 19: KINDNESS

224. looking at a set of pictures: Yael Millgram et al., "Sad as a Matter of Choice? Emotion-Regulation Goals in Depression," *Psychological Science* 26, no. 8 (2015): 1216–28; doi: 10.1177/0956797615583295.

229. what your brain looks like on kindness: Kathleen A. Garrison et al., "BOLD Signal and Functional Connectivity Associated with Loving Kindness Meditation," *Brain and Behavior* 4, no. 3 (214): 337–47; doi: 10.1002/brb3.219.

229. kindness—especially toward ourselves—can be scary: Paul Gilbert et al., "Fears of Compassion: Development of Three Self-Report Measures," *Psychology and Psychotherapy: Theory, Research and Practice* 84, no. 3 (2011): 239–55; doi: 10.1348/147608310X526511.

230. Here's how we described our findings: Ariel L. Beccia, et al., "Women's Experiences with a Mindful Eating Program for Binge and Emotional Eating: A Qualitative Investigation into the Process of Change," *Journal of Alternative and Complementary Medicine* 26, no. 10 (2020): 937–44.

CHAPTER 23. A NOTE ABOUT TRAUMA

240. years before paper was even invented: Judson A. Brewer, Hani M. Elwafi, and Jake H. Davis, "Craving to Quit: Psychological Models and Neurobiological Mechanisms of Mindfulness Training as Treatment for Addictions," *Psychology of Addictive Behaviors* 27, no. 2 (2013): 366–79; doi: 10.1037/a0028490.

243. 50 percent of our waking life: Matthew A. Killingsworth and Daniel T. Gilbert, "A Wandering Mind Is an Unhappy Mind," *Science* 330, no. 6006 (2010): 932; doi: 10.1126/science.1192439.

INDEX

Note: Page numbers in *italics* indicate figures.